The Dark Side of Liberalism

THE DARK SIDE OF LIBERALISM

Elitism vs. Democracy

ROBERT HOLLINGER

PRAEGER

Westport, Connecticut
London

Library of Congress Cataloging-in-Publication Data

Hollinger, Robert.
The dark side of liberalism : elitism vs. democracy / Robert Hollinger.
p. cm.
Includes bibliographical references and index.
ISBN 0-275-95334-3 (alk. paper)
1. Liberalism. 2. Democracy. 3. Elite (Social sciences)
I. Title.
JC574.H64 1996
320.5'1—dc20 95-40091

British Library Cataloguing in Publication Data is available.

Library of Congress Catalog Card Number: 95-40091
ISBN: 0-275-95334-3

First published in 1996

Praeger Publishers, 88 Post Road West, Westport, CT 06881
An imprint of Greenwood Publishing Group, Inc.

Printed in the United States of America

The paper used in this book complies with the Permanent Paper Standard issued by the National Information Standards Organization (Z39.48-1984).

10 9 8 7 6 5 4 3 2

For Pat and Lisa

Contents

Part III: Liberal Themes

Part IV: Current Developments

Acknowledgments

Many colleagues and friends have been of enormous help. David Depew invited me to participate in a conference on Philosophy and American Culture at California State University at Fullerton in March 1990. The result was an earlier version of chapter 5. Joe Margolis and Depew urged me to turn my paper on Rorty into a book, and made extremely helpful comments on earlier versions of the manuscript, as did Dick Bernstein and Tom McCarthy. My colleagues Tony Smith, Bill Robinson, and Dik Van Iten were of great help. Tony and Bill read and commented extensively on an early version of this book. Dik allowed me a semester without teaching responsibilities so that I could begin to write. I am grateful to them all. The late Konnie Kolenda made very helpful criticisms of my Fullerton paper on Rorty, and on my manuscript. He will be missed.

My colleague in the history department at Iowa State University, Alan I. Marcus, gave me the opportunity to lecture at an NEH Summer Institute he directed in Ames in 1990 and 1994 on the history of technology and science in America. He has taught me a great deal about American history and afforded me the opportunity to explore a wide variety of historical material. Much of this book could never have been written without this opportunity. I am also thankful to the National Endowment for the Humanities. I would like to thank Sheryl Kamps, Department of English, Iowa State University, for preparing the manuscript for publication and Karen Comstock for editing the final version of the manuscript.

My wife, Pat, and our daughter, Lisa, have, as always, been my haven in the world. The support I have received over the years from my late mother, Ruth Hollinger, and my parents-in-law, Virginia and Henry Pinkert, can never be adequately acknowledged.

Introduction: Liberalism, Democracy, and Elitism

Both liberalism and democracy, as theories and in practice, have had long, complex, and checkered histories. The idea of liberal democracy, which I shall focus on in this work, is perhaps even more subject to complexities, since its variations have been attempts to combine elements of liberal and democratic theories and practices in a number of different ways.

Liberal democracy has not suffered from a lack of critics, including liberal democrats, who often feel that liberal democracy is not living up to its own ideals or (what is not always the same thing) is not adjusting to the demands of the day.

More fundamental criticisms of liberal democracy come from the Left and the Right. The standard objection of the Marxist and socialist writers is that liberal democracy depends too much on economic individualism, capitalism, and some version of elitism. Not all writers on the Left argue that liberal democracy or liberalism has to be abandoned. Rather, according to writers such as C. B. MacPherson,[1] liberalism needs to be radicalized in the name of participatory democracy. According to the general left critique of liberalism, liberal democracy does not generate anything beyond what Benjamin Barber[2] calls "thin" democracy, that is, democracy is limited to a narrow realm of life—politics—and only then to such activities as voting. On this view, liberalism, and thus liberal democracy, undermines the classical ideals of democracy (direct democracy) that is supposed to have flourished in fourth-century Athens, during the Renaissance, in New England town meetings, and which was codified by Jean Jacques Rousseau, Karl Marx, and the New Left of the 1960s.[3] Liberal democracy is hardly real or genuine democracy at all, on this sort of view.

The conservative Right, following Edmund Burke and Alexis de Tocqueville, advocates a mixture of libertarianism and traditionalism. This unstable combination—it often breeds rampant economic individualism combined with repressive social policies and restrictions in the moral, social, and cultural spheres—is sometimes associated with populism.[4] Populism is said to express the will of the people better than liberalism or liberal democracy, because it is anti-elitist and liberalism and liberal democracy are not. Since anti-elitist populism has been embodied in both very reactionary and very radical socialist and anarchist movements, the relations between populism and democracy are no less complex than those between liberalism and democracy. A comprehensive investigation of the relations among populism, democracy, and liberalism will not be attempted here, and remains a much needed desideratum for research.

Some conservative liberals, such as Friedrich Hayek, argue that liberalism, as construed to give priority to individual rights and liberty, always takes priority to democracy, and must set limits to its scope. Some authors, such as Gottfried Dietze[5] argue that pure liberalism and pure democracy (liberalism and democracy "proper," as he calls them) are unacceptable; the former leads to chaos and the latter to mob rule. Liberal democracy, for Dietze, is a mixture of imperfect liberalism and imperfect democracy ("proper" liberalism and "proper" democracy).

Liberal democracy is thus seen as a compromise. It is designed to prevent mob rule and rampant individualism–egoism, rather than to foster the enlightened self-interest that liberals since the seventeenth century have wanted to defend in its place. For many liberals, liberal democracy is also designed to stave off conservative and reactionary elitism and government tyranny.

One result of this strategy has been what Alan Kahane calls "aristocratic liberalism."[6] This view attempts to combine the liberal values of freedom, diversity, and rational self-control with the ancient virtues of the civic republican tradition (and ultimately Aristotle), limited government, and a form of representative democracy that steers between the extremes of socialism and conservative aristocratic rule.

Aristocratic liberalism is the immediate forerunner of the liberal elitism I am interested in. It calls for minimal politics (keyed to a faith in the middle class of the nineteenth century in Western Europe). According to Kahane,[7] liberals were not democrats in the nineteenth century. They were (by definition) against universal suffrage. They were neither reactionary nor politically radical. As far as limited politics goes, Kahane says that "[m]any types of liberalism had very limited political demands, at least when judged from a democratic perspective. In this the aristocratic liberals are, I think, less on the margins of the liberal movement than may at first appear."[8]

Kahane goes on to argue that most versions of liberalism, including the aristocratic liberalism of John Stuart Mill, Tocqueville, and Jacob Burckhardt (the principle subjects of his study) were elitists: "The aristocratic liberals' elitism was a trait widely shared by liberals, no matter how differently they may construct their elites. . . . Liberal discourse, while preserving its democratic potential, tended to adhere to this elitist reality. In the case of the aristocratic liberals, this is expressed in the lesser place stressed, in practice but also in theory, on the more democratic potentials inherent in their modern humanistic language."[9]

I believe Kahane is right about liberalism. What I want to do in this book is trace the history of how a number of influential modern thinkers have furthered the cause of aristocratic liberalism. To do this I will focus on liberalism in philosophy (Immanuel Kant [1724–1804], John Stuart Mill [1806–1873],

Bertrand Russell [1872–1970]), in the social sciences (Max Weber [1864–1920] and Emile Durkheim [1858–1917]), and in the writings of leading American liberals of the twentieth century in politics, culture, and education.

The focus of my earlier historical sketches of liberalism is on the development of two kinds of elites: the knowledge or technocratic elite and the cultural elite. These two versions of the liberal elite have confined democracy (in both theory and practice) to a very limited domain, largely because of a distrust for the intelligence of most people—i.e., of people not in one or another of the acceptable elites. I am not going to defend a version of "power elite theory"[10] here. I am not discussing economic elites or politicians. I am going to focus only on the way in which the ideas of technocratic and scientific experts and of a high-cultural elite (from Matthew Arnold to Lionel Trilling) have argued against what Barber calls "strong democracy" (MacPherson and others call it "participatory democracy"). I am, in a phrase, focusing on the connections between liberal elitism and the theory of democratic elitism.[11] This theory, which finds canonical expression in Joseph Schumpeter's (1883–1950) *Capitalism, Socialism, and Democracy*[12] argues that the classical ideal of participatory democracy is based upon unrealistic assumptions. A political realist will claim that most people are politically irrational; that is, they are incapable of non-selfish rational judgments concerning public affairs, which is the essence of (rational, realistic) politics. Most people, therefore, should not be allowed to have a great deal of political influence, let alone power. The revisionist theory of democracy which Schumpeter defends (and many others, as will be seen), limits democratic participation to voting for competing elites (not just technocratic elites, who are usually just advisors to political elites), who will vie among themselves for power until the next elections. Further, thanks to liberals such as Walter Lippmann, even public opinion must be created by the elites, since most people have no intelligent opinions about public issues.

One of the ironies of this dark side of liberalism is that, beginning with the aristocratic liberals (even earlier, in fact), education was supposed to lift up the unwashed masses so that democracy could gradually be extended to all (but only in the limited sense of the vote). This is what Kahane and MacPherson call "developmental democracy." But as liberals become more pessimistic about the ability of people to become rational, even through education, the humanist values that education was to bring to the masses—high culture, rationality, self-control, respect for the value of diversity, the ability to make reasonable judgments—were thought to be values to which only a small minority could successfully aspire. These would be the people who qualified to be members of the cultural and knowledge elites. Once this vision emerged, and the social and behaviorial sciences move liberalism into the technocratic politics of social engineering, even thin democracy becomes too risky for many liberals, as I will indicate in more detail later.

The values of liberal humanism—autonomy, individuality, rational self-control, respect for diversity and culture, the cultivation of virtues and rational habits, of the intellect and sympathies of educated people—were supposed to be disseminated down to the masses so that democracy could work in ways that avoided the tyranny of the majority, chaos, socialism, anarchism, reactionary rule, and totalitarianism. But strong democracy requires political and economic equality, majority rule (not always), collective decision making, and a certain measure of social intelligence and rationality. Given the growing complexity and technocratic nature of social problems, problems such as poverty and a loss of faith in human potential, the prima facie tensions between liberal ideals and the agenda of democratic participation become more pronounced as time goes on.

In addition, certain philosophical assumptions about knowledge, rationality, and morality that derive from Plato, Aristotle, and the eighteenth-century European Enlightenment set limits on acceptable democracy within liberal thought. Democratic decisions must be rational, by dint of these universal criteria.

One possibility for reconciling liberalism and participatory democracy, which is particularly relevant today, would begin with a postmodernist rejection of these criteria, and of the idea that politics must be grounded in a foundational epistemology. Education for democracy in a multicultural postmodern world must be for a postmodernist liberal democracy. I shall discuss these matters in the last several chapters. Leading up to this conclusion, I will also discuss the versions of liberal democracy found in the writings of Richard Rorty and sketch a version of postmodern liberal democracy by drawing upon the works of recent writers such as John Rawls, Michael Walzer, Carole Patemen, and a variety of feminists, postmodernists, and radical democrats who are moving toward a postmodernist vision of participatory democracy. I shall also discuss the present political and educational climates, the cultural wars, and the latest version of populism, to distinguish them from what I, and others,[13] want to insist is not the sort of democracy that needs to be cultivated. (My own view is that John Dewey's conception of democracy as social intelligence for a shared good needs to be the starting point for a postmodern participatory democracy.) Rorty defends a thin Millian conception of democracy. The present revival of populism is not genuine democracy; not because it is conservative, but because it exhibits virtually no social intelligence, no dialogue, no respect for diversity or the notion of a common good or goal.

The populist reaction to the liberal elitism of our century does not guarantee participatory democracy in any sense that this term has been used by its advocates. It will not help us recognize what Kahane calls the democratic potential in the humanist tradition. Our universities are not producing students who are educated for this type of democratic participation either. I will discuss these issues in the final chapter.

In sum, parts 1 and 2 of this book are an attempt to sketch some of the history of modern liberal elitism in philosophy, the social sciences, and twentieth-century American society up to the liberalism of Rorty and the postmodernists. The third part of the book focuses on thematic issues that grow out of my historical sketches: liberalism and knowledge (i.e., science and technocracy), and liberalism, culture, and education. In the fourth part of this study, I give an impressionistic sketch of liberalism, democracy, elitism, and populism in the United States today. In the last chapter I discuss the state of higher education, the culture wars, and the danger to democratic education that many people rightly believe is threatening the future of our society. I end with a Deweyan theme, recently defended by Amy Gutmann in her book *Democratic Education*[14]: democratic education and a democratic society will either be developed in tandem or we will have neither education nor democracy in this society before very long.

Before proceeding, a few caveats are in order. First, I am neither a professional historian nor a sociologist, although I am a reasonably well read dilettante in the one and a longtime observer of sociological theory by avocation.[15] Specialists in these fields will probably be right to chastise me for rushing in where angels fear to tread. I am willing to take this risk to tell my story (which I do not believe has been told in quite the way I will be doing so).

Second, this book does not develop one long argument from *A* to *Z*. If it reads more like a series of overlapping and interconnecting essays on variations of a common theme or themes, this is how it was written. I do think the book has a certain kind of unity. But it is not an extended argument that begins in chapter 1 with the purpose of proving X in chapter 11. My aim has been to develop a series of well-known observations about liberalism, liberal democracy, and elitism and their implications for classical participatory democracy in a way that I think has not been done before. My hope is that my efforts will clarify the insights of major writers such as MacPherson and Barber by spelling out some details in ways that may be new; and that I can shed some light on contemporary issues in politics, education, and culture against the backdrop of the conflicts between liberalism, elitism, and democracy.[16]

NOTES

1. C. B. MacPherson, *The Real World of Democracy* (New York: Oxford University Press, 1966); idem, *The Life and Times of Liberal Democracy* (New York: Oxford University Press, 1977); idem, *Democratic Theory: Essays in Retrieval* (New York: Oxford University Press, 1975).
2. Benjamin Barber, *Strong Democracy* (Berkeley: University of California Press, 1984).
3. See James Miller, *Democracy in the Streets* (New York: Simon and Schuster, 1975).
4. See Michael Kazin, *The Populist Persuasion* (New York: Basic Books, 1995).
5. Gottfried Dietze, *Liberalism Proper and Proper Liberalism* (Baltimore: Johns Hopkins University Press, 1985).
6. Alan Kahane, *Aristocratic Liberalism* (New York: Oxford University Press, 1992).
7. Ibid., 140.
8. Ibid., 152–53.
9. Ibid., 157.
10. See Geraint Parry, *Political Elites* (Westport, CT: Praeger, 1969); and Eva Etzioni-Halevy, *The Elite Connection* (Cambridge, MA: Blackwell's, 1993).
11. See Peter Bachrach, *The Theory of the Democratic Elite* (Boston: Little, Brown and Company, 1967).
12. Joseph A. Schumpeter, *Capitalism, Socialism, and Democracy* (New York: Harper and Brothers, 1942).
13. See, e.g., Jean Bethke Elshtain, *Democracy on Trial* (New York: Basic Books, 1995).

14. Amy Gutmann, *Democratic Education* (Princeton: Princeton University Press, 1987).

15. See my book, *Postmodernism and the Social Sciences: A Thematic Approach* (Newbury Park, CA: Sage, 1994).

16. Among many books I have consulted, the most helpful are: Barry Holden, *Understanding Liberal Democracy* (Oxford: Philip Allan, 1988); David Held, *Models of Democracy* (Stanford: Stanford University Press, 1987); Anthony Arblaster, *The Rise and Decline of Western Liberalism* (New York: St. Martin's Press, 1982); Richard Bellamy, *Liberalism and Modern Society* (College Park: Pennsylvania State University Press, 1992).

A Note on Democracy and "Mob Rule"

According to classical democratic theory, citizens are entitled to participate in decisions that effect them both individually and collectively. In addition, many advocates of "strong" democracy believe that such participation is intrinsically valuable, since it is a manifestation of the human need for expression and self-development. On this sort of view, even if democratic participation is not the best way of achieving some bottom line, it is still important, since the human desire for self-expression is valuable for its own sake.

Liberalism is also interested in human self-development, but puts a premium on a set of ideas about knowledge, rationality, and self-control that implies that most people, even with optimum educational opportunities, cannot achieve the sort of rational development that is needed for self-government. Liberal democracy is one result of this view. Most people can be educated well enough to choose from among the select few who will act in their best interests, e.g., in representative assemblies. But democratic participation in any way that gives all citizens the power to deliberate, to reach collective decisions, and empowers them to enact those decisions is impossible, even if we waive crucial issues about size and complexity.

The theories of liberal democracy I examine in the chapters that follow are serious about only a very limited type of democratic involvement by citizens: political democracy, mainly voting for people who will then rule in the name of "the people." At the bottom of this idea, I believe, is the ancient equation, democracy = mob rule. My own preference is for some form of a stronger democracy, which goes even beyond Dewey's call for a ubiquitous democratic culture in all spheres of life, in that I believe that only a rejection of all foundational philosophies and political theories can make democracy in a multicultural, postmodern world a reality. In this book I do no more than sketch the bare bones of this sort of view.

This sort of democratic vision rejects the idea that politics, especially liberal politics, is merely a means to an end, some bottom line such as utility, efficiency, or whatever. Democracy is at least as much a process as a product. Indeed, even when people are terribly mistaken, their need and right to express themselves and to participate in decisions and actions is still of fundamental intrinsic value. Those who belittle this ideal because it does not have an impact on power politics miss the point and beg the question as to what democracy ought to count as success.

Still, there are many people, including lots of radicals, who worry about too much democratic participation. In what follows I will briefly touch upon what I take to be the key arguments against classical and participatory democracy, and shall try to rebut them.

1. Democracy means rule by the crowd or "the mob." The average person is a lover of sights and sounds, not truth and reality. People's animal drives and appetites rule their reason; therefore they cannot make wise decisions.

This argument clearly begs the question by assuming some sort of Platonic ideals of truth, knowledge, and reality, as well as a conception of politics that is modeled on an art, craft, or science that requires expert knowledge. In his book, *Democracy and Its Critics.*[1] Robert Dahl challenges this "guardianship" model of government. I will argue later that we must reject a guardianship model of liberalism and liberal democracy, in favor of a postmodernist liberal democracy.

2. History shows that democracy is dangerous. The French Revolution, the Reign of Terror, the Germans under Hitler, the counterculture of the 1960s, populism, labor union activity in the 1930s, and so on, make the masses very dangerous. Perhaps sometimes. But can the elite and the wise be absolved of violence, irrationality, and danger? Who was it that started most of the wars on this planet? Farmers? Whose ideologies have justified crusades, holy wars, colonial wars, Vietnam? Surely those of the "best and the brightest." In any event, these examples may prove to be dramatic but atypical cases. Moreover, the Terror did not prove that democracy must be dangerous or that the violent overthrow of centuries of oppression was not justified. Nor is it clear that democracy was at work in Hitler's Germany or that violence is always (or even ever) a sign that democracy is necessarily dangerous and irrational. Foucault once said that everything is dangerous. What conclusions should we draw about anything and everything, then? I frankly have never understood the force of this worry about democracy, as if other forms of human association were not equally tarnished by this charge.

3. Democracy means majority rule; and this is often tyrannical. To be sure. But one need not go as far as Rousseau (who claimed that the minority must "be forced to be free" when they demur from the general will) to defend participatory democracy. For one thing, democratic participation need not abandon representative government or checks and balances to protect minorities. For another thing, education, tolerance, and the appreciation of debate, dialogue, difference are ideas that have still to be instituted on a large scale. We cannot assume they cannot work, despite what we know from history. (Of course, sometimes they do work.)

4. Populism is often made up of ignorant, prejudiced folk whose values and ideals are not that of the liberal or socialist. Sometimes. Again, many very educated people also have prejudices and are racists, sexists, and so on. I do not

see how this undermines the desirability of an educated citizenship or democracy.

I, for one, am willing to bite the bullet on this issue. While my own political views and values are on the political Left, I believe that if democratic dialogue results in decisions I abhor or think are ignorant or worse, my job is to try to keep the conversation going and hope that my views and arguments will get debated and perhaps prevail, while also being open to modifying my own opinions and prejudices. (Maybe, e.g., political correctness and affirmative action *have* gone too far.) But even if they do not, even if democracy results in a very conservative society, I see no other viable alternative to more democracy. Elitism, totalitarianism, or the mindless disregard of others' views cannot compete with the idea of ongoing dialogue and critique of shared values and ideals.

5. Writers such as Alan Bloom chastise people for having low and crude tastes and values. Mass culture—sports, movies, pulp novels, TV, rock music, etc.—are signs of how stupid and ill prepared the masses are for wisdom and democracy. I agree with Bloom that lots of this stuff is mindless garbage. But I reject the elitist implications for politics. Besides, geniuses can like pop culture, too. (Ludwig Wittgenstein loved detective novels and Betty Grable movies.) Bloom just begs the question here. Besides, people are often not that taken in by garbage, and some of it may be healthy and politically astute, either as ironic criticism of society or as an expression of cultural diversity and democratic values. Mozart is no more the only musician worth listening to than Plato is the only writer worth reading, despite Bloom's contrary opinions.

6. Democratic revisionists follow Schumpeter in labeling most people as politically irrational, if not stupid or ignorant. On this view, politics requires that people look beyond their own noses in making political decisions. According to Schumpeter, most people, even some very intelligent ones, are incapable of doing that. I agree, but do not think humans are hard wired to be that way. More opportunity for empowerment, discussion, and education is still our best hope. Despite the fact that my students are cynical and seem to believe that everyone is really selfish, that community is impossible or dangerous, I still sense that this is a facade to avoid getting hurt and a manifestation of powerlessness, as well as a lack of opportunity to think about alternatives to the worldview and interpretation of American history of Ronald Reagan, George Bush, Newt Gingrich, and Rush Limbaugh.

7. Democracy is impossible in a large, complex world where our problems are global, and where science and technology are both the causes and cures of most of our problems.

I do not fully accept the premises. I do not, for example, believe that only technology and science can make things better. Further, the choice between democracy and technology is a false dilemma; we can and sometimes do have both. Sometimes democratic decisions about the uses or even the developments of technology occur. Nor do I believe that all of our problems are economic, technological, or scientific. We still do not have adequate ways of living in peace with people who are different; we still need to cling to dangerous religious beliefs and ideologies and to blame others for what happens to us. These are mainly problems of a very different order. It is only because the roles of science, technology, and greed seem so overwhelming and inescapable, only because politics has become little more than the manipulation of "human resources," that we tend to ignore the many options open to us for individual lives and societies that reject the mindless nostalgia of fundamentalist Christians, on the one hand, and technological utopians, on the other. In short, I reject both liberal democratic elitism and mindless populism, and advocate something closer to the classical ideal of democracy, but in a version that takes into account postmodernist insights, as well as elements in liberalism, feminism, and democratic socialism that can be woven together into a postmodernist democratic theory.

My view is that we must move beyond the assumptions and values that generate a cyclical movement from utopianism and optimism to pessimism, from religious and technocratic ideals of heaven on earth to nostalgic reactions to them, in order to seriously begin the job of growing up, in Freud's sense of the term. Aside from allowing people to express themselves and participate, a democratic culture must allow many voices to be heard, so that we can begin to move beyond the confines of this cluster of ideals to a society where unforeseen possibilities for human development can become realistic options.

NOTE

1. Robert A. Dahl, *Democracy and Its Critics* (New Haven: Yale University Press, 1989), chs. 4–5.

Part I

CHAPTERS IN THE HISTORY OF MODERN LIBERALISM

Chapter 1

Liberalism and Philosophy

In her challenging book, *The Pursuit of Certainty*,[1] Shirley Letwin makes the following remark about Mill: "He marked the birth of the 'liberal intellectual,' so familiar today, who with one part of him genuinely values liberty and recognizes the equal right of all adults to decide their lives for themselves, but with another wants the government, under the direction of the superior few, to impose what he considers the good life on all his fellows."[2] This, I submit, is the main dilemma of liberalism, in all its modern varieties, which can be seen as a response to this problem.

And where does this dilemma lead? Let us note the words of John Fitzgerald Kennedy:

> Most of us are conditioned for many years to have a political viewpoint—Republican or Democrat, liberal, conservative or moderate. The fact of the matter is that most of the problems . . . that we now face are technical problems, are administrative problems. They are very sophisticated judgments, which do not lend themselves to the great sort of passionate movements which have stirred this country so often in the past. [They] deal with questions which are beyond the comprehension of most men.[3]

It is not a coincidence that this remark is cited in a paper that argues that democracy in America is disappearing.

It may be true that world events make Kennedy's remark unavoidable, even if liberal democrats regret it. But do they? Or is this remark a manifestation, indeed an expression, of the end-of-ideology thesis that modern liberals see as the culmination of modern liberalism?

Here it might be worth recalling that the doctrine of education, begun with Mill and carried forward by Matthew Arnold, T. H. Huxley, Herbert Spencer, and William Clifford to John Dewey and Richard Rorty, was meant to overcome the dilemma described by Letwin. But modern liberal education more often than not cultivates a ruling elite, while also raising the cultural level of the masses, and thus the level of social intelligence needed for democracy. But given the growing conflict between technological civilization and democracy, it is not surprising to see liberalism's loyalties divided at best, and in favor of some form of "technocracy" at worst. Whether this is inevitable can be argued all day. It certainly is not obvious that it is; and even if it were, would that justify abandoning democracy? I do not think so. At any rate, it is interesting to note that Kennedy evidently thinks the technological imperative requires rational people, including liberals, to modify or abandon popular democracy for empirical reasons. This makes it look as if democracy is justifiable only on empirical grounds, e.g., as some sort of scientific hypothesis. Indeed, one type of liberalism (defended by Russell) maintains precisely this view. On this line of thought, liberalism itself is an empirical hypothesis, which can be "refuted" by empirical circumstances.

There are, to be sure, some liberals who argue that modern science, as opposed to modern technology, can be harnessed to serve liberal democratic forces.[4] But this is by no means obvious, given the history of the way science has either served antidemocratic forces in the United States and elsewhere, or at least served forces that favor an elitist conception of democracy.[5]

To return to Mill, one can cite, as Letwin,[6] Gertrude Himmelfarb,[7] and others have done,[8] a variety of factors to explain the dilemma of Mill's liberalism, namely, his belief in representative democracy combined with his distrust of the masses (which boils down to the fear of socialism, as well as the tyranny of the majority), and thus a belief in the need to give the minority of elites an influence disproportionate to their numbers. His vision was a class of scientists (sociologists) and elite legislators[9] who would bring to fruition his own merger of philosophic radicalism, the program of Auguste Comte and Claude Saint-Simon, and the cultural elitism and conservatism of Samuel Coleridge. It stems from his distrust of the masses, which colors his reformist recipe for bringing about a "liberal utopia," and results in a tension between the technocratic and romantic aspirations that his program for political and cultural education spawns. But the evidence that Mill defended doctrines that limit democratic participation for elitist reasons—that Mill was genuinely ambivalent about political democracy—is, I think, incontrovertible.

The evidence for my reading of Mill can be found in *On Liberty*, *Considerations on Representative Government*, his essay on Coleridge, and his writings on culture and politics. His attempt, in *On Liberty*, to defend individuality, eccentricity, and free speech must be seen in light of his distrust of the masses. The cultural elite must be protected from the masses and given a disproportionate share of power and influence. Mill argues that Parliament should be a debating society dominated by the intellectual elite. This is his rationale for Thomas Hare's weighted voting system that provided for a civil service exam that would give the educated classes more votes and a method of representation that would allow the minority elite to get elected to Parliament by counting votes from outside their home districts. Laws and policies would not be made by Parliament, but (as we would now say) by a managerial and technocratic elite appointed by the government.

What does Mill say in defense of these proposals?

1. A "rational democracy" is government by the wisest and the few; the masses can only vote to throw the rascals out.[10] This idea is defended later by Schumpeter and Weber to justify leadership of democracy by an elite.

2. Popular government is dangerous.[11]

3. Tolerance is only justified as an instrument to "mankind's convergence on the truth"; as we get closer to this, a new "contrivance" will be needed to defend tolerance of opinions that are known to be false.[12] Only "opinions" that are amenable to scientific evidence can be tolerated as knowledge marches on. Furthermore, democracy and liberalism are only partially true. Conservatism and aristocracy are also partly true. The great issues of politics must therefore always seek solutions that strike a balance between these two partial truths.

4. In Considerations on Representative Government,[13] "Thoughts on Parliamentary Reform," and "Democracy and Government,"[14] Mill argues that the educated elite should have a plurality of votes, which should be weighted more heavily than the votes of the less well educated. At one point Mill poses the following question: "ought everyone to have an equal voice?" and is categorically in favor of a negative answer, since the affirmative response is "palpably false."[15] This is not, as Dennis Thompson[16] and other defenders have argued,[17] merely a sign of Mill's ambivalence about popular representative democracy; it is symptomatic of his entire philosophy. This is not to say that Mill was not in many ways a democrat. But it is to raise the question of what sort of democracy is compatible with Millian doctrines, and with liberalism in general. More fundamentally, it raises the issue of the systematic ambivalence of modern liberals, not just Mill, toward democratic participation. I am claiming that "liberal democracy" in the twentieth century has not been in the service of certain elements in other models of democracy (such as participatory models) that deserve more weight in the public realm, but rather has undermined them.

5. The two core doctrines of his representative system are expertise in legislation and an intellectual elite in parliament to debate the issues of the day.[18] To repeat a point made earlier, the legislature will be a debating society in which the minority elite, whose election will be increased by the Hare Plan and by a system of weighted representation, will dominate the conversation, and laws will be drafted by experts appointed by the government.

6. The political expert alone can overcome the following problem: "[H]ow best to conciliate the two great elements on which good government depends; to combine the greatest amount of the advantage derived from the independent judgment of a specially instructed Few, with the greatest degree of the security for rectitude of purpose derived from rendering those Few responsible to the Many."[19]

That is, the only way of reconciling popular democracy and political elitism is via the role of the expert in guidance and education. So Millian liberalism takes a leaf from Kant and Rousseau and anticipates B. F. Skinner: Let people do what they want, but make sure the elite conditions their wants.

7. The masses can be "educated" to recognize and follow the lead of "superior intellect," who would rule in their name and under their ultimate control, using their cultural advantage and scientific knowledge to choose both ends and means in the service of democracy.[20]

8. Obedience to authority is right and necessary on matters of science and "scientific ethics," which even the educated nonexpert can never understand or adjudicate on rational grounds.[21] As Kant might put it, the masses can argue; but in the end they must "obey." Moreover, Mill believes that there is and must be a consensus among the elite[22]; there must be some things that for them, and thus for everyone, are "beyond discussion."[23] The "multitude" will be carried along by the authority of this elite consensus, for this is the only hope for "stable politics." Indeed, one commentator says: "Stable politics required unanimity amongst the intellectual elite; there can be no doubt at all that Mill eased his worries about the apparent inevitability of democracy by reminding himself of this agreement amongst 'all thinking and instructed persons.'"[24] It is interesting to note that Mill agrees with Tocqueville about one cause of the dangers of American democracy: the Americans have no ruling elite class.[25] It is only in "transitional," not "organic," periods (Comte's terms) that critical discussion and dissent are encouraged on a large scale, mainly because this is the only way to move to the next organic stage of stability, since the elite themselves are not unanimous in such periods. Organic ages are clearly more desirable for Comte and Mill (and also Durkheim).[26]

Here Mill, influenced by Comte and anticipating Durkheim, introduces the idea of an organic solidarity and consensus. So Mill already embodies what I shall call "romantic" and "corporate" liberalism in what I claim is an unstable mixture that, in the respective writings of Weber and Durkheim, falls apart and worsens the tensions (e.g., between romanticism and technocracy, liberalism and democracy), which Mill attempts to balance. For Mill, the requirement is that the "multitude" follow the lead of the "clerisy,"[27] of the intellectual elite, in order to enhance democracy. This proposal for resolving liberalism's ambivalence about popular democracy constitutes the dilemma of modern liberalism in a nutshell.

In the next chapter I want to show how Weber and Durkheim transform Millian liberalism into (respectively) romantic and corporate liberalism. I will discuss whether either of these modifications in liberalism avoids the problems we have just noticed in Mill. My argument is that the ambivalence toward democracy in Mill becomes more pronounced in Weber and Durkheim, to the point where Weber's loyalty to political realism and romantic choice and Durkheim's emphasis on the notion that modern society is an organic community push democracy closer to the margins of the liberal agenda.

At this point I want to talk briefly about Kant.

Kant and Mill are clearly the architects of modern liberalism. They differ in many ways: they have different epistemologies, different approaches to morality, and they differ about the relation between science and morality. Much of modern liberalism is a mixture of Kant and Mill. The notion that the state is morally neutral, and that justice is procedural, owes much to Kant, or at least Kantian influences, e.g., Weber. And while Kantian and Millian (e.g., utilitarian) versions of liberalism are often at odds, Kant and Mill have one thing in common: a distrust of genuine democracy. (Other relevant aspects of Kant's liberalism will be discussed in connection with Weber and romantic liberalism in the next chapter.)

In fact, Kant makes the same arguments against democracy that Mill does. In his political writings, especially his essay "An Answer to the Question 'What Is Enlightenment?'", in his *Contest of the Faculties*, and his essays on history,[28] Kant develops the idea that the intellectuals, philosophers in particular, need to promote Enlightenment from the top down. The public uses of reason—speaking truth to power—are the business of the philosopher, who makes a bargain with the enlightened despots. The philosophers will be allowed to speak the truth. This will make the enlightened despot more rational; and so rational government will eventually trickle down to the public, who will meanwhile become educated by the philosophers. But the private uses of reason, that is, in cases where one is playing a role, as teacher, civil servant, or whatever, are severely limited. Therefore, people must "shut up and obey" their leaders. Weber echoes these exact words, which amount to an early version of the theory of the democratic elite. Kant favors a form of republicanism, but not democracy. Despite the more radical, indeed subversive, elements in Kant's discussion of the faculties and the public uses of reason, brought out recently by Jurgen Habermas, Michel Foucault, Jean-François Lyotard, Jacques Derrida, and John Rawls,[29] there can be little doubt that Kant anticipates Mill in developing the liberal antipathy to participatory democracy by advocating a "top down" role for the intellectual elite to control what little democracy they allow. Thus, to cite but one illustration, the contemporary "liberal" sociologist Morris Janowitz defends the role of the social and policy sciences in advising the elite how best to control the masses on the grounds that it increases the rationality of those in power, and thus allows these disciplines to have a more sanguine effect on the real world.[30]

Liberalism as a philosophy is rooted in the twin ideas of individualism—negative liberty—and a distrust of government. The public-private divide, the division between civil society and the state, the separation of modern culture and life into "spheres"—science, art, morality (Kant)—all manifest, in Michael Walzer's words, "the liberal art of separation."[31]

In this context, anything and everything, including democracy, take second place. Gottfried Dietze captures this version of liberalism in his book *Liberalism Proper and Proper Liberalism*: "[L]iberalism created democracy. Democracy did not create liberalism, no matter how much the hope that democracy would promote liberalism may have been instrumental in the inception of liberalism. The priority of liberalism before modern democracy suggests that under that form of government, liberalism will continue to have priority before democracy, . . . It can also be argued that . . . democracy, established as a means for the realization of liberalism, must be less important than liberalism as its end."[32]

Dietze's logic is correct so far as it goes. But must we conceive of democracy as merely a means for the promotion of liberalism, even if modern democracy arose in such a context? What about other forms of democracy—classical or Athenian or, more generally, what MacPherson called "illiberal democracy"?[33] Perhaps liberalism should be seen as merely a means for the promotion of democratic practice.

How might one argue for the priority of democracy over liberalism? Or vice versa? Take the latter case first. The liberal value of individual (negative) freedom implies that collective decision making and democratic practice are inherently dangerous, and must be checked. If democracy has any intrinsic value, it is difficult to see how a "classical" liberal—e.g., a modern libertarian such as Hayek—could admit, let alone appreciate, it. In fact, Hayek claims that liberalism is more important than democracy. Specifically, he says this: "It is possible for a dictator to govern in a liberal way. And it is also possible that a democracy govern with a total lack of liberalism. My personal preference is for a liberal dictator and not for a democratic government lacking in liberalism."[34] Hayek may be right; but that is beside the point, which is that Hayek and Kant, two of the most prominent liberal theorists, both see a conflict between liberalism and democracy, and categorically favor the former when they do conflict.

But suppose that the liberal ideas of freedom, privacy, atomism, etc., are implausible, or less valuable—even only of equal value—to that of self-development in a community, or to the value of democratic expression and participation. Suppose that the market prevents certain other things that are considered at least as valuable as individual freedom, e.g., friendships construed along nonexchange theory lines (as in Aristotle). Suppose the liberal emphasis on knowledge, expertise, and high culture leads to a bottom-line mentality that culminates in a "Brave New World," where participation becomes unnecessary, even harmful, to the bottom line. Would liberalism still deserve priority over democratic practice?

Liberalism, when connected with the Enlightenment, has a built in distrust for the masses, for common sense, for tradition, and puts a premium on "rationality," science, scientific method, "empiricism," and so on. In optimistic periods the liberal believes that education into high culture and, say, scientific literacy will bring the masses up to a level where they can participate, although only minimally, in self-governance. As we shall see, developments in the social sciences move liberalism further along the path of government by experts. A distrust of citizens makes democratic practice very suspect in liberal eyes, if we mean by "democracy" participatory democracy.

Russell, for his part, wants to associate liberalism with empiricism, if not skepticism.

> The liberal creed, in practice, is one of live-and-let-live, of toleration and freedom so far as public order permits, of moderation and the absence of fanaticism in political programs. Democracy, when it becomes fanatical, as it did among Rousseau's disciples in the French Revolution, ceases to be liberal; indeed, a fanatical belief in democracy makes democratic institutions impossible, as appeared in England under Cromwell and in France under Robespierre. The genuine Liberal does not say "this is true," he says "I am inclined to think that under present circumstances this opinion is probably the best." And it is only in this limited and undogmatic sense that he will advocate democracy.[35]

On Russell's view, liberalism is undogmatic and open minded. I hope to show that Russell is wrong about this. Moreover, his characterization of democracy is unfair and slanted to the most extreme cases. For Russell and other liberals, democratic politics is bad because it is irrational. But it is precisely the attempt to substitute knowledge for politics that democratic practice cannot tolerate. Democracy should take political action seriously. The liberal, despite Russell's attack on Plato, is really taking up Plato's notion of the rule of the wise. But as Walzer and Rorty have argued, if we take democracy seriously, we need to move away from philosophy and the liberal notion of the rule of the expert, and the notion that participatory democracy, not liberalism, takes the values of "undogmatic empiricism" seriously.[36] This is in sharp contrast to the end-of-ideology views of social scientists, such as Robert Lane and Amiati Etzioni, who believe politics and "ideology" will and should disappear in a "knowledgeable society."[37] I hope to show that liberalism's emphasis on knowledge gives rise to a conception of politics that is antidemocratic and elitist.

In addition, since "democracy" is almost always modified by the adjective "political" within the liberal tradition—not by "cultural," "economic," or "social"—democratic practice means little more than representative government. This is all to the good; but is it enough? Is the ideal of democratic participation in all areas of life only an instrumental value? I think not.

Indeed, recent works by feminists and advocates of workplace democracy make it clear that liberalism does not foster democracy sufficiently, and that liberalism is quite compatible with all sorts of social, political, and economic inequalities. But, contrary to Hayek, these writers suggest that we must modify liberalism in order to promote more, not less, democracy in all spheres of life. Does liberalism rather sanction Hayek's view, so that, e.g., inequalities in the home or workplace—in the (for liberals) apolitical private sphere—are not out of kilter with liberalism or liberal democracy? If so, should we accept liberalism's priority to democracy when they conflict?

If not, can we argue for either the priority of democracy over liberalism, or its equal status, on the grounds that the noninstrumental values of democratic participation (for example, individual expression) are at least as important as liberal values, e.g., of liberty, and that liberalism cannot recognize these values, thus endangering an important dimension of democratic experience?

Russell compared liberalism in politics to scientific method. He said:

> The essence of the liberal outlook lies not in *what* opinions are held, but in *how* they are held: instead of being held dogmatically, they are held tentatively, and with a consciousness that new evidence may at any moment lead to their abandonment. This is the way in which opinions are held in science. . . . The scientific outlook, accordingly, is the intellectual counterpart of what is, in the practical sphere, the outlook of Liberalism.[38]

If Russell is right, then liberalism is not wedded to any particular political doctrines, including democracy or tolerance; and any doctrines that can be vindicated by science should be held by liberals, even if this means abandoning traditional liberal ideals, including democracy. Is liberalism just a method? Is democracy just a formal organizational arrangement, one which subserves liberalism so construed? Russell and others think so.

This is, in fact, just the problem. Liberalism qua scientific outlook applied to politics can perfectly well denounce democratic ideals and practices as outmoded, irrational, unscientific, or worse. This is really what underlies liberalism's dilemma. If liberal values are defined as the scientific outlook applied to politics, and thus yield only tentative solutions, why fight to preserve democracy if it is no longer pragmatically useful or empirically the best way of achieving the goals of liberalism, e.g., freedom in the private sphere combined with rational social engineering? In other words, if liberalism is just the political extension of scientific method, how does liberalism relate to democracy? What if there is a conflict between the two? Can liberal democratic projects, and indeed its very framework, be abandoned for empirical reasons? And if empiricism is itself part of the scientific-liberal outlook, is this not a vindication of Nietzsche's diagnosis of the will to truth, that it turns in on itself? One could try to construe liberalism as a sort of formal, procedural rules, in either Kantian or Rule Utilitarian fashion, as some liberals[39] have done. But then liberalism could still be compatible with quite illiberal and antidemocratic forces.

The issue is really whether liberals need to reject such a tentative allegiance to democracy. At the very least, this problem brings pragmatism and liberalism into direct conflict, and has often resulted in abandoning democracy to save liberalism. In a word, unless democracy is defended independently of liberalism, and in categorical fashion, as is done by Dewey and many social democrats, its justification will at best be tentative and secondary to those of liberal goals. This is especially important to note if we are after a participatory democracy that envisions democracy in cultural, and not merely narrowly political, terms. This is why, at the bottom line, Dewey wants to give democracy a philosophical justification; and why Rorty's refusal to do so runs the risk of reducing democracy to avoiding cruelty and obeying the law—a difference with Dewey that is as wide as the Grand Canyon. It may turn out that Dewey and George Mead, by equating scientific method with the method of social intelligence, and by holding fast to the notion that all educated members of a democracy are capable of the latter, can bridge the gap between liberal elitism and democracy, as Yehuda Erzahi suggests in his insightful book *The Descent of Icarus*.[40] At least they gave this problem serious attention. Even if they were unsuccessful, their vision of a democratic culture is still worth pursuing.

NOTES

1. Shirley Letwin, *The Pursuit of Certainty* (Cambridge, UK: Cambridge University Press, 1965); see also Alan S. Kahane, *Aristocratic Liberalism* (Oxford University Press, 1992).

2. Letwin, *Pursuit of Certainty*, 8.

3. Lewis H. Lapham, "Democracy in America?" *Harper's* 9 Nov. 1990, 47–56. The quote from Kennedy—taken from a May 1962 press conference—is on p. 54. See Lapham's more recent *The Wish for Kings: Democracy at Bay* (New York: Grove Press, 1992).

4. See here Paul Goldstene, *The Collapse of Liberal Empire* (San Francisco: Chandler and Sharp, 1977); idem, *The Bittersweet Century* (San Francisco: Chandler and Sharp, 1989); see also Yehuda Erzahi, *The Descent of Icaraus* (Cambridge: Harvard University Press, 1991), chs. 7–10.

5. For a recent argument to undermine "guardian democracy," see Robert Dahl, *Democracy and Its Critics* (New Haven: Yale University Press, 1989).
6. Letwin, op. cit., 8.
7. See Gertrude Himmelfarb, *On Liberty and Liberalism* (New York: Knopf, 1974).
8. Among the works I have consulted on these aspects of Mill, I found the following especially helpful: Stephen Holmes, "John Stuart Mill: Fallibilism, Expertise, and the Politics-Science Analogy," in *Knowledge and Politics,* ed. M. Dascal and O. Gruengard (Boulder: Westview Press, 1989), 125–44; Graeme Duncan, *Marx and Mill* (New York: Cambridge University Press, 1973), ch. 8, "The Elite and Liberal Politics"; Maurice Cowling, *Mill and Liberalism* (New York: Cambridge University Press, 1961); Dennis F. Thompson, *John Stuart Mill and Representative Government* (Princeton: Princeton University Press, 1976); J. B. Schneewind, ed., *Mill: A Collection of Essays* (Notre Dame: Notre Dame University Press, 1969); S. Jacobs, *Science and British Liberalism* (London: Avebury, 1991); Alan S. Kahane, *Aristocratic Liberalism* (New York: Oxford University Press, 1992); P. B. Kern, "Universal Sufferage without Democracy: Thomas Hare and John Stuart Mill," *Review of Politics* 34 (1972): 306–23; John Skorupski, "Liberal Elitism," in *Liberalism, Citizenship and Autonomy*, ed. David Milligan and William Watts Miller (London: Avebury, 1992), 134–53.
9. Duncan, op. cit., 277, quotation from Mill.
10. J. H. Burns, "J. S. Mill and Democracy, 1829–1861," in Schneewind, op. cit., 294.
11. Ibid., 311; cf. Duncan, op. cit., 260 for a citation in support of "Toryism."
12. See J. S. Mill, *Essential Works of J. S. Mill* (New York: Bantam, 1961), 293–94. I have discussed this issue in "The Limits of Tolerance: Mill vs. Feyerabend," *Southwest Philosophy Review* 2 (1985): 146–57.
13. See J. S. Mill, *Philosophy of J. S. Mill,* ed. M. Cohen (New York: Modern Library, 1961).
14. J. S. Mill, *Essays on Politics and Culture,* ed. G. Himmelfarb (New York: Anchor 1963); "Democracy and Government," in *John Stuart Mill on Politics and Society,* ed. G. L. Williams (London: Harvester, 1976).
15. Mill, *Essays on Politics and Culture*, 142–43.
16. Thompson, op. cit.
17. See J. Hamburger, *Intellectuals in Politics: John Stuart Mill and the Philosophic Radicals* (New Haven: Yale University Press, 1965).
18. William Thomas, *Mill* (New York: Oxford University Press, 1984), op. cit., 115f.
19. John M. Robson, *The Improvement of Mankind* (Toronto: University of Toronto Press, 1961), op. cit., 239. cp 190.
20. G. L. Williams, ed., *John Stuart Mill on Politics and Culture* (London: Harvester, 1976), op. cit., 182–85.
21. Richard B. Friedman, "An Introduction to Mill's Theory of Authority," in Schneewind, op. cit., 393.
22. R. J. Halliday, *John Stuart Mill* (London: Unwin, 1976), op. cit., 72ff.
23. Himmelfarb, *On Liberty and Liberalism*, 138.
24. Halliday, 73.
25. Mill, *Essays on Politics and Culture,* 210.
26. Himmelfarb, op. cit., 32ff.
27. See Ben Knights, *The Idea of the Clerisy in the Nineteenth Century* (Cambridge: Cambridge University Press), final cp.
28. See Immanuel Kant, *Political Writings*, 2d enl. ed., H. Riess (Cambridge: Cambridge University Press, 1991); idem, *Contest of the Faculties* (Lincoln:

University of Nebraska Press, 1992); idem, *Perpetual Peace and Other Essays* (Indianapolis: Hackett, 1989).

29. See Jurgen Habermas, *The Structural Transformation of the Public Sphere* (Cambridge: MIT Press, 1988); Michael Foucault, "Kant on Enlightenment and Revolution," *Economy and Society 14* (1986): 88–96; idem, "What Is Enlightenment?" in *The Foucault Reader,* ed. Paul Rabinow (New York: Random House, 1984), 32–51; Jacques Derrida, "The Contest of the Faculties," in *Logomachia: The Conflict of the Faculties*, ed. Richard Rand. (Lincoln: University of Nebraska Press, 1992), 1–33; Jean-Francois Lyotard, *The Differend* (Minneapolis: University of Minnesota Press, 1988); idem, "Judiciousness in Dispute: Kant after Marx," in *The Lyotard Reader*, ed. Andrew Benjamin. (Cambridge: Blackwell's, 1989), 324–60; John Christian Laursen, "The Subversive Kant: The Vocabulary of 'Public' and 'Publicity,'" *Political Theory* 13 (1986): 584–603; John Rawls, "The Idea of Public Reason," in Rawls, *Political Liberalism* (New York: Columbia University Press, 1993), 212–54; Onora O'Neill, "The Public Use of Reason," *Political Theory* 15 (1988): 523–51.

30. See the discussion in Richard Flacks, "The Sociology of Liberation Movements: Some Legacies and Lessons," in *Radical Sociologists and the Movement*, ed. Martin Oppenheimer, Martin J. Murray, and Rhonda F. Levine (Philadelphia: Temple, 1991), esp. 20ff; see also Morris Janowitz, *The Last Half Century* (Chicago: University of Chicago Press, 1978), ch. 1; Alan Wolfe, "Sociology, Liberalism, and the Radical Right," *New Left Review* 128 (1981): 3–27.

31. O'Neill, "Public Use of Reason," *Political Theory*, loc. cit.

32. Gottfried Dietze, *Liberalism Proper and Proper Liberalism* (Baltimore: Johns Hopkins University Press, 1985), 257–58.

33. C. B. MacPherson, *The Life and Times of Liberal Democracy* (New York: Oxford University Press, 1977).

34. F. A. Hayek, cited in Samuel Bowles and Herbert Gintis, *Democracy and Capitalism* (New York: Basic Books, 1986), 11–12.

35. Russell, cited in Benjamin Barber, *Strong Democracy* (Berkeley: University of California Press, 1984), 15.

36. Michael Walzer, "Philosophy and Democracy," in *What Should Political Theory Be Now*? ed. John Nelson (Albany: SUNY Press, 1983), 75–99.

37. See Robert E. Lane, "The Decline of Politics of Ideology in a Knowledgeable Society," *American Sociological Review* 30 (1966): 649–62; Amiati Etzioni, *The Active Society* (New York: Free Press, 1968); Daniel Bell, "Liberalism in the Post-Industrial Society," in Bell, *Winding Passages* (New York: Basic Books, 1983).

38. B. Russell, cited in Benjamin Barber, *Conquest of Politics* (Princeton: Princeton University Press, 1989), 41; see Bertrand Russell, "Philosophy and Politics," in Russell, *Unpopular Essays* (London: Unwin, 1968), 21–22.

39. See Ronald Dworkin, "Liberalism," in *Public and Private Morality*, ed. S. Hampshire (New York: Cambridge University Press, 1978), 113–42; idem, "The Foundations of Liberalism," in *Tanner Lectures on Values*, vol. II (Salt Lake City: University of Utah Press, 1990), 1-19.

40. Harvard University Press, 1990.

Chapter 2

Liberalism and the Social Sciences: Weber and Durkheim

The liberalism of Mill and Kant, which generates a conflict between elitism and democracy, undergoes major transformations in the writings of Max Weber and Emile Durkheim. This chapter discusses these transformations, with a view to exploring their implications for the dilemma of modern liberalism.

WEBER

Scholars are still debating the very basic question of whether Weber is a liberal at all.[1] Part of the difficulty is that Weber is clearly against democracy, except to allow citizens to vote for their leaders. After that, the people should "shut up and obey" the leader.[2] Parliamentary democracy, for Weber, is at best an instrumental means for achieving other goals he valued or thought necessary—e.g., diffusing the power of the bureaucracy and giving individuals in the iron cage the breathing space to pursue their own calling or personality, their personal values and life choices. Some writers conclude that Weber therefore cannot be a liberal.[3] But if the line of argument begun in the preceding chapter is correct, it should not be surprising that a writer can be a liberal and not be in favor of democracy. I believe Weber is such a writer.

One could still ask what kind of "liberal" he is. Some writers call him a "peculiar" liberal,[4] because he did not endorse many of the "typical" liberal programs, such as parliamentary government or certain economic practices associated with free-market capitalism. But Mill, whose liberalism is hardly an issue, was also against many aspects of capitalism, although he was not nearly as pessimistic about it as Weber. More importantly, Weber clearly does want to preserve the liberal vision of individual freedom and privacy, as well as the liberal values of autonomy and responsibility. He also wants to limit the power of the bureaucracy and the state, at least in the intervention of the lives of its citizens. Still others suggest he was a "liberal without liberalism."[5] I prefer this characterization because of its resonances with other themes in my argument (e.g., that Rorty is a Weberian).

Perhaps the best place to start a discussion of Weber's liberalism is with the crisis of modern culture. Generally speaking, the crisis is the culmination of a struggle between idealism, romanticism, and Kantian values, on the one hand, and the forces of capitalism, materialism, positivism, and modern science, on the other. Weber's transformation of liberalism is his attempt to come to grips with the disenchanted rationalized world that the crisis manifests. As Lawrence Scaff puts it, for Weber ". . . we are trapped in the paradox of a subjectivist culture of incessant stimulation and change on the one side and the objectivist constraint of the iron cage on the other. It is peculiarly the case that whichever side of the paradox we embrace—and it is essential to see that the modern individual must embrace *both* . . . [the] 'sublime values' of 'publicness' are driven from the stage in full retreat."[6] In Nietzschean terms, the will to truth (Weber's "rationalization") divests the world of values and meaning, by making public values 'subjective.'

Robert Eden echoes Scaff's remarks when he concludes his discussion of Weber's political views with the observation that Weber's attempt to preserve liberalism by transforming it into rule by an aristocratic Nietzschean elite of professionals, who adapt an ethical stance to give their life a mission—to limit the power of the bureaucracy in the iron cage—makes liberal politics a struggle between "democratic moralism" and "aristocratic nihilism."[7] Politics becomes the projection of the private wars of gods and demons onto the public arena, so as to preserve the liberal value of individual freedom in a modern technological civilization, and thus save the liberal democracies of the West from anarchy, socialism, reaction, and the tyranny of the majority in an age when public values have disappeared.

Weber's solution may in fact be the only viable one. For the moment, I want to reconstruct it in more detail, so as to bring out the ambivalences in his transformation of liberalism, and to further explore the view I have previously called "romantic liberalism." Two points need to be stressed. First, Weber, like Rorty, defends (a kind of) liberal democracy, but rejects a philosophical justification for liberalism.[8] This is impossible, for liberalism is only one of the many warring gods and demons. Only an arbitrary, ultimate, private choice—Weber uses Luther's "Here I stand, I can do no other" at the end of "Politics as a Vocation"—together with Machiavellian tactics can preserve liberal democracy.[9] Second, Weber's urgency about politics is combined "with a deep pessimism about its institutional possibilities."[10] In Wolfgang Mommsen's phrase, Weber is a "liberal in despair."[11] As a result, Weber's position tends to oscillate between romantic irony and political realism, between heroic efforts and pessimism and Machiavellian realism.

Mommsen's "A Liberal in Despair"[12] throws some interesting light on the Weberian roots of pragmatic liberalism, as can be seen below.

1. Weber wants to preserve Nietzsche's "aristocratic nihilism." I think this connects up with the influence of the Lutheran ideal of the calling, the Kantian or neo-Kantian emphasis on formalism, and the claim that ultimate values are matters of personal choice that one finds in Weber.

2. Weber abhors what Nietzsche calls "the last man" and thus democracy, but he does want to save liberal democracy. How can he do both? Mommsen claims he tried to "harmonize the doctrine of the Levellers with the message of Nietzsche."[13] This paves the way for his version of liberal elitism.

3. Weber's romanticism is a source of strength and political realism.[14] For Weber, the strong individual has the convictions that will allow her to face up to the demands of the day, which for Weber are not to be assessed in terms of philosophical ideals or values.

In fact, one commentator claims that Weber is a pragmatist. In a later chapter I argue that Rorty's version of liberalism is influenced at least as much by Weber as by Mill, and that the main difficulties in Rorty's political writings stem from this fact.

As Mommsen remarks:

> As a democrat, Weber was a pragmatic liberal. Democracy was a method and a means; it was not an end in itself. It was a method of selecting leaders, and it was a means of both giving their rule an aura of legitimacy and of including all politically significant segments of the population in the political affairs of the nation. However, it was not the proper means for deciding ordinary political issues. Such issues inevitably required *compromise* arrived at through negotiation rather than a vote. The classical democratic doctrine . . . was hardly one Weber could "believe" in. The theory of the "sovereignty of the people," the "will of the people," the "wisdom of the people," were all utopian fictions whose desire was the abolishment of the dominance of men over men—in Weber's view, a this-worldly impossibility.[15]

Liberalism, as construed by Weber, makes popular democracy not only virtually impossible, but irrational, even dangerous, if it goes beyond anything but voting for representatives to Parliament.

It is true that Weber's romantic ironism allows him a certain political distance, and an opportunity to play off various political factors for Madisonian ends. But Weber's romanticism is not the political romanticism of quietism, which both Weber and Carl Schmitt thought politically naive and therefore dangerous.

4. Weber's stance of value neutrality in politics and science is an effort to preserve individual autonomy, limit the scope of science, and create an atmosphere of pluralism, so as to preserve the autonomy of the individual in the iron cage. But for Weber this plurality of values is to be used in the political and social arena precisely because politics and science are value free. This is the public use of the wars of gods and demons, which could only be kept in check by strong leaders, and by the competition among them. Moreover, and here Weber and Rorty agree, the pluralist strategy is needed because in a disenchanted world "one should do everything possible to keep society as dynamic as possible."[16] But in Weber's case this moves him away from a democratic order.[17] The only way in which the private wars of gods and demons could preserve the Protestant liberal values of Luther and Kant, the aristocratic nihilism of Nietzsche, and the ethics of responsibility or consequences is by the abandonment of genuine participatory democracy. Weber requires a model of democracy in which the liberal-democratic values of democracy are abandoned in favor of a kind of Kantian thesis of the moral

neutrality of the state.[18] This allows Weber to combine political realism with ethical pluralism and a romantic emphasis on the individual's commitment to personal ultimate values.

As Roslyn Wallach Bologh argues in "Max Weber and the Dilemma of Rationality,"[19] Weber sees plebiscitary democracy as the only hope of bringing together the substantive rationality of charismatic leadership with the formal rationality of modern organization. Democracy and modern bureaucracy are in conflict, according to Weber.[20] One form this conflict takes is between formal and substantive rationality. Experts stand in the way of democracy. Weber distinguishes four types of democracy, according to Bologh: "collegiality," "immediate democracy," and two forms of representative democracy. One function of democracy is to legitimize power/authority by means of the vote. The other aim is to keep people as free from control by others as possible.[21] Democracy, in the first two senses, i.e., participatory democracy, is incompatible with modern bureaucratic society. Representative democracy becomes the only option. But this type of democracy ultimately paves the way for experts—professional politicians, bureaucrats, etc.—and thus genuine democratic participation becomes practically impossible. "So democracy, in either form (participatory or representative) is difficult to maintain in the modern state, except (according to Weber) by developing a system that incorporates certain features of participatory democracy (leaders, substantive values, voting) with that of modern bureaucracy (representation, professional politicians, etc.)."

Weber shares Nietzsche's venomous distrust of the last man, as is obvious from the very pessimistic conclusion of *The Protestant Ethic*. Weber believes that we can preserve the shared public ideals of that ethic—which Kant codifies in his philosophy—only by privatizing them. The iron cage has become totally secularized, and has abandoned those very values which made modern capitalism and the ambivalent rationalization and disenchantment of the world possible. Weber (as well as Rorty, and perhaps Francis Fukuyama) is willing to pay the price needed for the preservation of the aristocratic values liberalism shares with romanticism: the continued existence of the last man. But for Weber this in turn requires severe limits on democracy, as well as bureaucracy, to give a person Lebensraum. So Weber wants individuals who can "cope" with the realities of the iron cage to take seriously the Lutheran ideal of the calling and personality[22]; and this, in a way, is of a piece with Nietzsche's *Ubermensch*.[23] But Weber draws part of his inspiration from the neo-Kantian formal view of values and ideals that he learned from his teachers. Rejecting Kant's universalism, we get a purely formal notion of style and authentic choice—Weber is a kind of existentialist[24]—where each person commits herself to her own ultimate values and ideals, her "life choices," and develops the Nietzschean Spartan self-control and strength to hold on to them come what may. The modern person, and especially the scientist and the politician, must become responsible and autonomous, by making her chosen ultimate values the basis of her personality and her life calling in the absence of a public sphere. This is the essence of Weber's romantic liberalism. It aggravates the wars of gods and demons, even if, indeed precisely when, this very pluralism allows all persons to "become what they are," in Nietzsche's formulation of this ideal.

Yet for Weber this runs the obvious political risks of chaos, mediocrity, and the like, even though it does make possible a strategy for diffusing the powers in the iron cage that threaten the individual. So romantic privacy must be counteracted by political realism in a world without a common political culture. Weber accordingly maintains that this neo-Kantian type of ethic—the ethic of ultimate ends or "conviction"—must be combined with an ethic of responsibility or consequences to temper ideals and prevent the extremes of fanaticism and crass expediency to which each morality, if taken alone, respectively leads.[25] But this combination of Kantianism and utilitarianism is itself a matter of personal choice and conviction, that is, it is irrational, as Karl Popper, an unregenerate Weberian, insists upon in his own effort to combine social engineering and a neo-Kantian ideal of freedom.

Weber's romantic liberalism thus requires the preservation of the distinction between cultural spheres: art, science, and morality. The typical insistence on preserving these features of modernity that one finds in Rorty, Habermas, and others is a neo-Kantian strategy that modern liberals adopt to preserve their favored ways of drawing the distinctions between the private and the public and between knowledge and values.

This strategy will either reinforce fragmentation or require a purely formal and empty common core of values, responsibility, autonomy. It is designed to preserve plurality in order to enhance liberal values, but often requires Machiavellian realism or end-of-ideology, piecemeal social engineering to replace the lost public realm. Rorty's ideal of politics, "avoid cruelty," captures the resulting impoverished conception of politics that is light years away from the Deweyan conception of a democratic culture.

In fact, this Weberian strategy of combining romantic passion with scientific rationality and neutrality may in effect amount to an early version of the end-of-ideology thesis.[26] That is, the strategy of preserving the fragmented personal and social elements of modern life, yet playing them off against each other, amounts to James Madison's strategy for overcoming factionalism in *Federalist*, no. 10. Daniel Bell makes this point in a paper called "Passion and Politics in America":

> It has been one of the glories of the U.S. that politics has always been a pragmatic give-and-take rather than a series of wars-to-the-death. . . . "Politics . . . is a matter of adopting oneself to all sorts of people and situations, a game in which one may score but only by accepting the rules and recognizing one's opponents, rather than a moral crusade in which one's stainless standard must mow the enemy down." Democratic politics means bargaining between legitimate groups and the search for consensus. This was so because the historic contribution of liberalism was to separate law from morality.[27]

Bell then argues that it was Kant and Madison who made it possible for democracy, conceived (as in Weber) as a neutral but passionate struggle among interest groups—with its attendant distinction between individual passion and conscience, on one side, and the shared formal procedural rules of the game, on the other—to develop in this way.

Bell is undoubtedly right. But the questions are: Is this democracy? Is the price for democracy fragmentation? Must we abandon democracy to overcome fragmentation? This may not *be* a price, or at least it may be worth it, as Weber and Rorty maintain. But is Weber's Romantic liberalism, his "leadership plebicatory democracy," which paves the way for the interest group end-of-ideology pluralism Bell defends, the kind of democracy that lets citizens become involved in the political process? Or is it rather a way of curtailing such involvement, precisely in order to preserve the liberal values that Kant and Weber valued so highly? Does romantic liberalism, at least in Weber, if not in others,[28] give us anything more than a way of preserving factionalism, or rather devising policies that see the Madisonian solution to factionalism—in the guise of Weber's struggle between gods and demons as constrained by political realism—as the ultimate goal of liberal democracies?[29] But what happens to the Deweyan idea of a great communal democracy?[30] Can Weber's romantic liberalism, his mixture of Machiavellian power politics, technological rationality, and the romantic, Nietzschean ideals of self control and responsibility, be combined with the sort of democracy Dewey envisions? Can Weber's efforts to use Nietzsche to serve liberal democratic forces lead to anything other than either Rinehold Niebhur's (pessimistic) version of political realism or its mirror image, Richard Rorty's ironic version of political romanticism? If my claim that the vacillation between romanticism and technocracy is endemic to the liberalism of Mill and Weber is correct, I see no other basic alternatives within mainstream liberalism.

DURKHEIM

Durkheim's approach to modern industrial liberal democracies takes its point of departure from the traditions of French liberalism, republicanism, and rationalism, with a certain role accorded to direct democracy at the small group level (Weber sometimes advocates this same idea). Durkheim thus is the culmination of progressive French thought from the Enlightenment *philosophes* through Comte, Saint-Simon, and Tocqueville, and thus (indirectly) Hegel.[31] Despite his expressed hatred for Hegel, Durkheim, following Comte, is both a positivist and a Hegelian.

Durkheim views society as an evolving organism or system, whose parts or organs are related to each other in structural and functional terms. Hegel's realm of "objective spirit" becomes the realm of "social facts" and "social laws," which Durkheim believes can be discovered empirically through the use of Mill's methods and statistics.[32] Thus, unlike Weber, Durkheim is a social determinist, who rejects the "voluntarism" of Weber's action theory in favor of irreducible social explanations of social phenomena.

Durkheim believes that modern societies are evolving toward a form of social solidarity that he calls "organic solidarity" in *The Division of Labor in Society*.[33] Evolutionary changes, especially in size and population density, are moving liberal democracies to a new form of community, which will overcome the problems of modern culture that form the point of departure for Weber's political sociology. In a word, modern Western societies are becoming corporate states.

Durkheim in fact develops Hegel's corporate state idea in his own sociological and philosophical idiom, although his immediate point of departure is Comte, Saint-Simon and Spencer. But Durkheim tries to show that Spencer's defense of laissez-faire capitalism is fated to be surpassed, since the modern state will evolve into a social organism where economic individualism in civil society will be synthesized with a new form of "collective conscience" at the levels of both civil society and the national state. In fact, a science of morality, conceived in naturalistic terms,[34] will emerge and provide standards and rules that are at once descriptive and normative for what is necessary and proper in the new social order. The approach here is typical of functionalism: the dynamic adjustment and equilibrium the system requires for survival and evolution underwrite the moral standards, which in turn provide the system with its rationale. (The difference between the "normal" and the "pathological" is also spelled out in these functionalist terms by Durkheim.[35])

Each "occupational group" or profession will become, as in Hegel, an organ of the whole that functions in a relatively autonomous fashion, imbued with its own particularity, and yet also the universal collective conscience. The role of the professions is to transmit the particular ethos of that group to its members. When each occupational or secondary group performs its function, the net result will be the emergence of a national form of solidarity, which is, so to speak, an epiphenomenon of the new forms of integrating that emerge in the evolving structural-functional system.

The corporate state, and with it the ideology of corporate liberalism, emerged in the United States at about the same time Durkheim was giving its emergence in France canonical expression. (Hegel and Comte are not part of the liberal tradition, although they certainly have points of contact with that tradition, e.g., via Benjamin Constant and Tocqueville. In fact, the "corporate idea" turns out to be compatible with socialist, liberal and conservative developments.[36]) Corporate liberalism certainly rejects the laissez-faire elements in Millian liberalism. It defends the liberal and republican ideals of the French and American revolutions, the ideals of autonomy, dignity, and equality. But, drawing from the German idealist tradition, it sees the individual as essentially social, and thus as developing only in a social context, as in Aristotle and Hegel.

Durkheim clearly believes that democracy needs to be radically modified and curtailed in this new corporate *Gemeinschaft*. He distrusts the "mob" as much as his great heroes Comte and Saint-Simon, and makes use of Rousseau's dubious ideas about freedom and autonomy that are embodied in his notorious remark about forcing people to be free when their individual wills conflict with the general will. Indeed, Durkheim reconciles Kantian autonomy and social determination by appealing to the authority of the state and society's elite corps of professionals. The individual is free only when under rational control, and is abnormal when out of phase with the "conscience collective." Only control and "education" can correct these pathologies. Influenced by the Dreyfus affair and by Gustav Le Bon's *The Crowd*, the first modern treatise on mob psychology, Durkheim develops a form of liberal elitism in which the professional makes use of the science of morality to guide society in the direction that objective phenomena show it to be moving.

Durkheim, like Hegel, defies the modern state and makes it the embodiment of the new collective moral conscience. People who are not "normal," i.e., functional vis-a-vis the new order, are "pathological" as well as "undisciplined and irregular" and "morally incomplete."[37] Durkheim's Hegelian views are connected with his ideas on "religion" as the necessary shared agreement about certain basic ideals and values. In this respect he is an heir to Burke and a high priest of Comte's Religion of Humanity, and the forerunner of conservatives such as Lord Patrick Devlin.

From Charles Montesquieu, Tocqueville, Saint-Simon, and Comte, Durkheim inherits the idea of a well-ordered, hierarchical, and authoritarian social structure, ruled from the top down by objective experts. A modern society is pluralistic. Democracy in the modern world must be tied to the moral authority of the state and the collective solidarity it makes possible.[38] "The true characteristics of democracy are two-fold: (1) a greater range of the governmental consciousness and (2) closer communications between this consciousness and the mass of individuals."[39] This requires a strong state, authoritarian education, and professional groups to teach "civic virtues"[40] so as to mediate between the individual and the nation state. Unlike the "New Liberalism" of Leonard Hobhouse in England, and even, to some extent, of Herbert Croly and Lippmann in the United States, Durkheim's conception of the need for state intervention is very conservative. As Anthony Giddens sums it up, for Durkheim moral individuality depends upon a strong state, indeed, it is created by it; democracy requires a strong state; democratic participation must be limited; as an "organ of consciousness," the state determines what the needs of its people are, although it must still keep in contact with the people; the corporations protect the individual from the state, but also insure that "the people" will be educated in the "right" way. Democracy is equated with the rational opinions that form the dominant collective conscience—the "we conscience" that Rorty appeals to in his pragmatic ethnocentric defense of existing consensus by "we" liberal intellectuals. However, contrary to Rorty, for Durkheim appealing to the "we" conscience of the people is not democracy, since it appeals to untutored opinions, which are not part of Durkheim's organizational notion of democracy.[41]

Giddens claims that "Durkheim's sociology was rooted in an attempt to re-interpret the claims of political liberalism in the face of a twin challenge: from an anti-rationalist conservatism, on the one hand, and from socialism, on the other."[42] For Durkheim, "democracy" is a term for a certain kind of social organization, and does not involve majority rule, popular franchise, or the like. It rather denotes the relationship between the state as a corporate "moral" force, which protects the rights of its citizens (conceived as social units, not egoistic individuals), and civil society, a cluster of corporate organizations, mainly professional groups. The latter limit the power of the state, and educate the people for "genuine" democracy. A pluralist system of checks and balances prevents both an absolutist state and rule by the mob, and fosters equilibrium, adjustment, and change.

Here Giddens lets Durkheim speak for himself:

A minority must govern, in any developed society, and it makes little odds how this minority comes to power: for the rule of the aristocracy might often conform more closely to the will of the people than that of an elected elite. The difference between a system in which "the governing minority are established once and for all," and one in which "the minority that carries the day may be beaten tomorrow and replaced by another" is only "slight."

Democracy, for Durkheim, thus becomes a matter of the interplay of sentiments and ideas between government and mass; his discussion of democratic government contains no developed examination of the functioning of political parties, or of Parliament, or of the franchise, and indeed these considerations are regarded as of purely minor significance.[43]

For Durkheim, rational order and authority are primary, for only they can guarantee an evolving, adapting integrated system that preserves the necessary structural-functional properties that the modern division of labor requires. Democracy is a series of formal arrangements to make this happen: communication—but hardly dialogue, in Dewey's sense, or any other—between the state and civil society's secondary groups, *not* individuals; a managerial elite that keeps abreast of public opinion, but makes sure the secondary groups educate the people to hold the right opinions for the right reasons and develop in them an ethos of self-control and reasonableness and responsibility. As Giddens remarks, this is one step beyond even the theory of the democratic elite; it is a version of the totally administered state, anticipated by Saint Simon, emerging in the United States since the 1920s, and born again in the postindustrial new world order of today. The corporate entities do all the work.

Durkheim thus differs from Weber in believing that factionalism will allow conflict to result in a cooperative community, in which egoism and economic individualism give way to a Hegelian idea of the self as social. This self is molded by social factors that are driven by the demands of the system: equilibrium, adjustment, control. This comes to be the guiding idea of the corporate state in this century. Corporate liberalism provides that state with its blueprint and its rationale.

As was the case with other nineteenth-century liberals, notably Mill and Weber, the belief that liberalism can only be saved from the Left and the Right by moving away from popular democracy, while incorporating socialist and conservative elements, is an underlying feature of Durkheim's work.[44] This same motive was at work in late nineteenth- and twentieth-century America, as American liberalism became alternately Weberian, Durkheimian, and then a mixture of both under the pressures of American modernization. American political history from the Progressives to Daniel Bell can be seen as exemplifying these trends. While Weber transforms Millian liberalism by emphasizing its romantic elements, downplaying the scientific conception of politics, and Durkheim pushes the conservative, naturalistic, social-engineering elements found in Mill's appropriation of Comte, while de-emphasizing romantic concerns for individuality, the mixture of romantic and corporate liberalism in modern America produces a marriage between Weberian romantic liberalism, and the Durkheimian notion of a managerial elite. End-of-ideology liberalism, Rorty's romantic liberalism and Bell's conception of the postindustrial order are the offspring of this marriage.

To sum up: Weber transforms Millian liberalism in a number of ways. First, he rejects Mill's naturalism and combines a version of consequentialism with a radically subjective neo-Kantian formalism, infused with Nietzsche's elitist perspectivism. He thus makes the elitist romantic tendencies in Mill's and Kant's liberalism at once more pronounced and less democratic, as well as providing it with a noncognitivist framework that further weakens democracy and the idea of the public sphere. At the same time, Weber dilutes liberalism's commitment to democracy, and argues for the necessity of elitism in a culture that is at once nihilistic and technocratic.

Political realism is the only solution, since liberal democratic reformism, elitist or not, is just a matter of private taste, and arguably not in keeping with "the demands of the day." Liberal values and democracy become further separated, or at least their connections are subjectivized. Ironically, while this was designed to preserve them, it makes them appear unrealizable or at least unworkable, given the nature of the iron cage, the erosion of the public sphere, and the subjective nature of values. The result is a self-fulfilling recipe for both failure and eventual withdrawal from public space. As I hope to show, Weber anticipates most of Rorty's version of a liberal utopia.

Durkheim, on the other hand, further naturalizes the romantic elements in Mill's liberal humanism and rejects individualism in favor of a scientific reworking of Kantian and Hegelian notions of autonomy and self-determination, so as to push his political sociology in the direction of an administrative state that embodies the objective "social facts" he claims are emerging. The liberal virtues get embodied in corporate entities in an allegedly material and objective system—like structural and functional properties. The tradition of French rationalism, which combines the most illiberal elements in positivism and Hegelianism, appeals to (allegedly) scientifically verifiable social forces to defend the corporate state.

The combination of Weber's political realism and ethical subjectivism with Durkheim's administrative science of management has a complex and disturbing history in twentieth-century America. In closing this chapter it may be of interest to cite the words of an early American proponent of Durkheim's vision, Luther Lee Bernard, one of this country's founding sociologists. In a series of papers called "The Transition to an Objective Standard of Social Control" in the 1910–1911 *American Journal of Sociology*, in which Comte, Saint-Simon, Durkheim, and Spencer are discussed and their organic view of society defended, Bernard makes the following remark, which I quote at length:

> Experience is leading us in the United States toward the adoption of the policy of centralized administration by experts, who are made directly responsible to the people. Every social organization must be coercive to the extent necessary or it must break down. A social organization based upon a scientific analysis and control of social phenomena . . . involves the rule of an elite in no greater degree than is implied in the responsible direction of administrative details by experts, instead of more or less irresponsible control and exploitation by professional politicians. If we could conceive of a society in which all the individuals were equally informed on all social matters and all absolutely sincere, all traces of an elite composed of

experts, of aristocrats, or of professional politicians would disappear. But that is an impossibility.

Those activities not under a scientific social control and which need adjustment should be readjusted so far as possible on the basis of scientifically determined knowledge of social facts, which it is the business of the social organization to supply and enforce through whatever agencies are most effective—education, investigation, expert service.[45]

Bernard's vision can be read in retrospect as an accurate prediction of politics in twentieth-century America, as we shall see in more detail in the next two chapters.

NOTES

1. While I have read extensively in the secondary literature on Weber, I shall only note the writings that have proven the most helpful to me for present purposes. David Beetham, "Weber and the Liberal Political Tradition" in *The Barbarism of Reason: Max Weber and the Twilight of Enlightenment,* ed. Asher Horowitz and Terry Maley (Toronto: University of Toronto Press, 1994), 99–112.
2. Cited in David Beetham, *Max Weber and the Theory of Modern Politics* (Cambridge, UK: Polity Press, 1985), 236.
3. Regis A. Factor and Stephen P. Turner, "The Limits of Reason and Some Limitations of Weber's Morality," *Human Studies* 2 (1979): 301–34, 326ff.
4. Wilhelm Hennis, *Max Weber: Essays in Reconstruction* (London: Unwin 1988), 186.
5. Robert Eden, "Doing without Liberalism: Weber's Regime Politics," *Political Theory* 9 (1982): 379–407.
6. Lawrence A. Scaff, *Fleeing the Iron Cage* (Berkeley: University of California Press, 1989), 164; and Stephen P. Turner and Regis A. Factor, "The Disappearance of Tradition in Weber," *Midwest Studies in Philosophy* 15 (1990): 400–24.
7. Robert Eden, *Political Leadership and Nihilism* (Tampa: University of Florida Press, 1989), 209.
8. *Ibid*., 2.
9. See Max Weber, "Politics as Vocation," in *From Max Weber*, ed. Hans Gerth and C. Wright Mills (New York: Oxford University Press, 1946), 127.
10. Mark Warren, "Max Weber's Liberalism for a Nietzschean World," *American Political Science Review* 82 (March 1988): 32–50, 36.
11. Wolfgang Mommsen, *The Age of Bureaucracy* (New York: Oxford University Press, 1964), 95ff.
12. Ibid.
13. Ibid., 106.
14. Weber, "Politics as Vocation," 115.
15. Ernest Kilker, "Max Weber and the Possibilities for Democracy," in *Max Weber's Political Sociology*, ed. Ronald M. Glassman and Vatro Murvar (Westport, CT: Greenwood Press, 1984), 68.
16. Mommsen, *Age of Bureaucracy*, 112.
17. Ibid., 114.
18. Warren, op. cit., 37, 32.
19. In Glassman and Vatro, op. cit., 175–86, quote on p. 184.

20. Ibid., 182; See Max Weber, *Economy and Society* (Berkeley: University of California Press, 1978) 2: 987.
21. Discussed in Bologh, op. cit., 180–82; Weber, *Economy and Society* 1: 277.
22. See Harvey Goldman, *Max Weber and Thomas Mann* (Berkeley: University of California Press, 1988).
23. See William Shapiro, "The Nietzschean Roots of Max Weber's Social Science," Ph.D. diss., Cornell University, 1978.
24. See here L. M. Lachmann, *The Legacy of Max Weber* (London: Heineman, 1970).
25. See Weber, "Politics as a Vocation."
26. See David Beetham, *Max Weber and the Theory of Modern Politics* (Cambridge, UK: Polity Press, 1985), 242; and Daniel Bell, "Passion and Politics in America," *Encounter* 3 (1956): 54–60.
27. Bell, "Passion and Politics," p. 60. The words in quotes are from Edmund Wilson.
28. See Nancy Rosenblum's *Another Liberalism* (Cambridge: Harvard University Press, 1987).
29. See Eden, *Political Leadership and Nihilism*, op. cit., ch. 1. For a very different comparison between Weber and Dewey, see James T. Kloppenberg, *Uncertain Victory* (New York: Oxford University Press, 1988).
30. See Stephen P. Turner and Regis A. Factor, "The Disappearance of Tradition in Weber," in *Midwest Studies in Philosophy*, 15 (1990): 400–24.
31. I have consulted many secondary sources on Durkheim, but limit myself here to a few selected sources that have been most relevant to my argument.
32. Emile Durkheim, *Rules of Sociological Method* (New York: Free Press, 1982).
33. See Emile Durkheim, *The Division of Labor in Society* (New York: Free Press, 1933).
34. Emile Durkheim, *Moral Education* (New York: Free Press, 1961).
35. See Durkheim, *Rules*; and idem, *Suicide* (New York: Free Press, 1951).
36. See James Gilbert, *Designing the Industrial State* (New York: Quadrangle, 1972).
37. Emile Durkheim, *Sociology and Philosophy* (New York: Free Press, 1974), 64–65: and Lewis Coser, "Durkheim's Conservativism" in *Emile Durkheim on Philosophy and Society*, ed. Kurt Wolff (New York: Harper, 1957), 220.
38. See Anthony Giddens, ed., *Durkheim: Selections* (New York: Cambridge University Press, 1979), 197ff; and Robert Bellah, ed., *Emile Durkheim on Morality and Society* (Chicago: University of Chicago Press, 1973), 58–61.
39. Giddens, *Durkheim: Selections*, 199.
40. Emile Durkheim, *Professional Ethics and Civic Morals* (1957; reprint, New York: Routledge, 1992).
41. See Anthony Giddens, *Emile Durkheim* (New York: Penguin, 1978), 64ff.
42. Anthony Giddens, "Durkheim's Political Sociology," *Sociological Review* LS Vol. 1 (1971): 477–519, 513.
43. Ibid., 509–10. The quoted words are from Durkheim, *Professional Ethics and Civic Morals*, op. cit., 78; see also Melvin Richter, "Durkheim's Politics and Political Sociology," in Wolff, op. cit., 170–210, esp. 192f.
44. Frank Pearce, *The Radical Durkheim* (London: Unwin, 1989), ch. 3.
45. *American Journal of Sociology* 11 (1910–1911): 533–34; cf. Frank Fischer, *Technocracy and the Politics of Expertise* (Newbury Park, CA: Sage, 1990), chs. 3–4. For a recent (left of center) defense of elite democracy, see Eva Etzioni-Halevy, *Fragile Democracy* (Totowa: Transaction Publishers, 1989); and idem, *The Elite*

Connection: Problems and Potentials of Western Democracy (Cambridge: Blackwell's, 1993).

Chapter 3

American Liberalism: Durkheimian Trends

The modernization of America, which began in the 1890s, transformed the country in a variety of ways. "Upheaval" would not be too strong a term to use in this connection. The key development, so far as my argument is concerned, is the abandonment of Millian liberalism and laissez-faire capitalism in favor of corporate liberalism and the corporate state.[1] These developments, which also took place in England, and came to be called the "New Liberalism,"[2] with T. H. Green and Hobhouse as its main architects, in this country soon advocated the abandonment of Jeffersonian democracy and its emphasis on political individualism and the minimal state.

From a sociological and psychological perspective, the changes were enormous: urbanization, an increase in crime, illness, and unemployment, and the maladjustment which changes bring. A number of distinct responses to these problems arose, beginning perhaps with the attitudes of the industrialists—sometimes called the "robber barrons"[3]—who by and large defended Social Darwinism, a term coined by Spencer, who was brought to New York by Andrew Carnegie and soon became a folk hero.[4] For Spencer, laissez-faire capitalism and the society it sustained constituted the highest stage of human evolution. Social Darwinism became popular in this country, mainly through the sociologist William Graham Sumner.[5] Part of this movement included versions of the "Science of Race" and Eugenics (an invention of Darwin's cousin Francis Galton).[6] According to this view, those who were suffering from the new upheaval were weak and deserved whatever they got, and in any case must be controlled if they were not to infect the entire society. The Eugenics movement, which culminated in Nazism, has a fairly long history in this country. Even at its most benign, it paved the way for the development of psychological testing and cradle-to-grave control in the name of adjustment and normalcy, a story that could be, and, in fact, has been, told through Foucaultian eyes.[7] The development of scientific management by Frederick Taylor, as progressive as it might have been at the time, is bound up with this response to industrialism. To be sure, a milder, non-Spencerian form of evolutionism took hold before too long.[8] As we shall see, however, this Durkheimian model of social evolution, which culminates in the structural-functional conservatism of Talcott Parsons and his followers, still puts a premium on the need for "architects of adjustment," equilibrium, and the absence of criticism of the "system" in order to assist in the total control of individuals under the name of human resource management, industrial psychology, the School movement, etc.

Another response to industrialization begins with the Social Gospel movement (whose main architect was Walter Rauschenbusch, Rorty's maternal grandfather).[9] This movement, espoused by members of the American Protestant elite, was connected with their need to retain power and moral leverage in an increasingly secularized society[10]; and is, thereby, connected to the professionalization of the humanities, the social sciences, and the growth of social service professions, and even Hull House.[11] A well-meaning group of individuals, who ranged from very liberal reformers to Christian socialists, spawned a group of activists who attacked laissez-faire capitalism and sought to improve the lot of the poor, especially in urban areas, notably Chicago, where this reformism was connected to the Chicago Sociologists and to Dewey, who was in Chicago at the time.

Many of the early social scientists, e.g., Albion Small and E. A. Ross, were either one-time ministers or the sons of ministers who wanted to wed the social sciences to social reform. (The connections between this movement and populism are complicated by the variety of interpretations placed on the latter by historians and social theorists. The stories about populism range from those of the radical and democratic enemies of the robber barons and the elite to those of the very reactionary, antisemitic, anti-Black defenders of the worst in American nativism and antimodernism.[12]) The American Social Science Association (ASSA), founded in 1865, was designed to institutionalize these goals.[13] In many respects this group mirrored the Verein fur Sozialpolitik in Germany, a roughly contemporary group whose members were also reformist journalists, ministers, and social scientists (but generally more conservative than the ASSA members). The Germans were bent on getting the state involved in economics and in some ways expressed the same ideals as the New Liberals in England. But Max Weber, a more liberal younger member of this group, who were dubbed "the sociologists of the chair," tried to constrain the advocacy and reformism (as well as the conservatism) of the members by articulating his views about science as a vocation and the moral neutrality of the social sciences, that is, by making the social sciences "objective" and "professional," to defuse the legitimacy of the Verein.[14] Weber was not against social reform, but he was against the connection between it and scientific research, which was to be objective and value free.

A similar history attends the ASSA, which was usurped in 1884 by the establishment of the American Economic Association (founded by Richard Ely, a Social Gospel activist who was one of America's leading economists and reformists) and the American Historical Association (founded by, among others, Woodrow Wilson) and, in 1903, by the American Sociological Association and the American Political Science Association. The drift of these developments was to temper the reformism of ASSA members by urging the professionalization and, therefore, (until 1923 when the Social Science Research Council was formed) the fragmentation of the social sciences. This trend, which Mary Furner calls the movement from "advocacy to objectivity"[15] did not, at first, abandon the radical reformist spirit, but sought to underwrite it with "real" social science. This, too, echoed debates in Germany and Austria, namely the so-called *Methodenstreit*, basically a conflict between neoclassical economists (such as Carl Menger) who advocated a positivist, value-free conception of the social sciences, and neo-Kantians and idealists (such as Wilhelm Windleband, and Weber's teacher Herman Rickert), who advocated a historical, value-laden approach to human culture and society.[16] Weber played a key role in adjudicating this debate (the *Weruteilstreit*) too, by synthesizing these two views in his own work and methodological writings.[17] His connection between value relevance and objective research may in fact have convinced the Americans—many of whom studied in Germany—that one could combine advocacy and objectivity. But later events, including the dismissal of E. A. Ross and Ely, two of the foremost advocates of this position (which led Dewey and A. O. Lovejoy to found the American Association of University Professors), seems to have dampened the spirit of reform, by setting its limits to disagreements among scholar-experts about means, not ends. Criticism and reform were constrained by the idea that the system is in order as it is, and requires only a bit of tinkering here and there.[18]

These events were connected to the rise of the modern American university, and the growth of professionalism that attended it.[19] This combination of events is a key to understanding developments in this country. The American penchant for practicality and education gave the development of science, technology, professional training, and scientific management a new impetus in this century. Writers such as Samuel Haber[20] have shown the connections between the notions of efficiency and moral progress (the "gospel of efficiency") that moved the nation in a Durkheimian direction beginning with the Progressives. In moving away from laissez-faire doctrines to corporate doctrines and practices,[21] science and technology were wedded to education and professionalization, which in turn were wedded to the new corporate structures and ideals. As James Gilbert argues in *Designing the Industrial State*, these developments were consistent with socialist, liberal-progressive, and conservative managerial trends[22]—perhaps one source of the ambivalences in modern American liberalism, which, like its European forerunners, manages to combine elements of these modern philosophies in sometimes dangerous (and unforeseen) ways. The concern, indeed obsession, with bigness, efficiency, integration, and organization leads to the growing emphasis on technological management by an elite, to what Herbert Croly in *The Promise of American Life*[23] calls the "New Nationalism," a combination of Jeffersonian (i.e., democratic) ends and Hamiltonian (i.e., nationalist, corporate, and elitist) means. Democracy can only be advanced by an elite corps of scientists, technocrats, educators, social workers, and bureaucrats, using the techniques pioneered by Henry Ford and Frederick Taylor, not by participatory democracy. Indeed, the 1933 slogan of the Chicago Centenary of Progress International Exposition—"Science finds, industry applies, man conforms"[24]—can already be seen in inchoate form before the turn of the century. However, contrary to Croly's (prewar) optimism, the relationship between the new social order and the participatory democracy of Jefferson, Jackson, and populism was hardly expedited by the movement toward a corporate liberal state.[25]

The rise of the American university was surely connected to the problems and needs of the newly modernized society. Until late in the nineteenth century, American colleges were predominantly church related, and were primarily concerned with making their students good Christian gentlemen. (By the same token, American science was fairly primitive until about the time of the Civil War.[26]) The democratic movements prior to industrialization did spawn the Land Grant institutions, which attempted to wed the liberal and practical arts and to make higher education both more practical and more available to the masses than did Harvard or Princeton. Some education leaders tried to reconcile Darwin and religion, while others, as we recently saw, tried to marry Christianity to radical reform, even socialism.

In the meantime, the perceived need for advances in science, technology, engineering, social welfare, health, law, etc., pushed in the direction of research, common and standard curricula, certification requirements (and thus connections among state, business, and education), professional behavior, specialized organization (motivated not the least by the desire for power and prestige), and, finally, a new type of bureaucracy to hold the new universities together. Under the impetus of Harvard's President Elliot, who argued for a public service orientation to science, research, and education, and thanks to the creation of graduate centers at Chicago, Johns Hopkins, and Cornell, and later at Wisconsin, the new university became a forerunner of Clark Kerr's "multiuniversity," where research, classical scholarship, and social service were intermixed and quickly became antagonistic to each other. These conflicts led to the development of a professional corps of university administrators. Further moved by Thorstein Veblen's belief that the modern engineer could move the country forward to a technological utopia by defeating the pecuniary, interest-driven capitalists and providing a model of service to professors and other professionals, and the prospect of making a technological America both democratic and efficient, the newly emerging universities began to play a major role in the "new" America.[27]

The role of professionalization tells a story that is both more complex and less straightforward. It is almost too easy to look around today, to see how much of a "credential society" we have become,[28] and to provide a genealogy of these developments that sees them as uniformly advantageous. But the notions of social control and adjustment, of value-neutral social engineering, or at any rate of social engineering designed to further liberal democracy,[29] are double-edged swords. The connections, at least the intended connections, between professionalization and democracy have been real enough in many cases. But the results have often been otherwise, thanks in part to the well-known phenomenon of the unintended consequences of intentional action. So a few issues about professionalism will be worth closer scrutiny.

At first blush, indeed, there seems to be a conflict between professionalism and democracy, as Nathan Hatch points out in the introduction to his collection on the professions in American history.[30] Professionalism requires a knowledge elite, who have the training and the authority to undertake certain tasks, often indeed, a monopoly sanctioned by the state. But all of the professions at least claim that their primary mission is service to the public, and, in fact, promotion of the common good. This certainly was the motivation for American engineers, who saw themselves as the saviors of democracy as far back as the Jacksonian era.[31] The narrative is more complicated in the case of scientists, who have had a love-hate affair with popular democracy since the 1840s, yet who have always claimed to be serving the public by their research and proposals.[32] It is true that, as Daniel Kevles argues, the National Science Foundation was a victory for elitism, not democracy.[33] But there were times when large groups of scientists, e.g., shortly before World War II and during the Vietnam era, have tried to disengage science from advanced capitalism and the military-industrial complex (and thus, to some extent, the universities).[34] Such movements are relatively rare and have been largely unsuccessful for any extended period. But that, of course, is beside the point. (What may be to the point is the question of whether science is a democracy writ small, as Karl Popper, Polanyi, Merton, and others have argued. I cannot discuss this issue here.) Yet by and large there have been conflicts between expertise, in science and elsewhere, and participatory democracy. The case for a tension is clearer in some professions, e.g., the behavioral and policy sciences, not to mention law and medicine. In any event, it seems clear that, generally speaking, the process of professionalization split the new professionals from the majority, and decreased the incentives for democratic participation, much less criticism or reform.

It is necessary to mention a number of features of the "New Nationalism/Freedom," which I have been calling "corporate liberalism": e.g., its growing emphasis on a class of experts to provide social control and adjustment, combined with its growing distrust of the masses (especially after World War I); its dislike for politics; and its almost Panglossian optimism about the benefits of a scientific society. These tendencies reinforced the growing pessimism about popular democracy. Whether this tension was intended or not, whether advocates of the New Liberalism were in favor of democracy or not, whether they believed in elitism for democracy or not, whether they wanted to combine "objectivity"—with or without Weberian value neutrality—with advocacy and reform, and how this impinged on beliefs about how much and what kind of democracy was feasible in the newly industrialized society are issues that are, and will likely remain, essentially contestable. In any case, capitalism was attacked only in so far as advocates of the New Liberalism believed laissez-faire did not promote the "search for order." But some form of capitalism was considered desirable and necessary. The idea of "industrial democracy" only promotes more worker participation within an industrial capitalist system that would be guided by experts in industrial psychology and Taylorism—hardly a harbinger of participatory democracy.

The significance of the Progressive Movement is still being debated.[35] On the view I am defending, the Progressives, by whom I mean Croly, Lippmann, Woodrow Wilson, Charles Beard, and a host of other later liberal intellectuals and activists (including, some would argue, Franklin Delano Roosevelt),[36] wanted to serve the forces of the New Liberalism, and of American democracy, by using knowledge, especially science, to reorganize society, and to solve many social and political problems. This attitude is not particularly controversial, so far as it goes. The obvious questions are: How far was it meant to go? How far does it go? and What are its effects on democratic practice?

To begin with, especially after World War I (the Progressives' endorsement of American involvement in this war is a chapter all its own),[37] the Progressives lost faith in the masses, and thus in democracy. But even before then, the reform spirit of these writers was fused with an elitist mentality, as seen in the writings of Lippmann and Croly,[38] and the noblesse-oblige attitudes of Wilson, who can be seen as embodying Weber's notion of a strong charismatic leader, thus giving the American presidency its impetus toward the Caesarism that Weber admired.[39] Lippmann and Croly in particular pushed for the idea of a plutocratic educated elite to control things for the common democratic good. But it was democracy in the minimal sense that we saw in Mill, Weber, and Durkheim. The uneducated masses are incapable of self-rule. Indeed, for Lippmann the public is a "phantom"; and popular opinions must be cultivated by the ruling elite.[40]

Combined in these writers, and in politicians such as Theodore Roosevelt and Woodrow Wilson, were the forces that sprung out of Frederick Taylor's scientific management movement. The ideas of "efficiency and uplift" sustained the impetus toward a corporate state, which was canonized by Veblen's call for a technocracy governed by reformist engineers and professionals who emulated them. Veblen and Taylor wished to put these social engineers in the service of the common good, and not directly in the service of the growing corporate capitalism. But their hopes were not to be borne out, despite the best intentions.[41]

In view of the fact that Lippmann and Croly founded and edited the *New Republic*[42] and that progressivism has had an influence second to none on subsequent American liberals[43] who often tried to emulate and glorify them, it is important to raise the question of whether, at the "crossroads of liberalism," American democracy got run over.

To be sure, there were Progressives such as Beard and Bentley, who were really quite radical in their concern for popular democracy, and who combined the reformist fervor of Croly and Lippmann with a conception of the social sciences that tried to harmonize objectivity and advocacy in the interests of an enlarged democracy. Dewey had more in common with them than with Progressives such as Croly and Lippmann. Indeed, Dewey's *Public and Its Problems* is a direct attack on Lippmann's antidemocratic *Public Opinion* and *The Phantom Public*.[44] Bentley, Beard, and Dewey managed to avoid the scientism of Croly, Lippmann, and Durkheim and the romantic liberalism, including its cleavage between advocacy and objectivity, of Weber.

The development of the professionalized social and behavioral sciences, whose mottoes were "social control"[45] and "adjustment,"[46] can serve to illustrate some of the difficulties and Janus-faced aspects of the Progressive movement.

As noted already, the early social scientists in the ASSA were reformists, who advocated health care, education, improved sanitary conditions, and the like for the urban poor. The first generation of professionals, Albion Small, Lester

Ward, E. A. Ross, Richard Ely, furthered these goals, and tried to study social conditions more scientifically, so as to take measures to prevent and control the problems, while helping people adjust to the new order.

World War I provided an opportunity for scientists to help the war effort, and, not incidentally, to gain more power and prestige with the federal government, which up to that point had not funded scientific research that was not directly practical. This policy caused scientists and engineers to get involved with corporations and the newly created "philanthropic" foundations of Andrew Carnegie and John Rockefeller. (The corporations saw scientists as providing the tools to make corporations more competitive in the international arena.) This in turn dampened any criticism of corporate capitalism, while moving scientists and engineers further away from democratic aspirations or control.

All the while, the scientific community pressed for more recognition and funding by the federal government. World War I (as well as World War II) provided them with the opportunity. One element in the activity of scientists during World War I was the Psychological Mental Testing movement that was used to examine soldiers, and that paved the way for the whole mental-testing movement, for industrial psychology, for school counseling, and for various efforts in the direction of common schooling and child rearing. The assumption was that people needed to become adjusted from birth in order to become more efficient and productive workers in the new corporate order.[47] The growth of industrial psychology[48] and various applied branches of psychology (counseling, etc.) can be seen as carrying on the tradition of Social Darwinism, albeit in its allegedly more benign form. Urbanization spawned Behaviorism and the Psychological Corporation, a group that worked for industry to test workers and help them adjust, i.e., become more productive and efficient.[49] It is even arguable that these developments were outgrowths of the Eugenics movement.[50]

In the social sciences, beginning with the establishment of the Social Science Research Council in 1923, efforts were made to make sociology and political science more "objective." Founded by Charles E. Merriam, it was an effort to unify the social sciences for purposes of doing empirical and statistical research for greater social control. Merriam and the Chicago Sociologist William Ogburn (the inventor of the [Durkheimian] notion of "cultural lag," which was used to justify social control to adjust America to new developments in science and technology) worked with Herbert Hoover, the embodiment of the Veblen-Taylor engineer as savior model, and produced a two-volume study called *Recent Social Trends in the United States* in 1933, with a preface by former President Hoover.[51] The stage was set for national planning, the administrative and policy sciences, and the managerial revolution.

Merriam, a major figure in American political science and a key player in these developments,[52] effectively incorporated Durkheim's notion of a science of politics with Weber's vocation for politics, and thus combined advocacy and reform with objectivity. But the fact remains that the Carnegie Foundation funded research on behavioral approaches to the social sciences to improve ways of "adjusting" workers to make them more productive,[53] and that, at least for a time, Merriam and his followers endorsed Durkheim's view of democracy as an organizational framework controlled by an elite class of experts, with a minimum of popular sovereignty. Saint-Simon had finally arrived in America.[54]

Harold Lasswell, Merriam's brightest student, became convinced that problems of politics required the introduction of Freudian ideas and techniques to forward the goals of social control and integration, adjustment and accommodation. In his book *Psychopathology and Politics*,[55] he anticipates American Ego Psychology by arguing that anybody who cannot or will not adjust to the system, let alone complains about it, is neurotic and must be dealt with accordingly. (In later years Lasswell becomes a proponent of Weberian political realism and power politics.[56]) "Normality" is defined in terms of accommodation to a system that is all right as it is, and which is always in a process of dynamic equilibrium—an idea first put forward by Durkheim in *Suicide* and *The Rules of Sociological Method*, where "the normal" and "the pathological" are characterized in functionalist terms.[57]

To be sure, members of the Chicago School, which included George Herbert Mead and Dewey,[58] tried to introduce less positivistic, more hermeneutical approaches to social science and human interaction (e.g., Mead's "symbolic interactionism") and thus had a different idea of what adjustment, accommodation, and control meant.[59] But Mead's theory of social behaviorism, an attempt (like Weber's) to synthesize positivism and idealism, while it seemed to be more benign than, say Merriam's approach, still defined "normality" in terms of adjustment and accommodation. True, Mead, like Dewey, rejected scientism, and favored human interaction and dialogue as a vehicle for social, cultural, and political analysis and action. And the Chicago School in general was involved in progressive social reform and a critique of capitalism. So the ideals of accommodation, adjustment, integration, and social harmony may also be double-edged swords, that can either sustain or undermine popular democracy.

These efforts by the Chicago School were also accompanied by activities designed to clean up corrupt government and politicians, institute a professionalized civil service, make the law more responsive to social needs, and so on. But, as sane as this outlook was and is, Dewey's remark that the best cure for the faults of democracy is more democracy was evidently not thought to be a viable option by the Progressives and their followers in the social and behavioral sciences.

Part of the picture is that the United States is in some ways basically conservative, never having gone through the social history that spawned radical movements in Europe.[60] This is the germ of truth in Louis Hartz's work on liberalism in America. It therefore follows that our system is basically in order, that, as Rorty also believes, America has always been dominated by a liberal consensus, so that political radicalism is both unnecessary and un-American. Our disagreements are only about means, not ends. This, combined with the way the newly professionalized, university-trained experts became tamer and less reformist, made it natural to assume that a genuine social science, infused with this liberal ideology, would move the country further and further to the realization of our common ideals and goals. *Recent Social Trends* maintained that national planning by a managerial elite, controlled by a strong leader, would be a natural development toward greater democracy. Aside from the fact that this vision now seems overly naive and optimistic, one gets the feeling that the experts had a very minimal vision of what constitutes the good life or the common good. Rorty's onetime (tongue-in-cheek) "bluff philistinism," the idea that liberal America was the pinnacle of world history because we have better plumbing than anybody else, justified this impoverished technological utopian vision of where America then stood.

The not unrelated notion that experts are morally superior human beings, who can only make empirical errors in calculation (which leads to the idea that the only acceptable criticisms of society by academics are about matters revolving around empirical disagreements by experts)[61] is supported either by some naturalistic ethics (such as Mill's or Durkheim's) or by Weber's view that the scholar and the politician have the moral virtues of affirmation, responsibility, and integrity. In addition, Weber's decisionistic views about values was misinterpreted by the positivists and behavioralists to suggest that knowledge is the only thing that matters, and that values can be made more intelligent and responsible, if not more objective, as science teaches us more about ourselves and the world. At the very least—and here is where people like Lasswell come in—scientific knowledge will provide the scientists, policy advisors, and leaders with the ability to change people's minds and actions through social control and adjustment techniques. After all, if our only problems are instrumental, not ideological, people who are maladjusted will be immoral and can only by made normal, and therefore acceptable, by being taught how to adjust to a system that can only further everybody's good if properly adjusted. As we have been recently told by Samuel Huntington and others, our country will be better off without too much democracy.[62] This is the gist of the civic culture idea of politics, behavioralism, interest group liberalism, and the end-of-ideology thesis, all of which are discussed in the next chapter.

America from the 1920s to the present is largely the story, for better or for worse, of this technocratic, managerial elite mentality. The antidemocratic but also anticapitalist technocracy movement of the 1930s (rejected by Dewey)[63]; the involvement of physicists and psychologists in two world wars; the rise of the therapeutic state; the managerial revolution; the increasing partnerships among government, corporations, and universities; the growing disparity between the expert and the majority of common folk; the growing dominance of positivism in research and the applied and policy sciences; the involvement of social scientists in the National Science Foundation and allied government agencies (including the Central Intelligence Agency)—instigated by Parsons during the cold war to allow American social scientists to do their part as cold war liberals)[64]; the general refusal of research scientists to be subject to political control by the people or their elected president[65]; and the emphasis on the end of ideology, complacency, conformity, and optimism in the face of genuine social and economic problems have all conspired to justify the technocrats' vision of what modern American democracy should be.

To assume that all of our problems are amenable to objective, morally neutral piecemeal social engineering is to take Rorty's bluff philistinism only too seriously. After the Persian Gulf War, *Time* magazine had an article that proclaimed that our technological victory over Iraq proved that our educational system and everything else in our society is really working just fine, thank you. Only a few chronic malcontents[66] think otherwise; but these negative, ideological types can be dismissed. This rhetoric, used against the social and cultural critics of the 1930s, 1950s and 1960s, has recently been attacked by Christopher Norris, in a book about neopragmatism and the war in the Persian Gulf.[67]

The obvious questions this bottom-line mentality raises are: What are the costs for democracy that we have paid for our success in technology and material comfort? Are "ideology" and nontechnological values really irrelevant to today's world, or to what used to be called "the good life" and "the commonweal"? Is Dewey's view that democracy is a way of life, where human interaction is an end as well as a means, an outmoded idea now that bluff philistinism has triumphed in our society? What, if anything, can we learn from the radicals of the 1930s and the 1960s, perhaps even from their populist and Wobblie forerunners?

We can perhaps begin to get our bearings here by considering another outgrowth of the progressive tradition, one which has some continuity with the first generation of reformers we looked at before. I have in mind Randolph Bourne, Charles Beard, Arthur Bentley, and, above all, John Dewey.

Bourne, a student of Dewey and a genuine American radical who was not a Marxist (along with Veblen and C. Wright Mills, and of course, Dewey, one of the very few to be in this class) had very serious reservations about American involvement in World War I, and, in particular, the support of the war by Dewey, *The New Republic*, liberals, and pragmatists in general. (Van Wick Brooks and Lewis Mumford, Progressives, but never as committed to pragmatism, concurred with Bourne, as did, incidentally, Walter Rauschenbusch.[68]) Bourne[69] accused Dewey of letting pragmatism become a philosophy of acquiescence, a charge echoed by Mumford,[70] and later by leftist critiques of Dewey, that saw in his philosophy a defense of politics as engineering and adjustment.[71]

While Bourne did remain faithful to the radical elements in Dewey's pragmatism, and while Dewey came to regret his endorsement of U.S. involvement in World War I and was not exactly thrilled with our involvement in World War II (nor with many aspects of the New Deal), it is arguable that these general criticisms of Dewey are misplaced.[72]

In their book, *Disenchanted Realists: Political Science and the American Crisis, 1884–1984*,[73] S. Seidelman and R. Harpham distinguish the progressivism of Beard, Bentley, and (to a lesser extent) Merriam, from that of Croly, Lippmann, and others. Bentley, who was later to collaborate with Dewey on *The Knower and the Known*,[74] and had a long correspondence with him, is, according to Seidelman and Harpham, "the best representative of a tendency to link a radical liberal social science with an equalitarian politics."[75] For Bentley, an objective social science is needed to serve reform forces, by making the American public aware of what is really going on as a preface to radical reform from the bottom up. In this way, he combined Weber's idea of politics as a moral vocation with Durkheim's view of politics as a science.[76]

A similar program is associated with the work of Charles Beard, at least until the liberal disillusionment (that even affected Croly) after World War I.[77] Beard, as a muckraker, tried to marry populism and progressivism, and assumed the American public would rise up and engage in reformist activity upon learning all about the seedy side of democratic America. Again, social science was used to serve radical democracy.[78] For Merriam, Weber's iron cage was rather "a perfect union of democracy and bureaucracy"[79]; so he was more sanguine than Beard and Bentley about the Durkheimian imperative. Yet, on occasion, he also believed that the American public was capable of accepting the truth and participating in the "new politics" he advocated, which in his later years was a version of democracy very close to Dewey's.

During the 1930s, while many erstwhile liberals (including Stuart Chase and George Soule[80]) were advocating some version of the Technocracy movement—a series of utopian schemes for eliminating capitalism and placing a Saint Simonean ruling elite of scientists and engineers in power—a number of more radical Progressives, including Edmund Wilson and Matthew Josephson, debated Progressive liberals who were less radical, such as Soule, Kenneth Burke, and Benjamin Ginzburg, on the future of Progressive liberalism in the pages of *The New Republic*.[81] So the radical liberal wing of the Progressive tradition was still active in the 1930s, along with the Marxists and other cultural critics of capitalist America, including the Trotskyists.

As for Dewey, he was quite clearly more radical than many of his detractors *and* defenders want to admit. Consider the following remarks from *Liberalism and Social Action*.[82]

> [T]here is no opposition in principle between liberalism as social philosophy and radicalism in action, if by radicalism is signified the adoption of policies that bring about drastic instead of piecemeal social changes. It is all a question of what kind of procedures the intelligent study of changing conditions discloses. These changes have been so tremendous in the last century, yes, in the last forty years, that it looks to me as if radical methods were now necessary. But all that the argument here requires is recognition of the fact that there is nothing in the nature of liberalism that makes it a milk-water doctrine, committed to compromise and minor "reforms." It is worth noting that the earlier liberals were regarded in their day as subversive radicals.[83]

Dewey closes the chapter on the future of liberalism with these words: "Any liberalism that does not make full cultural freedom supreme and that does not see the relation between it and genuine industrial freedom as a way of life is degenerate and delusive liberalism."[84] That is, capitalism and laissez-faire individualism, and therewith Millian liberalism, have to be set aside for a "renascent liberalism." As writers such as James Campbell[85] and Alphonse D'Amico have shown,[86] Dewey's general politics and specific proposals were quite radical, and were associated with a call for a new public philosophy. Moreover, it has been convincingly argued that Dewey, while often vague and ambivalent about politics, never pushed for the kind of political practices that were associated with the Durkheimian mentality of other Progressives such as Lippmann, Croly, Merriam, and Lasswell.[87]

I believe that Dewey tried to avoid the scientific politics of these writers, the romantic privacy and political defeatism of Weber, and wanted a genuine democracy, which he calls "the Great Community" in *The Public and Its Problems*.[88] He never rejected science and its social relevance, nor expertise as such, but these factors were always to be harnessed to public dialogue and action under the auspices of social intelligence and communication.

These democratic loyalties come out clearly in the following passages:

> A class of experts is inevitably so removed from common interests as to become a class with private interests and private knowledge, which in social matters is not knowledge at all. . . . No government by experts in which the masses do not have the chance to inform the experts as to their needs can be anything but an oligarchy managed in the interests of the few. And the enlightenment [of the masses] must proceed in ways which force the administrative specialists to take account of the needs. The world has suffered more from leaders and authorities than from the masses.
>
> The essential need, . . . is the improvement of the methods and conditions of debate, discussion and persuasion. That is *the* problem of the public . . . this improvement depends essentially upon freeing and perfecting the processes of inquiry and of dissemination of their conclusions. Inquiry, indeed, is a work which devolves upon experts. But their existence is not shown in framing and executing policies, but in discovering and making known the facts upon which the former depend. They are technical experts in the sense that scientific investigators and artists manifest *expertise*. It is not necessary that the many should have the knowledge and skill to carry on the needed investigations; what is required is that they have the ability to judge of the bearing of the knowledge supplied by others upon common concerns.[89]

There are many reasons why Dewey has been misunderstood, and why his project failed.[90] But it still has its potential, as does Habermas's similar project.[91] It is needed today more than at any time in memory, although it must be modified in certain ways, as I indicate in chapter 6.

A number of reasons might be offered for why Dewey's project failed. His refusal to take Marxism more seriously; his unwillingness to criticize all forms of capitalism; perhaps a certain kind of political naiveté; and the fear that he was too much of a positivist and technocrat have all been suggested, as have, indeed, their opposites. Perhaps Dewey's version of liberalism, while compatible with progressive democracy and a synthesis of romanticism and social engineering, does not avoid the dilemma of Millian and romantic liberalism, although I think he came close to succeeding, while avoiding the excesses of Weber's romanticism and Durkheim's scientism and elitism. As Joseph Featherstone puts it: "Dewey attempted to harness technology, science and cultural standards to communal, Populist and egalitarian ends, instead of private, elite interests. As a reformer, . . . he often found himself [in] opposition to the American reform tradition, which has been for the most part profoundly elitist. His was a typically complex utopian balancing act, and it did not always work. Yet a marriage of cultural standards and Populism was consistently his aim."[92] This strikes me as right, which puts Dewey one major step ahead of Kant, Mill, Weber, and Durkheim, in so far as he rejects the excesses of elitism, romanticism, and scientism, and places his faith in democracy as a way of life, with its roots in social intelligence and citizen participation. If anybody has the last word, "at the level of theory," it should be Dewey. *Our* problem is how to revitalize this vision for today and tomorrow.

In any event, I think that events, more than Dewey's philosophical and political shortcomings, explain the failure of his program: World War II and its aftermath; the cold war and McCarthyism; the cold war liberalism of onetime radicals and even Deweyites, such as Sidney Hook, James Rorty, and Daniel Bell; the managerial revolution and its successor, the end-of-ideology thesis; and the dominance of positivism and behavioralism in academics and the policy sciences. I want to turn to these and other phenomena, such as interest group liberalism and the controversies about the "power elite" in the next chapter, both to contrast Dewey's program with them, and to assess these recent developments, which in some important respects mark a shift from corporate to Weberian liberalism.

NOTES

1. Robert Wiebe, *The Search for Order: 1877–1920* (New York: Hill and Wang, 1967).

2. See Michael Freeden, *The New Liberalism* (New York: Oxford University Press); James T. Kloppenberg, *Uncertain Victory* (New York: Oxford University Press, 1988). Dewey and Royce were defenders of this New Liberalism, which combined Hegelian and Millian themes; see, e.g., John Dewey, "The Ethics of Democracy" in Dewey, *The Early Works*, vol. 1, 1882–1898 (Carbondale: Southern Illinois University, 1969), 227–49; and John Dewey, *Lectures on Psychological and Political Ethics: 1898*, ed. Donald F. Koch (New York: Hafner, 1976).

3. See Alfred D. Chandler, *The Visible Hand* (Cambridge: Harvard University Press, 1977).

4. On Spencer in New York, see Richard Hofstadter, *Social Darwinism in American Thought* (Boston: Beacon, 1955), 45ff., and Paul F. Boller, Jr., *American Thought in Transition: The Impact of Evolutionary Naturalism, 1865–1900* (Chicago: Rand McNally, 1969), 54ff.

5. Hofstadter, op. cit.; and Boller, op. cit.

6. Hamilton Cravens, *The Triumph of Evolution* (Baltimore: Johns Hopkins University Press, 1988); Daniel Kevles, *In the Name of Eugenics* (Berkeley: University of California Press, 1985).

7. David Rothman, *The Discovery of the Asylum* (Boston: Little Brown, 1971); idem, *Conscience and Convenience* (Boston: Little Brown, 1980); M. J. Wiener, ed. *Humanitarianism or Control?* (Houston: Rice University Press, 1981); Donald Napoli, *Architects of Adjustment* (Port Washington, NY: Kennikat Press, 1981); Michael Sokal, ed., *Psychological Testing in American Society: 1890–1930* (New Brunswick: Rutgers University Press, 1987); A. R. Buss, ed., *Psychology in Social Context* (New York: Irvington, 1979); Matthew Hale, *Human Science and Social Order* (Philadelphia: Temple University Press, 1980); Paul Boyer, *Urban Masses and Moral Order in America* (Cambridge: Harvard University Press, 1978); Donald K. Pickering, *Eugenics and the Progressives* (Nashville: Vanderbilt University Press, 1968); Mitchell G. Ash and William R. Woodward, eds., *Psychology in Twentieth Century Thought and Society* (New York: Cambridge University Press, 1988); Michael Sokal, "Origins of the Psychological Corporation," *Journal of the History of the Behavioral Sciences* 16 (1981): 54–67; David Bakan, "Behaviorism and American Urbanization," *Journal of the History of the Behavioral Sciences* 2 (1966); John C. Burnham, "On the Origins of Behaviorism," *Journal of the History of the Behavioral Sciences* 3 (1968): 143–51; Thomas M. Camfield, "The

Professionalization of American Psychology, 1870–1917," *Journal of the History of the Behavioral Sciences* 8 (January 1973); John M. O'Donnell, *The Origins of Behaviorism* (New York: New York University Press, 1985).

8. Cravens, op. cit.; William Fine, *Progressive Evolutionism and American Sociology: 1890–1920* (Ann Arbor: UMI Research Press, 1975); Napoli, *Architects of Adjustment*, op. cit.; Cynthia Eagle Russett, *The Concept of Equilibrium in American Thought* (New Haven: Yale University Press, 1966).

9. See David W. Noble, *The Paradox of Progressive Thought* (Minneapolis: University of Minnesota Press, 1958); Donald B. Meyer, *The Protestant Search for Political Realism* (Berkeley: University of California Press, 1960); and Christopher Lasch, *The True and Only Heaven* (New York: Norton, 1991). According to Lasch, Rauschenbusch combined theological conservatism—he believed in original sin—and political radicalism and was not against political violence, which he viewed in nonmoral terms, 379ff., esp. 380 note. David W. Noble makes some interesting observations about Rauschenbusch, as does Robert T. Handy. Noble claims that Rauschenbusch believed that once evil was recognized through education, our basically healthy society would be fine; see David Noble, *The Progressive Mind: 1890–1917* (Chicago: Rand McNally, 1979), 76. In his book *The Social Gospel in America: 1870–1920* (New York: Oxford University Press, 1966), Handy says this about Rauschenbusch: "His method was to begin with the descriptive and the comparative, . . . and then . . . move on to the prescriptive . . . both as a social prophet and as a herald of the coming kingdom. In calling for concrete action, Rauschenbusch drew heavily on the progressive, reformist, and socialistic thinking of his time. He was willing to be labeled a Christian socialist; but his socialism was evolutionary, non-doctrinaire, and in fact non-political. Distrusting the materialistic philosophy and the moral laxity of the movement, he never became a party member."

10. Richard A. Hofstadter, *The Age of Reform* (New York: Vintage, 1955) and books on the Social Gospel movement, cited above.

11. Laurence Veysey, "The Plural Organized Worlds of the Humanities," in *The Organization of Knowledge in Modern America, 1860–1920*, ed. A. Oleson and J. Voss (Baltimore: Johns Hopkins University Press, 1979), 51–106; and Bruce Kuklick, "The Emergence of the Humanities," *South Atlantic Quarterly* 89 (Winter 1990): 195–206. See also Arthur Vidich and Sanford M. Lyman, *American Sociology* (New Haven: Yale University Press, 1985); H. Schwedinger and J. Schwedinger, *Sociologists of the Chair* (New York: Basic Books, 1974); Joel Spring, *Education and the Rise of the Corporate State* (Boston: Beacon Press, 1972); Clyde W. Barrow, *Universities and the Capitalist State* (Madison: University of Wisconsin Press, 1990); Roy Lubove, *The Professional Altruist* (Cambridge: Harvard University Press, 1966); Dennis Smith, *The Chicago School: A Liberal Critique of Capitalism* (New York: St. Martin's Press, 1988); Lawrence A. Cremin, *The Transformation of the School* (New York: Vintage, 1961); see Hofstadter, op. cit., and idem, *Anti-Intellectualism in American Life* (New York: Vintage, 1962); Lawrence Goodwyn, *Democratic Promise* (New York: Oxford University Press, 1976).

12. Dorothy Ross, "The Development of the Social Sciences," in Oleson and Voss, op. cit., 107–39; and idem, *Origins of American Social Science* (New York: Cambridge University Press, 1991); Vidich and Lyman, op. cit., Schwedinger and Schwedinger, op. cit.; Mary Furner, *From Advocacy and Objectivity* (Lexington: University of Kentucky Press, 1975); Thomas L. Haskell, *The Emergence of Professional Social Science* (Urbana: University of Illinois Press, 1977); and idem, ed., *The Authority of Experts* (Bloomington: Indiana University Press, 1984); Luther Lee Bernard and Jesse Bernard, *Origins of American Sociology* (New York:

Crowell, 1943); Stephen Turner and Jonathan Turner, *The Impossible Science: An Institutional Analysis of American Sociology* (Newbury Park, CA: Sage, 1990); Roscoe C. Hinkle and Gissela Hinkle, *The Development of Modern Sociology* (New York: Random House, 1954); Geoffrey Hawthorn, *Enlightenment and Despair* (New York: Cambridge University Press, 1976); Don Martindale, *The Scope of Social Theory*, vol. 1 (Boston: Cap and Gown Press, 1984); Anthony Oberschall, "The Institutionalization of American Sociology" in *The Establishment of Empirical Sociology*, ed. A. Oberschall (New York: Harper, 1972), 187–252; Roger C. Bannister, *Sociology and Scientism* (Chapel Hill: University of North Carolina Press, 1983); Hamilton Cravens, "History of the Social Sciences" in *Historical Writing on American Science*, ed. M. Kohlstedt and M. Rossiter (Baltimore: Johns Hopkins University Press, 1986), 183–207.

13. On the *Verein*, see W. Mommsen, ed., *Max Weber and His Contemporaries*, (London: Unwin, 1987); Kloppenberg, op. cit.; D. Ross, op. cit.; and Furner, op. cit.; Reinhard Bendix and Guenther Roth, ed., *Scholarship and Partisanship: Essays on Max Weber*, (Berkeley: University of California Press, 1971).

14. Furner, op. cit.; Haskell, op. cit.; Ross, op. cit.; and *The Authority of Experts*, op. cit.

15. Furner, 323; cf. Ross in Oleson, op. cit.

16. See Christopher Bryant, *Positivism in Social Theory and Research* (New York: St. Martins, 1984).

17. Ibid.

18. See Furner, op. cit.; and Ross in Oleson, op. cit.

19. David F. Noble, *America by Design* (New York: Knopf, 1977); Nathan Hatch, ed., *The Professions in American History* (Baltimore: Johns Hopkins University Press, 1987); Margali Sarfatti Larson, *The Rise of Professionalism* (Berkeley: University of California Press, 1977); Burton Bledstein, *The Culture of Professionalism* (New York: Norton, 1976); Randall Collins, *The Credential Society* (New York: Academic Press, 1979); Charles Derber, William A. Schwartz, and Yale Magrass, *Power in the Highest Degree* (New York: Oxford University Press, 1990); Wiebe, op. cit.

20. Samuel Haber, *Efficiency and Uplift: Scientific Management in the Progressive Era, 1890–1920* (Chicago: University of Chicago Press, 1964); Samuel Hays, *Conservation and the Gospel of Efficiency* (Cambridge: Harvard University Press, 1959); Thomas Hughes, *American Genesis* (New York: Viking, 1989).

21. Sidney Fine, *Laissez Faire and the General Welfare State* (Ann Arbor: University of Michigan Press, 1967); James Weinstein, *The Corporate Ideal in the Liberal State* (Boston: Beacon Press, 1972), R. Jeffrey Lustig, *Corporate Liberalism* (Berkeley: University of California Press, 1984).

22. David F. Noble, op. cit., Larson, op. cit.; Bledstein, op. cit.; James Gilbert, *Designing the Industrial State* (New York: Quadrangle, 1972).

23. Herbert Croly, *The Promise of American Life* (New York: Macmillan, 1907); and idem, *Progressive Democracy* (New York: Macmillan, 1914); Charles Forcey, *The Crossroads of Liberalism* (New York: Oxford University Press, 1961).

24. Merritt Roe Smith, "Technology, Industry, and the Idea of Progress," in *Responsible Technology: Impact of Technology on Society*, ed. Kevin B. Byrne, Nobel Lectures, no. 21 (New York: Harper, 1986), 1.

25. Wendell Berry, *The Unsettling of American Agriculture* (San Francisco: Sierra Club, 1977); Daniel Boorstein, *The Lost World of Thomas Jefferson* (Boston: Beacon, 1948); and idem, *The Republic of Technology* (New York: Harper, 1978); cf. *America by Design*, op. cit.

26. Robert V. Bruce, *The Launching of Modern American Science* (Ithaca: Cornell University Press, 1987); Charles E. Rosenberg, *No Other Gods* (Baltimore: Johns

Hopkins University Press, 1976); George Daniels, *Science in American Society* (New York: Knopf, 1971).

27. Laurence Veysey, *The Emergence of the American University* (Chicago: University of Chicago Press, 1967); on Veblen, see Donald Stabile, *Prophets of Order* (Boston: South End Press, 1984); and David Riesman, *Thorstein Veblen* (New York: Scribner's, 1953). See also Edwin Layton, *The Revolt of the Engineers* (Baltimore: Johns Hopkins University Press, 1967); Bruce Sinclair in Hatch, op. cit.

On the idea of technological utopia and the marriage of the poet and the engineer see Harvey Segal, *Technological Utopianism in American Culture* (Chicago: University of Chicago Press, 1985); and Cecelia Tichi, *Shifting Gears* (Chapel Hill: University of North Carolina Press, 1987). Technocracy and literary criticism went their own ways in the 1930s, when engineers got hooked into business and literary types became involved in various counterculture movements, including Marxism. See Daniel Aaron, *Writers on the Left* (New York: Harcourt, 1961); and James Gilbert, *Writers and Partisans* (New York: Wiley, 1968).

28. Randall Collins, op. cit.; and *Power in the Highest Degree*, op. cit.

29. Sidney Kaplan, "Social Engineers as Saviors: The Effects of World War I on Some American Liberals," *Journal of the History of Ideas* 16 (1956): 347–69; Morris Janowitz, *The Last Half Century* (Chicago: University of Chicago Press, 1978); Dusky Lee Smith, "Sociology and the Rise of Corporate Liberalism," *Science and Society* 38 (1974): 401–18; Charles Page, *Class and American Sociology* (New York: Dial, 1940).

30. Nathan Hatch, op. cit.

31. Layton, op. cit.; Sinclair in Hatch, op. cit.; Segal, op. cit.

32. Daniel Kevles in Hatch, op. cit.

33. Daniel Kevles, *The Physicists* (Cambridge: Harvard University Press, 1971).

34. Peter J. Kuznick, *Beyond the Laboratory* (Chicago: University of Chicago Press, 1984); David Dickson, *The New Science of Politics* (Chicago: University of Chicago Press, 1990).

35. John Buenker, John Burnham and Robert Crunden, *Progressivism* (Boston: Schenkman, 1977); Robert Crunden, *Ministers of Reform* (New York: Basic Books, 1982); Arthur Ekrich, *Progressivism in America* (New York: New Viewpoints, 1974); Lasch, op. cit.

36. For good discussions, see Peter Novick, *The Objectivity Question* (New York: Cambridge University Press, 1989); Richard A. Hofstadter, *The Progressive Historians* (New York: Vintage, 1968); David Noble, *The End of American History* (Minneapolis: University of Minnesota Press, 1985).

37. Carol S. Gruber, *Mars and Minerva: World War I and the Uses of Higher Learning in America* (Baton Rouge: Louisiana State University Press, 1975); Stuart I. Rochester, *American Liberal Disillusionment in the Wake of World War I* (College Park: Pennsylvania State University Press, 1971); Casey Nelson Blake, *Beloved Community* (Chapel Hill: University of North Carolina Press, 1990); Daniel Levine, "Randolph Bourne, John Dewey and the Legacy of Liberalism," *Antioch Review* 28 (Summer 1969): 234–44. For a collection of Bourne's essays, see *Radical Will*, ed. Olaf Hanson (New York: Urizon, 1977).

38. Walter Lippmann, *Drift and Mastery* (New York: Holt, 1914); idem, *A Preface to Politics* (Boston: Mitchell Kennerley, 1914); idem, *The Phantom Public* (Boston: Harcourt, 1925), *Public Opinion* (New York: Macmillan, 1922); *The Good Society* (Boston: Little Brown, 1937), and Croly, op. cit.

39. See Robert Eden, op. cit., ch. 1; see also John Chamberlain, *Farewell to Reform* (London: Liveright, 1932); and Martin Sklar, "Woodrow Wilson and the

Political Economy of Modern U.S. Liberalism," in *A New History of Leviathan*, ed. R. Radosh and M. Rothbard (New York: Dutton, 1972).

40. See works by Lippmann cited in note 38 above.

41. James Weinstein, *The Corporate Ideal in the Liberal State* (Boston: Beacon Press), argues that the Progressives in effect, if not intent, strengthen the corporations and thus the corporate state.

42. David Seidelman, *The New Republic* (Westport, CT: Praeger, 1986).

43. See also Forcey, *Crossroads of Liberalism*, op. cit.

44. John Dewey, *The Public and Its Problems* (New York: Holt, 1927); see Lasch, op. cit., 363ff.

45. E. A. Ross, *Social Control* (1901; reprint, Boston: Beacon, 1959); Julius Weinberg, *Edward Alsworth Ross and the Sociology of Progressivism* (Madison: University of Wisconsin Press, 1972); Janowitz, op. cit.; Bannister, op. cit.; and Joseph S. Roucek, ed., *Social Control for the 1980s: A Handbook for Order in a Democratic Society* (Westport, CT: Greenwood, 1987). Note the revealing subtitle!

46. *Architects of Adjustment*, op. cit.

47. Ronald Tobey, *The American Ideology of National Science: 1919–1930* (Pittsburgh: University of Pittsburgh Press, 1971); Kevles, op. cit.

48. *Architects of Adjustment*, op. cit.; *Psychological Testing and American Society*, op. cit.

49. Loren Baritz, *Servants of Power* (New York: Wiley, 1969); *Human Science and Social Order*, op. cit.; Gene M. Lyons, *The Uneasy Partnership* (New York: Russell Sage, 1969); Matthew Hale, *Human Science and Social Order* (Philadelphia: Temple University Press, 1980).

50. Bakan, op. cit.; Camfield, op. cit.; *Psychological Testing and American Society*, op. cit.; *Eugenics and the Progressives*, op. cit.; and Garland E. Allen, "The Role of Experts in Scientific Controversy," in *Scientific Controversies*, ed. Tristam Engelhardt and Arthur L. Caplan (New York: Cambridge University Press, 1987), 169–202; see also, David M. Kennedy, "The Progressive Era: An Overview," *Historian* 37 (1975): 453–68.

51. Charles Merriam and W. Ogburn, *Recent Social Trends in the United States*, 2 vols. (New York: McGraw Hill, 1933).

52. Barry Karl, *Charles Merriam and the Study of Politics* (Chicago: University of Chicago Press, 1974); idem, *Executive Reorganization and Reform in the New Deal* (Cambridge: Harvard University Press, 1963); idem, *The Uneasy State* (Chicago: University of Chicago Press, 1981); S. Seidelman and R. Harpham, *Disenchanted Realists* (Albany: SUNY Press, 1985); Charles Merriam, *New Aspects of Politics* (Chicago: University of Chicago Press, 1925); Mark C. Smith, *Social Science in the Crucible* (Durham: Duke University Press, 1994). In a late book, *The New Democracy and the New Despotism* (New York: McGraw Hill, 1939), Merriam moves closer to Dewey, and away from the guardian idea of an administrative elite.

53. Robert Arnove, ed., *Philanthropy and Cultural Imperialism* (Chicago: G. T. Hall, 1980) (esp. the essays by Donald Fisher on the social sciences and conservative ideology and Peter Seybold on the Ford Foundation's efforts to make behavioralism the dominant ideology in American political science after World War II); Jerry Israel, ed., *Building The Organizational Society* (New York: Free Press, 1972); Donald Fisher, "American Philanthropy and the Social Sciences," 233–68; and Peter J. Seybold, "The Ford Foundation," 268–304.

54. Frank Fischer, *Technocracy and the Politics of Expertise* (Newbury Park, CA: Sage, 1990), ch. 4.

55. Harold Lasswell, *Psychopathology and Politics* (New York: Viking, 1930).

56. Harold Lasswell and Abraham Kaplan, *Power and Society* (Yale University Press, 1950); Harold Lasswell, *Politics: Who Gets What, When, How* (New York: Meridian, 1951).

57. Emile Durkheim, *Suicide* (New York: Free Press, 1951); idem, *The Rules of Sociological Method* (New York: Free Press, 1962).

58. Dennis Smith, op. cit.

59. Dmitri N. Shalin, "G. H. Mead, Socialism and the Progressive Agenda," *American Journal of Sociology* 93 (1988): 913–51.

60. Louis Hartz, *The Liberal Tradition in America* (New York: Harcourt, 1955). Cf. Hawthorn, 193; Oberschall, 242–4; Martindale, 62; Daniel Boorstein, *The Decline of Radicalism* (New York: Random House, 1967); and idem, *The Genius of American Politics* (Chicago: University of Chicago Press, 1953).

61. Furner, 324, cp. 228, 163; Ross in Oleson.

62. Michel Crozier, Samuel P. Huntington, and Joji Wantanuki, *The Crisis of Democracy* (New York: New York University Press, 1975). See chapters 4 and 8 below for discussion of end of ideology and cold-war liberalism.

63. William Aken, *Technocracy and the American Dream* (Berkeley: University of California Press, 1977); cf. Alan Lawson, *The Failure of Independent Liberalism* (New York: Capricorn, 1971).

64. S. Klansner and V. Lidz, eds., *The Nationalization of the Social Sciences* (Philadelphia: University of Pennsylvania Press, 1986); Anthony Arblaster, *The Rise and Decline of Western Liberalism* (New York: St. Martin's, 1982), on cold-war Liberalism. See also Irving Louis Horowitz, ed., *The Rise and Fall of Project Camelot* (Cambridge: MIT Press, 1982); and Peter Coleman, *The Liberal Conspiracy* (New York: Free Press, 1989).

65. Kevles, *The Physicists*, op. cit.

66. Sidney Hook, "Civilization and Its Malcontents," *National Review* 13 (October 1989).

67. Christopher Norris, *Uncritical Reason* (Amherst: University of Massachusetts Press, 1992).

68. See *Beloved Community*, op. cit., for Bourne, Brooks, and Mumford; and *The Protestant Search for Political Realism*, op. cit., for Rauschenbusch. See also Paul F. Bourke, "The Social Critics and the End of American Innocence: 1907–1921," *Journal of American Studies* 3 (1968): 57–72; and idem, "The Status of Politics: 1909–1919," *Journal of American Studies* 8 (1974): 171–202.

69. Michael Walzer, *In the Company of Critics* (New York: Basic Books, 1988); Christopher Lasch, *The New Radicalism in America* (New York: Vintage, 1965); *Beloved Community*, op. cit.; Daniel Levine, "Randolph Bourne, John Dewey, and the Legacy of Liberalism," *Antioch Review* (Summer 1969): 234–44; and Tom Curtis, "Bourne, MacDonald, Chomsky and the Rhetoric of Resistance," *Antioch Review* (Summer 1969) 245–52.

70. Gail Kennedy, ed., *Pragmatism and American Culture* (Boston: Heath, 1952); Arthur E. Murphey, "John Dewey and American Liberalism," *Journal of Philosophy* 57 (1960) 420–36; Ernest Sutherland Bates, "John Dewey: America's Philosophic Engineer," *Monthly Review* 122 (1933): 387–396, 404.

71. George Novack, *Pragmatism vs. Marxism* (New York: Pathfinder, 1975).

72. See John Patrick Diggins, "Dewey on Peace and War," *American Scholar* 49 (1981): 213–30; idem, *Mussolini and Fascism: The View from America* (Princeton: Princeton University Press, 1972); and idem, "Ideology and Pragmatism: Philosophy or Passion?" *American Political Science Review* 64 (1970): 889–900; cf. James Campbell, "Dewey's Method of Social Reconstruction," *Transactions of the C. S. Pierce Society* 20 (1983–84): 263–93.

73. (Albany: SUNY Press, 1988).

74. John Dewey and Arthur F. Bentley, *The Knower and the Known* (Boston: Beacon, 1949).

75. S. Ratner and J. Altman, eds., *John Dewey and Arthur F. Bentley: A Philosophical Correspondence, 1932–1951* (New Brunswick: Rutgers University Press, 1964).

76. Seidelman and Harpham, *Disenchanted Realists*, 69.

77. Merriam sometimes had a similar position, but was more favorably inclined toward a positivist view of science. See Avery Leiserson, "Charles Merriam, Max Weber and the Search for Synthesis in Political Science," *American Political Science Review* 69 (March 1975): 175–85; see also Merriam, op. cit.

78. Stuart I. Rochester, *American Liberal Disillusionment in the Wake of World War I*; and Carl Gruber, *Mars and Minerva*, op. cit.

79. Stuart I. Rochester, *American Liberal Disillusionment in the Wake of World War I*: 92–94.

80. Ibid., 115.

81. See *Failure of Independent Liberalism*, op. cit. For the role of ethical naturalism, see Edward Purcell, *The Critics in Democratic Theory* (Lexington: University of Kentucky Press, 1973).

82. Edmund Wilson, "Appeal to Progressives," *New Republic*, 14 January 1932: 234–38; George Soule, "Hard-boiled Radicalism," *New Republic*, 12 Jan. 1931: 261–65; Robert Hallowell; "Americanize America!" *New Republic*, 4 Feb. 1931: 324–36, Kenneth Burke "Boring from Within," *New Republic*, 4 Feb. 1931: 326–29; Matthew Josephson, "The Road to Indignation," 18 February 1931, 13–15; Benjamin Ginzburg, "Against Messianism," ibid., 15–17; see also Lewis Mumford, "The Corruption of Liberalism," ibid., 1940, 568–73. Mumford and others accuse Dewey of not being against capitalism, but only in favor of harnessing its excesses.

83. John Dewey, *Liberalism and Social Action* (New York: Capricorn, 1935); reprinted in idem, *Problems of Men* (New York: Philosophical Library, 1946); see also *Individualism Old and New* (New York: Capricorn, 1930); idem, *The Public and Its Problems* (New York: Holt, 1927); idem, "Creative Democracy—The Task before Us," in *Classic American Philosophers*, ed. Max Fish (New York: Appleton, 1951), 389–95.

84. Dewey, *Problems of Men*, 138.

85. Ibid., 142.

86. James Campbell, op. cit.; and idem, "Rorty's Use of Dewey," *Southern Journal of Philosophy* 21 (1984): 175–87.

87. A. D'Amico, "Impractical America: Reconsideration of the Pragmatic Lesson," *Political Theory* 13 (1986): 83–104; idem, *Individuality and Community* (Tampa: University of Florida Presses; 1978); idem, "Analysis and Advocacy, Pragmatism and the Study of Politics," *Polity* 6 (1974): 193–208; idem, "The Politics after Deconstruction: Rorty, Dewey, and Marx," in *Context over Foundation: Dewey and Marx*, ed. William Gavin (Boston: Reidel, 1988), 177–205. See the other essays in this book, especially by Garry M. Brodsky, "Politics, Culture, and Society in Marx and Dewey," 77–119; James Campbell, "Dewey's Understanding of Marx and Marxism," 119–47; Peter T. Manicas, "Philosophy and Politics: A Historical Approach to Dewey and Marx," 147–77. See also A. D'Amico, "Dewey and Marx: On Partisanship and the Reconstruction of Society," *American Political Science Review* 75 (1981): 654–66. Also see Peter Manicas, "Dewey and the Class Struggle," in *Values in Twentieth Century America*, ed. A. Edel (Philadelphia: Temple University Press, 1988), 67–81; idem, "John Dewey and the Problem of Justice," *Journal of Value Inquiry* 14 (1981): 279–91; and idem, "John Dewey: Anarchism and the Political State," *Transactions of the C. S. Pierce Society* 18 (1982): 133–58; Arthur Lothstein, "Salving from the Dross: John Dewey's

Anarcho-Communism," *Philosophical Forum* (1978): 55–110; Gary Bullert, *The Politics of John Dewey* (Buffalo: Prometheus, 1983); and A. H. Somjee, *The Political Philosophy of John Dewey* (New York: Teachers College Press, 1968). Finally, see William W. Brickman, "Dewey's Social and Political Commentary," in *Guide to the Works of John Dewey*, ed. Jo Ann Boydston (Carbondale: Southern Illinois University Press, 1970), 218–256; and, above all, the recent work by Robert B. Westbrook, *John Dewey and American Democracy* (Ithaca: Cornell University Press, 1991), far and away the best book on Dewey. See two fine papers on this topic by Timothy V. Kaufman-Osborn: "John Dewey and the Liberal Science of Community," *Journal of Politics* (1984): 1143–64; and idem, "Pragmatism, Policy Science, and the State," ibid. (1986): 827–48. See also Charles W. Anderson, *Pragmatic Liberalism* (Chicago: University of Chicago Press, 1990); and Alan P. Grimes, "The Pragmatic Course of Liberalism," *Western Political Quarterly* (1956): 633–40.

88. Dewey, *The Public and its Problems*, op. cit.

89. These remarks by Dewey are reprinted in James Gouinlock, ed., *The Moral Writings of John Dewey* (New York: Hafner, 1976), 245–46.

90. *The Failure of Independent Liberalism*, op. cit.

91. John Keane, *Public Life and Late Capitalism* (New York: Cambridge University Press, 1984).

92. Joseph Featherstone, "John Dewey and David Riesman: From the Lost Individual to the Lonley Crowd," in *On The Making of Americans: Essays in Honor of David Riesman*, ed. H. Gans, N. Glazer, J. Gusfield, and C. Jencks (Philadelphia: University of Pennsylvania Press, 1979), 3–40, 32.

Chapter 4

American Liberalism: Weberian Trends

In my discussion of Weber, I cited David Beetham's claim that Weber was the first end-of-ideology theorist,[1] and tried to explain how his brand of liberalism fits in with this position. In this chapter I want to glance at some Weberian trends within post-World War II American liberalism[2]: cold war liberalism,[3] the end-of-ideology thesis,[4] political realism,[5] empirical democratic theory,[6] and pluralism.[7] To round out my discussion and bring it up to the present, I glance at the end-of-history thesis,[8] the politics of postindustrial society,[9] and the neoliberalism of writers such as Huntington.[10] My claim is that there is a common Weberian motif in all of these recent versions of liberalism.

It seems fairly clear that American liberalism after World War II, until about 1960, differed from earlier corporate liberalism in two ways: it was less optimistic, and (to perhaps reformulate the same point) it was based upon what sociologists call "conflict" models of society.[11] More precisely, the conception of politics envisioned by many postwar American liberals was confined to a narrowly defined range of legitimate issues and conflicts, between and among interest groups or elites, who are all committed to the same "nonideological" brand of "liberalism," and differ only about which means best promote the common good of the system. In short, post–World War II liberalism turns away from the optimistic, even utopian, activist mood of prewar corporate liberalism toward an end-of-ideology politics that advocates complacency and glorifies the American system as it is.

This strategy required these liberals to distinguish their own role as critical intellectuals from the position of those who (they believed) deservedly fell under the axe of Joseph McCarthy.[12]

But the fear of Stalin and McCarthy is only part of the story. Accompanying this fear was the growing fear of the masses, the so-called mass society.[13] Indeed, writers such as Daniel Bell and Talcott Parsons argued that McCarthyism was rooted in the same mass mentality that gave rise to populism, which they correctly viewed as a popular distrust of the elite, and which clearly had admixtures of antisemitic and anti-Black sentiments, as well as isolationism and an America-first nativism that in some quarters continue to this day.[14] While this interpretation of McCarthyism, populism, and their connections has been vigorously criticized,[15] the main point is that the Weberian postwar liberals feared and distrusted the masses as much as the Progressives and corporate liberals of earlier years. Indeed, some of the movements I will soon examine combine Weberian and Durkheimian trends in a number of ways.

But this fear of "mass society" took different forms after the war. Gone was the optimistic utopianism of the social engineers and technocrats, whose faith in a Durkheimian *Gemeinschaft* was undermined by the anxiety over totalitarianism—which was associated with utopianism by writers such as Hannah Arendt and the historian J. L. Talmon,[16] and even with certain features of the New Deal, e.g., national planning, by Hayek and Popper.[17]

The liberal strategy was to adopt some form of Madisonian politics, often in its Weberian form. The fears about mass society, on the one hand, and the perceived dangers of both "ideology" and "utopia," on the other, could be alleviated by the adoption of an end-of-ideology conception of politics, combined with some mechanism for turning factionalism into what Daniel Boorstein called "the genius of American politics."[18] End-of-ideology piecemeal social engineering became the order of the day.

In general, Weber's conception of politics, his sharp fact-value dichotomy, with its emphasis on value neutrality, decisionism, and positivism, his emphasis on bureaucracy and status groups, his pluralism and relativism, the preservation of the three cultural spheres (with the attendant limits on science together with the need for a strong executive and expert advisors), his political realism and pragmatism, and the Protestant work ethic all come into play in postwar American liberalism.

One somewhat disturbing tendency that usually accompanied these Weberian trends was a growing emphasis on "pragmatism," which was often just another label for some form of allegedly value-neutral political realism. This almost always justified a "nonideological" conflict model of American politics that served the function of achieving consensus against the background of the (ideology of a) taken-for-granted basic agreement about liberal America, as worked out by Louis Hartz,[19] Arthur Schlesinger,[20] and Boorstein.[21] This was unfortunate, since it neglected Dewey's version of pragmatism, including his vision of a democratic culture, and endorsed a "pragmatic" politics that actually undermined Dewey's vision.

Thus, the political realism of Hans Morgenthau, Reinhold Niebuhr, and Harold Lasswell emphasizes Weber's *Realpolitik*, which they based upon the pessimism of Weber. Niebuhr turned it into a philosophy of history in such works as *Children of Light and Children of Darkness* and *The Irony of American History*.[22] Morgenthau, in his books *Scientific Man vs. Power Politics* and *Science: Servant or Master?*,[23] carries forward Niebuhr's arguments, emphasizing the Weberian arguments about the limits of science and the necessity of responsible political realism, especially in the international arena during the cold war, owing to the tragic vision of life that, according to Niebuhr, Dewey neglected. Lasswell, in books such as *Power and Society* (coauthored with Abraham Kaplan) and *Politics: Who Gets What, When, How*,[24] focuses on the domestic scene, where power politics is seen as a value-neutral strategy justified by empirical analysis.

Other approaches to politics adopted by liberals emphasize Weber's doctrines about value neutrality and "professionalism," i.e., the view that the science of politics must be value free. Gone in these views is the romantic, perhaps heroic, pessimism of Weber; instead, the scholar's task of being a morally neutral, responsible specialist or technician is emphasized. The most thoroughgoing efforts in this direction were by proponents of the empirical democratic theory[25] and the "economic" theory of democracy, which emphasized studies of voting behavior and other empirical, value-neutral phenomena, allegedly subject to rigorous empirical analysis. On this view, research in the social and behavioral sciences shows that democracy, conceived as a process, works more efficiently when the politically uninformed remain uninvolved. This conclusion, which Schumpeter had already rehearsed—he uses the term "irrational" to characterize the opinions of the politically uninformed—is at once an attack on "the politic of mass society" and a precursor to the crisis-of-democracy theorists of the 1970s, whose target was what for them is another chapter in the politics of mass society: the New Left of the 1960s. The innuendo is clear: nineteenth-century populism and twentieth-century democratic socialism and radicalism are all dangerous, irrational, and undermine democratic processes. The question of what this view takes for granted by way of political, methodological, and ideological assumptions (e.g., rational choice theory, methodological individualism, the view that politics is only the quest for power) has been addressed elsewhere,[26] and I shall not pursue these issues further.

Still another variation on Weberian liberalism takes the form of pluralism, or "interest group liberalism," which emphasizes the conflict model of society in Weber and others, so as to justify the idea that democratic consensus is the result of some sort of bargaining process among interest groups including—sometimes almost exclusively—elite groups. Robert Dahl, the most forceful proponent of this view,[27] develops an updated Madisonian strategy, that focuses on competition among elites—which Dahl calls "polyarchy." The masses choose the elites, who then control the political arena. This idea goes back to Schumpeter and ultimately to Weber, as we saw in chapter 2, and is defended by writers such as Giovanni Sartori[28] in basically elitist models of democracy, often in allegedly "value-neutral," "empirical" terms. (In fairness to Dahl, he has recently argued against the "guardianship" view of democracy, in *Democracy and Its Critics*.[29])

C. Wright Mills[30] and William Domhoff[31] argue that this "interest group pluralism" is really a defense of the "power elite," which many American liberals, carrying out the logic of the cold war, end-of-ideology vision of American politics tried to sustain on "scientific" grounds.

I have tried to argue that it is dangerous to ground democracy on empirical or procedural criteria, just as it is worrisome to define liberalism in methodological terms. Conceiving democracy along empirical lines, e.g., as an organizational system of a certain sort (as in Durkheim) or as an instrument for achieving certain liberal ideals such as individual freedom in the iron cage (as in

Weber) makes democracy and even liberalism very tenuous, since democracy is then warranted only on the condition that certain other forces are in place. But then democracy, as well as traditional liberal values such as privacy, can be drastically modified or given up if the "empirical evidence" seems to warrant it; or else democracy and liberal society have a minimal content, e.g., voting for officials and formal procedural guarantees, which are compatible with very undemocratic and illiberal practices.

A case in point is the way some corporate leaders of today's postindustrial society want to erode privacy, on the grounds that nothing people do in the new order is irrelevant to their job performance, and thus to the public good. Some advocates of this view, which harks back to the calls for adjustment and control during the days of "efficiency and uplift," go on to argue that this politicalization of everything will allow the corporations to win the war on drugs—presumably by keeping anybody on drugs out of work. I think liberal democrats should resist this, and be very reluctant to eliminate privacy for "empirical" reasons. But on the approach to democracy I am now criticizing, this obvious move seems difficult to make.

Many political theorists and historians[32] have shown that these empirical, value-neutral conceptions of liberal democracy are nothing of the sort; they are attempts to defend the ideology of the cold war liberals, whose distrust of the masses, whom they always associate with ignorant conservatism, pushes them in the direction of one or another version of the theory of the democratic elite.[33] To be sure, these interpretations, which derive from Mills, have been countered; and the debates may be undecidable for hermeneutical reasons, even if we discount the ideological stakes on all sides.[34] But I still maintain that unless we follow Dewey in defining democracy as a way of life[35] that is intrinsically valuable in the first instance, widespread democratic participation, and the preservation of the liberal value of, say, privacy, will be precarious at best. The "decline of political philosophy" movement, defended by empirical political theorists, strikes me as continuous with the end-of-ideology thesis and with Rorty's postmodernist defense of American liberalism. We just assume there is a widespread liberal consensus among the only people who count, and make all other groups deviant, i.e., "ideological," so that politics becomes an empirical, nonideological search for the best means of keeping the "system" in dynamic equilibrium. But the system might achieve equilibrium in unfair ways.

To recognize empirical democratic theory as but another version of democratic elitism,[36] one need only consider the so-called crisis-of-democracy argument of Samuel Huntington,[37] which echoes the earlier "behavioralist" argument of empirical democratic theorists[38] that our "system," or "civic culture," is suffering from an "overload," and that democracy functions best when there is a minimum of democratic participation by citizens. Here is what Huntington says:

> The vulnerability of democratic government in the United States . . . comes not primarily from external threats, . . . nor from internal subversion from the left or the right, . . . but rather from the internal dynamics of democracy itself in a highly educated, mobilized, and participant society. "Democracy never lasts long," John Adams observed. "It soon wastes, exhausts and murders itself. There never was a

democracy yet that did not commit suicide." That suicide is more likely to be the product of overindulgence than of any other cause. A value which is normally good in itself is not necessarily optimized when it is maximized. We have come to recognize that there are potentially desirable limits to economic growth. There are also potentially desirable limits to the indefinite extension of political democracy. Democracy will have a longer life if it has a more balanced existence.[39]

And what constitutes a "more balanced existence"? We must strike a balance between "creedal passion," i.e., ideology, and "creedal passivity," or too little involvement. However we strike this balance, "the effective operation of a democratic political system requires some measure of apathy and noninvolvement on the part of some individuals and groups."[40] Which groups should be marginalized?

Huntington continues:

In the past, every democratic society has had a marginal population, of greater or lesser size, which has not actively participated in politics. In itself, this marginality on the part of some groups is inherently undemocratic, but it has also been one of the factors which has enabled democracy to function effectively. Marginal social groups, as in the case of the blacks, are now becoming full participants in the political system. Yet the danger of overloading the political system with demands which extend its functions and undermine its authority still remains. Less marginality on the part of some groups thus needs to be replaced by more self-restraint on the part of all groups.[41]

This all sounds quite reasonable, until we ask what it means. It is worth noting, for instance, that Nietzsche makes a similar argument in assessing the ways in which the will to truth undermines itself: it creates "rising expectations" on the part of the masses that cannot be fulfilled, but will rather make nihilism a greater reality.[42] Huntington's worries about "too much democracy" seem to echo Nietzsche's fears. Are the marginalized of our society, e.g., women, people of color, gays and lesbians, and members of the so-called underclass to conclude that they are really doing well, or take seriously the claim that, by insisting on their just due they will throw the system out of balance and thus hurt everybody? The import of Huntington's argument should be obvious. At the very least, it suffers from the same glaring and, I think, unconscionable assumption of interest group and elitist liberalism: the "system" is fair, power and influence are divided equitably, and the consensus achieved benefits everybody, since it preserves a fair system, even if one's own interests are overridden by good utilitarian considerations.

I do not think Daniel Bell's efforts to deal with these sort of questions is much more promising than Huntington's solution. True, Bell argues against the excesses of the market and against technocracy in *The Coming of Postindustrial Society* and *The Cultural Contradictions of Capitalism*.[43] But Bell blames the "liberal culture of modernism" for the disequilibrium of our society, much as Huntington blames too much democratic politics.[44] But surely the writers he mentions are just as much against the excesses of the market and technocracy as he is. As Habermas points out,[45] this strategy neglects the way in which the capitalist system is the root of the problem. The problem, for Bell, is that we have lost a sense of solidarity, which requires the Durkheimian expedient of a revitalization of religion and tradition.[46] For Bell, a postindustrial society—the natural culmination of the end-of-ideology conception of politics—is socialist in the economic realm (he defends equality of opportunity), liberal in the political realm, and conservative in the cultural realm.[47] But what does he mean by "liberalism"? As early as *The End of Ideology*, he invokes Weber's "ethic of responsibility" to argue for "nonideological," piecemeal reformist politics.[48] But Bell neglects to mention that, for Weber, the ethics of responsibility combines a consequentialist outlook with an ethic of ultimate ends, or values. Without convictions, politics, even "realistic" politics, becomes a dangerous expediency for Weber, just as convictions alone lead to fanaticism. But Bell elides this important point by construing "ideology" as either fanatical Marxism or extreme right-wing populism, and then by distinguishing, despite what he is really saying, between "ideology" and "philosophy." Moreover, for Bell it is a constraint on politics that all proposals involve a detailed accounting of all costs and benefits. But this is unduly restrictive, since valuable political reform need not be able to answer all such questions immediately; in any case, not all legitimate practical reform boils down to technology and accounting. Further, social engineering + accounting does not guarantee justice, or even Weber's ethics of responsibility. The Nazi gas chambers were a very well thought out political program, which might very well have met Bell's "pragmatic" requirement. I do not, in any case, see the connection between Bell and Dewey, despite Bell's insistence that Dewey is a great influence on his own thought. I have no doubt that this is so; but the end-of-ideology conception of politics is pretty clearly un-Deweyan. It would restrict, perhaps even prohibit, the kind of politics Dewey sometimes practiced. Moreover, Bell's tendencies toward scientism and the knowledgeable elite—the hallmark of his account of postindustrial society—are anti-Deweyan, and are derived more from Veblen, who advocated the sort of technocracy Dewey always rejected.

What, then, are Bell's liberal convictions? Here is what he says: "Liberalism accepts the tension of the public and the private, the dual roles of person and citizen, individual and group. The questions are: how to find common purposes, yet retain individual means of fulfilling them; and how to define individual (and group) needs and find common means of meeting them."[49] What is needed is a new "public philosophy"—the philosophy of the "public household," which combines Millian liberalism, Weber's political realism, a corporate-based knowledge elite, and traditional values, by which Bell clearly means the Protestant ethic. It is one step from this strange brew to the "neoliberal" effort to use the market of postindustrial society to solve all social problems; a step backwards to the nineteenth-century liberalism of Spencer.

So Bell makes the move of the neoliberals; indeed, he is one of the architects of this view,[50] which infuses Millian liberalism and market capitalism with a Durkheimian faith, or, what amounts to the same thing, combines an all powerful Weberian executive with a Durkheimian knowledge elite of bureaucrats and technicians. But, as Bell admits, the politics of the postindustrial society, where this public philosophy will be realized, still leaves us with the problems of majority rule and the conflict between elites and masses, as well as the division of culture into spheres, which I claim is a root cause of the dilemma of modern liberalism.[51] Bell really does not address these issues, but assumes that a society in which more people become members of a knowledge elite will move in the direction of a Durkheimian community, where pluralism will yield cooperation, not conflict. Other advocates of this sort of view, especially Amiati Etzioni,[52] Robert Lane,[53] Heinz Eulau,[54] Zbigniew Brzezinski,[55] and the "neoliberals" merely carry the cold war liberals' end-of-ideology politics one step further, while incorporating many of the other postwar liberal doctrines discussed above. A growing "knowledge elite" will make politics unnecessary, while simultaneously bringing the liberal tradition to its allegedly logical completion in a politics of "competence," not "ideology."

The fact that the programs and vision of liberal democracy are becoming things of the past is evidently not a problem.[56] Nor is this new "public philosophy" (dubbed "Reaganism with a human face"[57]), which claims that the market can achieve Bell's Durkheimian ends, in any way remotely akin to Dewey's great community, which focuses on democracy as a way of life. Moreover, Bell accuses foes of the elite of "resentment" and denies the existence of a "new class" of elites.[58] Indeed, the neoliberals who follow Bell and the other postindustrial theorists equate liberalism with a market economy and a "pragmatic" politics of competence.

The knowledge elite of postindustrial corporate society is combined with the logic of the end-of-ideology thesis: as Robert Lane argues, "ideology *and* politics" will be unnecessary in a "knowledge society." Others, notably Christopher Lasch in his recent *The True and Only Heaven*,[59] argue that modern liberalism is the cause of all our problems because it has been too optimistic. On my view it is closer to the truth to say that it has not been optimistic enough about the possibilities of Deweyan democracy.

The end-of-history thesis of Francis Fukuyama[60]—a Straussian "liberal" with affinities to contemporary conservatives such as Newt Gingrich and William Bennett (see *New York Times* Sunday *Magazine*, 29 January 1995)—claims that liberalism has triumphed, that communism is dead, and that a postindustrial world in which human rights are universally secured is upon us. This is merely the globalization of the end-of-ideology thesis, despite Fukuyama's denials. His claim that we are witnessing "an unabashed victory of economic and political liberalism" really means a victory for global capitalism, consumerism, technological and economic problem solving: "the satisfaction of sophisticated consumer demands." Our new world order, where capitalism and communism have been *aufgehoben* by postindustrial utopia, is liberalism triumphant. As the U.S. secretary of defense (cited in *Time* Magazine) maintained,[61] after the Gulf War, our swift and decisive technological victory in the Persian Gulf also shows liberalism triumphant, and proves that our educational system and our society really are in pretty good shape, after all. The fact that the United States can now conduct Orwellian technological warfare without dissent or moral discussion; that Durkheimian ends can only be achieved by the crudest form of patriotism; that institutionalized and individual racism, sexism, and poverty (the "underclass") are getting worse by the day while society manifests the most virulent forms of Social Darwinism since Spencer; and that liberal education and universities are being destroyed by the extreme Right and Left, and, above all, by corporate America, make the proclaimed victory of liberalism empty indeed. Indeed, if this is liberalism triumphant, I shudder to think what its defeat might look like.

If liberalism *has* triumphed, then it has surely done so at the cost of even the last pretense of democracy in the United States of America. The recently proclaimed "betrayal of American democracy"[62] is but the final chapter in the dark side of liberalism. To revitalize democracy, to the extent that this is possible, we may have to radically transform or even abandon much, if not all, of the liberal tradition. For liberalism's "triumph" comes on the heels of a tradition that successfully eliminates any criticism, radical or not, that is incompatible with the elitist liberal project.

As a step toward an articulation of a conception of liberalism that is friendlier to democratic participation, I turn next to Richard Rorty's "postmodernist" liberalism. I shall argue that Rorty's own version of liberalism can defend only a very thin conception of democracy, since he is caught between Mill and Weber, and has incorporated what I regard as the worst of both these strands of liberalism. Yet his defense of a postmodernist approach to liberalism, together with his own radicalization of theory, can be made part of a postmodernist approach to radical democracy—a task whose full elaboration is beyond the limits of this book. But I will at least begin to move in this direction in chapters 6 and 11.

NOTES

1. See Beetham, *op. cit.*, 242.

2. See Terence Ball, "The Politics of Social Science in Postwar America," in *Recasting America*, ed. F. May (New York: Routledge 1990), 76–92; and William Buxton, *Talcott Parsons and the Capitalist Nation-State* (Toronto: University of Toronto Press, 1985).

3. See David Ricci, *The Tragedy of Political Science* (New Haven: Yale University Press, 1984); Marion J. Morton, *The Terrors of Ideological Politics* (Cleveland: Case Western Reserve University Press, 1972); Robert Booth Fowler, *Believing Skeptics* (Westport, CT: Greenwood, 1978); William J. Newman, *The Futilitarian Society* (New York: George Braziller, 1961); Philip Abbott, *Furious Fancies* (Westport, CT: Greenwood, 1980).

4. See Daniel Bell, *The End of Ideology*, with an 1988 afterward, "The End of Ideology Revisited" (Cambridge: Harvard University Press, 1989); Seymour Martin Lipset, *Political Man* (Garden City: Anchor, 1963); M. Rejai, ed., *Decline of Ideology*? (New York: Atherton, 1971); Chaim I. Waxman, ed., *The End of Ideology Debate* (New York: Funk and Wagnalls, 1968); James P. Young, *The Politics of Affluence* (Boston: Chandler, 1968).

5. See Michael Joseph Smith, *Realist Thought from Weber to Kissinger* (Baton Rouge: Louisiana State University Press, 1990); and Stephen Turner and Regis Factor, *Max Weber and the Dispute about Reason and Value* (New York: Routledge, 1984), ch. 7.

6. See Charles Cnudde and Dean Neubauer, eds., *Empirical Democratic Theory*, (Boston: Markham Publishing, 1969); Albert Somit and Joseph Tanenhaus, *The Development of American Political Science* (New York: Irvington Publishers, 1982); Charles A. McCoy and John Playford, eds., *Apolitical Politics* (New York:

Crowell, 1967); Bernard Crick, *The American Science of Politics* (Berkeley: University of California Press, 1960). For a defense of Schumpeter's version of elite pluralism, see Giovanni Sartori, *The Theory of Democracy Revisited* (New York: Chatham House, 1987). See also Etzioni-Halevy, *The Elite Connection: Problems and Potentials of Western Democracy* (Cambridge: Blackwell's, 1993).

7. See J. David Greenstone, "Group Theories," in *Micropolitical Theories*, vol. 2; *Handbook of Political Science*, ed. Fred I. Greenstein and Nelson W. Polsby (Boston: Addison-Wesley, 1975), 243–319; William Alton Kelso, *American Democratic Theory: Pluralism and Its Critics* (Westport, CT: Greenwood, 1978); Theodore J. Lowi, *The End of Liberalism* (New York: Norton, 1969).

8. See Francis Fukuyama, *The End of History and the Last Man* (New York: Macmillan, 1991).

9. See Daniel Bell, *The Coming of Post-Industrial Society* (New York: Basic Books, 1973); idem, *The Cultural Contradictions of Capitalism* (New York: Basic Books, 1976); Alain Touraine, *The Post-Industrial Society* (New York: Random House, 1971); and idem, "What Is Daniel Bell Afraid Of?" *American Journal of Sociology* 77 (1972): 469–73; Christopher Lasch, "Toward A Theory of Post-Industrial Society" and Dusky Lee Smith "Scientific Liberalism: Ward, Galbraith, and the Welfare State," both in *Politics in the Post-Welfare State*, ed. M. Donald Hancock and Gideon Sjoberg (New York: Columbia University Press, 1972), 36–50, 51–65; Samuel P. Huntington, "Postindustrial Politics: How Benign Will It Be?" *Comparative Politics* 6 (1974): 163–91.

10. Randell Rothenberg, *The Neo-Liberals* (New York: Simon and Schuster, 1984); Samuel P. Huntington, *American Politics: The Promise of Disharmony* (Cambridge: Harvard University Press, 1981); Michel Crozier, Samuel P. Huntington, and Joji Watanuki, *The Crisis of Democracy* (New York City: New York University Press, 1975); Samuel P. Huntington, "Paradigms of American Politics: Beyond the One, the Two, and the Many," *Political Science Quarterly* 89 (1974): 1–26; idem, "The Democratic Distemper," in *The Public Interest* 25 (1962): 10–36.

11. See Randall Collins, *Three Sociological Traditions* (New York: Oxford University Press, 1985).

12. See, e.g., Michael Paul Rogin, *The Intellectuals and McCarthy: The Radical Specter* (Cambridge: MIT Press, 1967); Daniel Bell, ed. *The Radical Right* (New York: Anchor, 1964); and the symposium "Our Country and Our Culture" in *Partisan Review* 52 (1952).

13. See William Kornhauser, *The Politics of Mass Society* (New York: Free Press, 1959).

14. See Richard Hofstadter, *Anti-Intellectualism in American Life* (New York: Vintage, 1962); and John Higham, *Strangers in the Land* (New Brunswick: Rutgers University Press, 1955).

15. See Rogin, op. cit.

16. See Hannah Arendt, *The Origins of Totalitarianism* (New York: Penguin, 1951); and J. L. Talmon, *The Origins of Totalitarian Democracy* (Westport, CT: Praeger, 1952).

17. See e.g., Friedrich von Hayek, *The Road to Serfdom* (Chicago: University of Chicago Press, 1944); Karl Popper, *The Poverty of Historicism* (New York: Harper, 1957).

18. Daniel Boorstein, *The Genius of American Politics* (Chicago: University of Chicago Press, 1953).

19. Louis Hartz, *The Liberal Tradition in America* (New York: Harcourt, 1955).

20. Arthur Schlesinger, Jr., *The Vital Center* (New York: Houghton Mifflin, 1949).

21. Boorstein, *The Genius of American Politics*; idem, *The Decline of Radicalism* (New York: Random House, 1969).

22. Rinehold Niebuhr, *Children of Light and Children of Darkness* (New York: Scribner's, 1944), *The Irony of American History* (New York: Scribner's, 1952).

23. Chicago: University Chicago Press, 1946; New York: Harper, 1952. For a good recent discussion of political realism, see Joel H. Rosenthal, *Righteous Realists* (Baton Rouge: Louisiana State University Press, 1991). See also Daniel F. Rice, *Reinhold Niebuhr versus John Dewey* (Albany: State University of New York Press, 1993).

24. Lasswell, loc. cit.

25. Lasswell, op. cit.

26. See, e.g., Ricci, op. cit.

27. See Robert Dahl, *A Preface to Democratic Theory* (Chicago: University of Chicago Press, 1956); idem, *Pluralist Democracy in the United States* (Chicago: Rand McNally, 1967), *Dilemmas of Pluralist Democracy* (New Haven: Yale University Press, 1982).

28. See Sartori, op. cit.

29. New Haven: Yale University Press, 1988.

30. C. Wright Mills, *The Power Elite* (New York: Oxford University Press, 1956); idem, *Power, Politics and People* (New York: Oxford University Press, 1960). See also Irving Louis Horowitz, ed., *The New Sociology* (New York: Oxford University Press, 1964); and William Domhoff and F. Ballard, eds., *C. Wright Mills and the Power Elite* (Boston: Beacon Press, 1968). On the general topic of the power elite, see Kenneth Prewitt and Alan Stone, *The Ruling Elite* (New York: Harper, 1973); Peter Bachrach, *The Theory of the Democratic Elite* (Boston: Little, Brown, 1967); Geraint Parry, *Political Elites* (Westport, CT: Praeger, 1969); Tom Bottomore, *Elites and Masses* (New York: Basic Books, 1964); Eva Etzioni-Halevy, *Fragile Democracy* (Totowa: Transaction Books, 1990).

31. For Domhoff, see his *The Power Elite and the State* (New York: Aldine De Gruyter, 1990); idem, *The Powers That Be* (New York: Random House, 1969). For a good discussion of the debate between defenders of Dahl's pluralism and Mill's power elite theory see William Alton Kelso, *American Democratic Theory: Pluralism and Its Critics* (Westport, CT: Greenwood, 1978).

32. See, e.g., Morton, op. cit.; Newman, op. cit.; Ricci, op. cit.

33. See especially Morton and Ricci, works cited above.

34. For an interesting recent discussion, see Robert F. Alford and Roger Friedland, *Powers of Theory* (New York: Cambridge University Press, 1985).

35. See Dewey, "The Ethics of Democracy," op. cit; and idem, "Creative Democracy—the Task before Us," op. cit; and idem, *Freedom and Culture* (New York: Capricorn, 1939), esp. last chapter. For two defenses of the methodological version of democracy I am worried about, see Sidney Hook, "The Centrality of Democracy" and "The Justification of Democracy," both in *The American Pragmatists*, ed. Milton Konvitz and Gail Kennedy (New York: Meridian, 1960), 379–403; and Paul Kurtz, "The Democratic Ethic," in *Journeys through Philosophy*, ed. Nicholas Capaldi, Eugene Kelly and Luis E. Navia rev. ed. (Buffalo: Prometheus, 1982), 285–301.

36. See Barry Holden, *Understanding Liberal Democracy* (London: Philip Allan, 1988); Keith Graham, *The Battle of Democracy* (London: Harvester, 1986); David Ricci, *Community Power and Democratic Theory* (New York: Random House, 1971); Lee Ann Osbun, *The Problem of Participation* (Landham, MD: University Press of America, 1985); Charles Cnudde and Deane Neubauer, eds., *Empirical Democratic Theory* (Boston: Markham, 1969); Charles A. McCoy and John Playford, eds., *Apolitical Politics* (New York: Crowell, 1967); Quentin Skinner, "The Empirical

Theorists of Democracy and Their Critics: A Plague on Both Their Houses," *Political Theory* 1 (1973): 287–306.

37. Huntington, *Crisis of Democracy*, op. cit. As an antidote to Huntington, see Walter Dean Burnham, *The Current Crisis in American Politics* (New York: Oxford University Press, 1982).

38. See Ricci, op. cit., 144ff.; and Heinz Eulau, ed., *Behavioralism in Political Science* (New York: Atherton, 1969).

39. Huntington, op. cit., 115.

40. Ibid.

41. Ibid., 114.

42. Friedrich Nietzsche, *The Birth of Tragedy*, in *Basic Writings of Nietzsche*, ed. Walter Kaufmann (New York: Modern Library, 1966), 111 (sec. 18).

43. Bell, op. cit.

44. Bell, *The Cultural Contradictions of Capitalism*, xvii–xxi.

45. See Jurgen Habermas, "Neo-Conservative Cultural Criticism in the United States and West Germany" in *Habermas and Modernity*, ed. Richard Bernstein (Cambridge: MIT Press, 1985), 78–94.

46. In addition to the two books cited, see the essays in Daniel Bell, *The Winding Passage* (New York: Basic Books, 1980).

47. See Bell, *Cultural Contradictions*, xi.

48. See Daniel Bell, "Afterward," *The End of Ideology*, p. 416, *op. cit.*

49. Bell, *Cultural Contradictions*, 279.

50. See the essays by Reich and Sandel in *The Power of Public Ideas*, ed. Robert B. Reich (Cambridge: Harvard University Press, 1988). See also Michael Sandel, "Democracy and Community: A Public Philosophy for American Liberalism," *New Republic*, 22 February 1988, 20–23; Sandel, "The Political Theory of the Procedural Republic," in *The Power of Public Ideas*, op. cit., 109–22; and Robert B. Reich, "Policy Making in a Democracy," in *The Power of Public Ideas*, op. cit. 123–56.

51. As I have argued throughout, the sharp division between politics and culture is a characteristic feature of modern liberalism. But this division produces many of the conflicts between democracy and elitism I have been discussing.

52. Amiati Etzioni, *The Active Society* (New York: Free Press, 1968).

53. Robert E. Lane, "The Decline of Politics and Ideology in a Knowledgeable Society," *American Sociological Review* 31 (1966): 649–62.

54. Heinz Eulau, *Technology and Civility* (Stanford: Hoover Institution Press, 1977).

55. Zbigniew Brzezinski, *Between Two Ages* (New York: Viking, 1970).

56. See Lapham's *Harper* article on the decline of democracy, *loc. cit.*

57. See Randall Rothenberg, *The Neo-Liberals* (New York: Simon and Schuster, 1984), 21. Neo-liberalism is the latest version of nineteenth-century free market liberalism, I believe.

58. See the essays in B. Bruce Briggs, ed., *The New Class?* (New York: McGraw-Hill, 1979). For an interesting overview of the debates, see Charles Derber, et al., "Postscript: The New Class and Social Theory," in *Power in the Highest Degree* (New York: Oxford University Press, 1990), 211–26.

59. See Lasch, op. cit.; and Louis Menand, "Man of the People," *New York Review of Books*, 11 April 1991, 39–44; cf. Robert Bellah, et al., *The Good Society* (New York: Knopf, 1991).

60. See Francis Fukuyama, "The End of History," *National Interest* 16 (Summer 1989) 3–18; responses and Fukuyama's reply in ibid. (Winter 1989–90). The citations are from "The End of History?" 3, 18. See also Francis Fukuyama, *The End of History and the Last Man* (New York: Macmillan, 1991); compare p. xi with Richard Rorty, *Contingency, Solidarity, and Irony* (New York: Cambridge

University Press, 1989); 63. For comments on Fukuyama, see Perry Anderson, *A Zone of Engagement* (New York: Verso, 1992).

61. "Bush's Republican Guard," *Time*, 11 March 1991, 54–55.

62. See William Greider, *Who Will Tell the People: The Betrayal of American Democracy* (New York: Simon and Schuster, 1992).

Part II

RECENT DEVELOPMENTS IN LIBERALISM

Chapter 5

Rorty's Pragmatic Liberalism: Between Mill and Weber

Richard Rorty's defense of what he once called "postmodernist bourgeois liberalism"[1] is motivated by his pragmatic metaphilosophy,[2] which leads him to defend liberal society in exclusively historicist and ethnocentric terms. No metanarrative, theory of human nature, metaphysics, or theology can ground such a society; only hope and the desire to see it continue are needed. Yet, Rorty frankly admits that bourgeois liberalism is no longer relevant to contemporary concerns,[3] while also insisting that Mill has said the last word, at the level of theory, about the basic order of such a society.[4] Despite all his recent talk about the need to continuously change "final vocabularies" in order to (*inter alia*) "break the crust of established tradition" and to make us realize we are not living up to our country's ideals, he rejects even Dewey's renascent liberalism,"[5] or at any rate interprets Dewey's "Hegelianized liberalism"[6] in metaphilosophical, not political terms. He emphasizes a kind of Weberian romantic individualism and neglects the radical democratic potential in both Dewey and his own metaphilosophy by defining the public sphere to mean little more than avoiding cruelty. Thus, his concern for privacy leads to a conception of liberalism that stresses Mill and Weber to the exclusion of Dewey's conception of democracy. Indeed, since for Rorty there is nothing in between a metaphysically grounded politics and piecemeal social engineering, the Deweyan ideal of the public intellectual, who can launch general criticisms of, say, institutionalized racism and sexism, finds no place in Rorty's thinking. Given his loyalty to Thomas Kuhn's methodological conservatism (we should not reject a paradigm unless we have a better one to put in its place) and to Bell's end-of-ideology thesis,[7] Rorty leaves one with very little room for maneuver in the political sphere.

Generally speaking, Rorty seems to assert the following:

a. Millian liberalism provides the last word "at the level of theory"[8] about our political order.

b. Strong poets and utopian revolutionaries must invent new vocabularies to break the crust of established tradition.
c. Immanent critique of our society, even by the Left, is desirable and even necessary.[9]

It is not obvious that the above are mutually consistent. First, it is not clear what, if any, the restrictions on strong poets and revolutionary utopians are. This issue is complex, since it involves Rorty's sharp private-public distinction, and the paradoxical claim that the revolutionary writer invents new private "final vocabularies" that gradually change our public discourse through education.[10] Yet radical social critics such as Nietzsche and Foucault are relegated to the private sphere by Rorty. Who, then, is a revolutionary thinker on his view? Writers such as Ralph Waldo Emerson and William Blake, I suppose. In any case, why does Rorty not consider the possibility that revolutionary utopians will come up with a final vocabulary that sets Mill's liberalism aside? And why can the immanent critique he allows the Left (and others, notably Dewey) not lead us to call Mill's liberalism into question?

Rorty's views are extremely puzzling. Perhaps it will help to work through some of his writings on politics to see if we can make more sense of what he is arguing.

In "The Priority of Democracy to Philosophy,"[11] he claims that Jefferson wanted to privatize religion so that it became a matter of personal development, not political citizenship. This is a version of Rorty's "epistemological behaviorism"[12] applied to politics. In a liberal society what is in your heart of hearts is irrelevant to your status as a citizen. Obeying the law and being an atheist are compatible. Of course, Rorty is right: there is ample historical evidence that the origins of the private- public split is the consequence of religious toleration. Presumably Mill's defense of this split is based upon the same idea. According to Rorty, Mill and Jefferson "wanted to resolve the tension between these two sides," the private and the public, by recourse to some metaphysical or theological doctrine about rights, truth, human nature. Since Rorty will have none of this (he sometimes criticizes Dewey for defending democracy in metaphysical and theological terms), there is no way, "at the level of theory," of resolving the tension except the expedient adopted by Max Weber: we moderns must have the strength to live a bifurcated existence, just as modern society must be divided into the spheres of culture, politics, and science.[13]

Rorty clearly exhibits his Weberian loyalties in the following passage:

> Instead of . . . suggesting that philosophical reflection, or a return to religion, might enable us to re-enchant the world, I think that communitarians should stick to the question of whether disenchantment has, on balance, done us more harm than good, or created more dangers than it has evaded. For Dewey, communal and public disenchantment is the price we pay for individual and private spiritual liberation, the kind of liberation that Emerson thought characteristically American. Dewey was as well aware as Weber that there is a price to be paid, but he thought it well worth paying. He assumed that no good achieved by earlier societies would be worth recapturing if the price were a diminution in our ability to leave people alone, to let them try out their private visions of perfection in peace. He admired the American

habit of giving democracy priority over philosophy by asking, about any vision of the meaning of life, "Would not acting out this vision interfere with the ability of others to work out their own salvation?"

The danger of re-enchanting the world, from a Deweyan point of view, is that it might interfere with the development of what Rawls calls "a social union of social unions," some of which may be (and in Emerson's view, should be) very small indeed. For it is hard to be both enchanted with one version of the world and tolerant of all the others.[14]

Notice how Rorty pairs Weber and Dewey. While this may not be totally wrong,[15] it is crucially misleading, and indeed borders on being disingenuous. I think Dewey was a Hegelian, whose romantic leanings were always subservient to a Hegelian ideal of community, while Weber abhorred Hegel and rejected any such idea of a community. In an earlier essay, "Method, Social Science, and Social Hope," Rorty claimed that Mill and Dewey were kindred spirits, and that Dewey synthesized Hegel and Mill, just as Mill synthesized Jeremy Bentham and Samuel Coleridge. Perhaps Rorty is trying to synthesize Mill and Emerson with Dewey. In any case, this comparison between Mill and Dewey, like that between Dewey and Weber, is at least as misleading as it is true. The fact that Dewey rejected Millian liberalism in *Individualism Old and New*—a point Rorty refuses to admit—including the sharp public-private distinction that Rorty and Weber both insist upon, seems to make Rorty's taxonomy an instance of what he himself defends (following Harold Bloom) as a "strong misreading." But in this case the strong misreading is grossly misleading, and does little more than tell us who Rorty's heroes are. Rorty's claim[16] that Dewey and Weber together invented the vocabulary of social democracy ignores crucial differences in their political outlooks. He also downplays the similarities between Dewey and Habermas, the latter of whom raises important criticisms of Weber.[17]

The Weber-Rorty strategy of liberalism without philosophy rests upon the hope that the technocrats, bureaucrats, and political leaders will do their best to enhance utilitarian ends while leaving people alone in the private sphere. Worse still, the Weber-Rorty strategy oscillates between romantic withdrawal and pessimism and adjustment to the status quo, since this strategy arguably forces an either/or choice between the individual's own self-development and involvement in the public realm. In the realm of the social and policy sciences, the Weber-Rorty strategy generates a conflict between private ideals and technocratic politics, or an end-of-ideology notion of politics as social engineering, with its attendant strategy of "adjusting" the individual and her ideals to the system. It is important to recognize the sharp differences on these matters between Weber and Dewey,[18] and between the latter and Rorty, who really is a Weberian and closer to William James than to Dewey on political and cultural matters.

Weber's romanticism, his desire to save privacy and values in the iron cage, leads him to severely restrict democratic participation in order to achieve this goal. The war between the gods and demons is a strategy of Madisonian factionalism: power politics limits democracy while preserving the value pluralism that enhances freedom. The converse is equally true for Weber: value pluralism limits the power of the bureaucracy, but at the price of democratic participation. Rorty wants more of the latter. But his own romanticism is, in effect, an attempt to give the individual free space, but at the cost of involvement in politics. This is why Rorty severely restricts the political to "avoiding cruelty," and why utopian revolutionaries are modeled on Emerson, for whom individual genius will legislate democratic political changes. The public sphere all but disappears; political democracy will not remain intact when this happens.[19]

But Weber's strategy is combined with a Machiavellian political realism, where a charismatic leader rules by virtue of personality and strength. Rorty, however, comes closer to being a political romantic, in Carl Schmitt's sense of the term.[20] Rorty's ironism is a version of that form of aestheticism that withdraws from the political. "Romanticism is subjectified occasionalism," Schmitt says; and "the romantic subject treats the world as an occasion and opportunity for his romantic productivity." Schmitt elaborates: "The romantic withdraws from reality. . . . He ironically avoids the constraints of objectivity and guards himself against being committed to anything. The reservation of all infinite possibilities lies in irony . . . everything—society and history, the cosmos and humanity—serves only the productivity of the romantic ego . . . every event is transformed into a fantastic and dreamlike ambiguity, and every object can become anything."[21]

Alex Callinicos glosses Schmitt's remarks in his recent *Against Postmodernism*[22] as follows:

> Schmitt argues that this aestheticization of the relationship between individual and reality was possible only in a "bourgeois world," "where it is left to the private individual to be his own priest, his own poet, his own philosopher, his own king, and his own master builder in the cathedral of his own personality." Moretti takes this explanation a step further. Modernism is "a crucial component of that . . . transformation that has taken place in modern Western societies: the meaning of life is sought no more in the realm of public life, politics . . . instead, it has migrated into the world of . . . private life" . . . . Modernism's "unbelievable range of political choices can be explained only by its basic political indifference."[23]

This type of political strategy *could* be a form of political resistance; but it is much less constructive than Weber's strategy, even though both minimize democratic participation to save the individual. Similarly, Rorty's attempt to democratize Nietzsche's *ubermensch*, construed as a romantic ironist, has the same effect as Weber's privatization of Kant: both amount to the sort of political romanticism that, as Schmitt saw, paves the way for, indeed requires, the Machiavellian political realism that he and Weber saw as an inevitable outgrowth of political romanticism in a pluralist liberal democracy. For Schmitt, indeed, this romantic-liberal strategy avoids political realities—the need to decide and act—which is why liberal democracies need strong charismatic leaders.[24] Rorty is much too sanguine, perhaps naive, about the compatibility of private romanticism and social democracy. Besides, as Callinicos points out, Rorty's desire to democratize the *ubermensch* is hardly likely to occur in today's economic and political climate.[25] The Weberian strategy adopted by Rorty has the effect of minimizing real democracy, furthering elitist and Caesarist politics, and increasing political withdrawal. To save the values of liberal humanism, we must give up participatory democracy and rely on Madison's strategy to limit the political power of the modern state and civil society to interfere in private life. But democracy is only sometimes a means to these ends[26]; and strong democracy, of the Deweyan type, is a threat to romantic privacy.

Rorty may very well be distinguishing the private and the public in another way. I suspect that his reference to the imagination and other romantic themes is directed toward severing the private from the public by some strategy that preserves the inner personality that Weber was defending. But then Rorty's romantic ironists can escape the iron cage, not by trying to modify it, but only by withdrawing into the realm of fantasy, once they have done their minimal duty not to be cruel to others in the public arena. If this is not political defeatism, I do not know what is.

I am convinced that the Weber-Rorty strategy is an attempt to form an alliance between two mutually exclusive and antagonistic ideas: romantic fantasy and technological power politics. This requires us to live the life of a Kierkegaardian: to be a knight of faith in private and a petty bourgeois bank clerk in public. Rorty defends just this view in a paper I will discuss presently.

Sometimes Rorty claims that the bifurcation between private romantic cultivation and the public aspect of our lives can be overcome. At the end of his *London Review of Books* lecture, "The Contingency of Community," he says:

> If the ideal culture of the ideal liberal society ever comes into existence, if Nietzsche, Wittgenstein, Freud and Bloom become part of common sense, then the battle between moralism and romanticism will be over, because the language in which the issue between them was stated will be obsolete. But in the meantime, we should side with the Romantics and do our best to aestheticize society, to keep it safe for everybody else.
>
> Romanticism is thus a vehicle for democratization. But what sort of political culture does aesthetic politics—political romanticism—lead to, and with what results?[27]

In a more recent paper, "Foucault/Dewey/Nietzsche,"[28] Rorty tries to further his goal of defusing and marginalizing more radical uses of revolutionary thought by privatizing them. He also makes clear how narcissistic—and very un-Deweyan—his liberal ironist is when he approvingly cites Blake, "I must create my own system, or be enslaved by another man's."[29] Heretofore the need to create one's final vocabulary, and thus one's world *de novo*, which Rorty tries to democratize via his interpretation of Freud and Nietzsche,[30] need not cut the romantic off from the social bonds that unite one with "one's fellow citizens," or their shared vocabulary. But in this paper the romantic should not desire that his vocabulary be adopted by others. Rorty is now even more extreme in the way he privatizes novel visions than he was heretofore, since elsewhere the revolutionary vocabularies would alter the crust of established traditions and languages in the services of immanent reform and critique. Thus, in some places he suggests that if the utopian revolutionary's final vocabulary is nonsexist, this can help change public discourse.[31] But in the paper under discussion, the "banal"[32] public discourse should not be affected by revolutionary visions of autonomy. So these visions do not, in this paper, have *any* social purchase. He talks about not offering "philosophical grounds for being on your side in public affairs" and equates this with his private ideals, as if my preference for Dostoyevsky over Sartre is on all fours with my preference for civil rights over institutional racism.[33] Here is where Rorty's tacit assumption that the abandonment of foundationalism leaves us without any shared criteria, that there is no space for the criticism of common opinion or existing consensus—i.e., for public space and dialogue—degenerates into nihilism. And what if "standing with one's fellow citizens" puts you in the camp of the racist? Contrary to Rorty's distinction between being radical and being useful,[34] sometimes being useful and being radical are one and the same. I believe we now live in such a time.

As I have indicated in a number of places, Rorty's version of liberalism is a mixture of Millian and Weberian motifs, which resemble those exemplified in cold war liberals such as Sidney Hook and Daniel Bell. Rorty's conception of democracy is very thin, and his romantic liberalism is an obstacle to participatory democracy. His romantic liberalism is, in effect, although not in intent, elitist and politically naive; it borders on what Nietzsche calls "the pessimism of weakness," and rests upon the kind of sharp private-public distinction that, at best, justifies thin, minimal, procedural democracy, and along with it a purely formal notion of community. There is no room for public intellectuals who want to make general criticisms of society if they do not also have viable concrete proposals for reform. This implies that if I can not figure out a way of eliminating institutional sexism and racism, I cannot launch any general criticisms of our society's failures in these areas without becoming a theologian. I am afraid that I do not see this at all. In any event, it is hard to find any important similarities in the realm of politics or culture between Rorty and Dewey. Dewey's notions of democratic culture, community, politics, and renascent liberalism are either dismissed or ignored by Rorty.

However, Rorty's antifoundationalist, post-metaphysical pragmatism amounts to a kind of postmodernism about politics, ethics, and communication that can be made an element in a version of liberalism that is compatible with, indeed, partly constitutive of, a more radical conception of democratic participation. In the next chapter I sketch one version of such an ideal.

NOTES

1. Richard Rorty, "Postmodernist Bourgeois Liberalism," *Journal of Philosophy* 80 (1983): 583–89.

2. Richard Rorty, *Philosophy and the Mirror of Nature* (Princeton: Princeton University Press, 1979); idem, *Consequences of Pragmatism* (Minneapolis: University of Minnesota Press, 1982); idem, *Contingency, Irony, and Solidarity* (New York: Cambridge University Press, 1989).

3. See Rorty, *Consequences*, 209–10, n. 16.

4. Rorty, *Contingency*, 63; "Philosophy as Science, as Metaphor, and as Politics," *The Institution of Philosophy*, ed. A. Cohen and M. Dascal (LaSalle: Open Court, 1989), 13–33; idem, "Anti-Representationalism, Ethnocentrism, and Liberalism," in Rorty, *Objectivity, Relativism and Truth*, vol. 1 (New York:

Cambridge University Press, 1991); idem, "The Priority of Democracy to Philosophy" in *Reading Rorty*, ed. Alan Malachowski (Cambridge: Blackwell's, 1992), 279–302; idem, "Two Cheers for the Cultural Left," *South Atlantic Quarterly* 89 (1990): 227–34, idem, A Post-Philosophical Politics?," an interview with Danny Postel, *Philosophy and Social Criticism* 17 (1990): 199–204.

5. John Dewey, *Individualism Old and New* (New York: Capricorn, 1929); idem, *Liberalism and Social Action* (New York: Capricorn, 1935).

6. "Postmodernist," and "Method, Social Science, and Social Hope," in Rorty, *Consequences*, 191–210.

7. See Richard Rorty, "Thugs and Theorists," *Political Theory* 16 (1989).

8. Rorty, *Contingency, Irony, and Solidarity*, xiv.

9. Ibid., chs. 3-4; Rorty, "A Post-Philosophical Politics?" op. cit., 200; idem, "Two Cheers for the Cultural Left," op. cit.

10. See here Richard Rorty, "Education without Dogma," *Dissent* 36 (Spring 1989): 198–204; idem, "The Opening of American Minds," *Harper's*, July 1989, 18–21; idem, "The Humanistic Intellectual," in *Viewpoints* (American Council for Learned Societies Occasional Papers, no. 10, 1989), 9–12.

11. See Richard Rorty, "The Priority of Democracy to Philosophy," in *Reading Rorty*, ed. Alan Malachowski (Cambridge: Blackwell's, 1989).

12. Richard Rorty, "Epistemological Behaviorism and the De-transcendentalization of Analytic Philosophy," in *Hermeneutics and Praxis*, ed. R. Hollinger (Notre Dame: University of Notre Dame Press, 1985), 89–121.

13. See here Max Weber, "Science as a Vocation," in *From Max Weber*, ed. H. Gerth and C. Wright Mills (New York: Oxford University Press, 1946).

14. Rorty, "Priority," 294, 295. In his earlier "Habermas and Lyotard on Postmodernity," *Praxis International* 3 (1984): 32–44, Rorty associates Dewey with the re-enchantment of the world when he says: "Dewey's suggestion that the way to re-enchant the world, to bring back what religion gave our forefathers, is to stick to the concrete," p. 42, and even links this goal with postmodernism: "Those who want beautiful social harmonies want a postmodernist form of social life, in which society as a whole asserts itself without bothering to ground itself," p. 43. This last phrase is taken by Rorty from Hans Blumenberg, *The Legitimacy of the Modern Age* (Cambridge: MIT Press, 1985). Rorty has been becoming more pessimistic of late, or at least has changed his mind. For a good recent discussion of these issues, see Ernst Behler, *Irony and the Discourse of Modernity* (Seattle: University of Washington Press, 1991).

15. See here James T. Kloppenberg, *Uncertain Victory* (New York: Oxford University Press, 1986) for a stimulating interpretation of Weber as a social democrat and Progressive.

16. See Rorty, "Method, Social Science, and Social Hope," op. cit., 209–10, n. 16; cf. idem, "Postmodernist Bourgeois Liberalism," op. cit.

17. Rorty, "Philosophy as Science, as Metaphor, and as Politics," op. cit., 28.

18. Ibid., 23f.

19. Jurgen Habermas, *The Theory of Communicative Action*, 2 vols. (Boston: Beacon Press, 1984, 1987): idem, *Philosophical Discourse on Modernity* (Cambridge: MIT Press, 1988).

20. See here Michael A. Weinstein, "Western Liberalism Goes Postmodern: Rorty's Pragmatism," in *Canadian Journal of Political and Social Theory* 9 (1986): 10–19, esp. 14–16; and Dieter Misgeld, "Modernity, Democracy, and Social Engineering," *Praxis International* 7 (1987–88): 268–85; cf. James Kloppenberg, *Uncertain Victory* (New York: Oxford University Press, 1988), for an attempt to assimilate Weber to the Progressives and social democracy.

21. See Carl Schmitt, *Political Romanticism* (Cambridge: MIT Press, 1986). For comparisons between Weber and Schmitt, see G. L. Ulmen, "The Sociology of the State: Carl Schmitt and Max Weber," *State Culture and Society* 1, no. 2, (1985): 3–57.

22. Alex Callinicos, *Against Postmodernism* (New York: St. Martin's, 1990), 48.

23. Ibid. The reference is to Schmitt, op. cit., 17, 71–72, 75–76.

24. Ibid., 49. The reference is to F. Moretti, "The Spell of Indecision," in *Marxism and the Interpretation of Culture*, ed. C. Nelson and L. Grossberg (Urbana: University of Illinois Press, 1988), 339, 341.

25. Ibid., 117.

26. Ibid., 90.

27. Beetham, op. cit., 136, 142.

28. Rorty, *Contingency*, 54, 56.

29. *Raritan* 9 (Spring 1990) 1–8; cf. Rorty, "Method, Social Science and Social Hope."

30. *Raritan*, 1; cf. his remarks against MacIntyre on the rich aesthete, Richard Rorty, "Freud and Moral Reflection," in *Pragmatism's Freud: The Moral Disposition of Psychoanalysis*, ed. Joseph H. Smith and William Kerrigan (Baltimore: Johns Hopkins University Press, 1986), p. 16, where Rorty says: "I would welcome a culture dominated by 'the Rich Aesthete, the Manager, and the Therapist' so long as *everybody* who wants to gets to be an aesthete (and, if not rich) as comfortably off as most—as rich as the managers can manage, guided by Rawls' Difference Principle."

31. Ibid., 1–27. This is vol. 9 of the Psychiatry and the Humanities Series.

32. *Raritan*, 5.

33. Ibid., 7.

34. Berkeley Lecture, September 1989, Applied Heidegger Conference.

Chapter 6

Liberalism and Participatory Democracy

In this chapter I would like to sketch a conception of participatory democracy. In particular, I want to explore the issue of whether anything in the modern liberal tradition can be made compatible with this conception of democracy, or perhaps even become an essential ingredient in it.

This question is important for a variety of (perhaps obvious) reasons. My argument has been that modern liberal thought and practice undermines participatory democracy, which shares with "classical" democracy a trust in people, at least as citizens, to arrive at reasonable consensus on common projects. But I also believe that there are no logical or conceptual incompatibilities between liberalism and democracy: the term "liberal democracy" is not a contradiction in terms. Some way of combining elements of liberalism with participatory democracy should therefore be possible.

Thus, I will not consider more radical proposals, on the part of both those Marxists who think liberalism must be totally rejected if we are to have democracy,[1] and those who believe that participatory democracy must be abandoned altogether if liberalism is to survive. These views may be right. But I am committed here to an immanent critique of liberalism, and thus to the question of whether an immanent reconstruction of liberalism can redeem the democratic promise of the radical elements of the liberal tradition.

The most natural way for me to proceed is to see whether any trends within liberalism that point in the direction of participatory democracy, or are at least congenial to it, can be identified. These should involve either the rejection or the severe modification of the elitist dimensions of liberalism that generate the dilemma of modern liberalism. Then we can explore the extent to which these elements in liberalism can be made part of a model of participatory democracy, or at least be developed in tandem with such a model.

One important example of just such a view is the work of Dewey, who tried to combine the need for experts with the ideas that they should not play a decisive, let alone determinative, role in public life, and that education could instill in citizens the kinds of skills and habits that would make the faith in common inquiry, necessary for democratic culture and participation, more effective.[2]

Of course, for Dewey "democracy" was a name for an entire culture, for practices and institutions that range over the departments of human life. Dialogue and conversation were the means to actualize such a unified culture. As a number of writers have pointed out, Dewey anticipates Habermas's own attempt at reconstructing participatory democracy, although Habermas is in many ways still too caught up in views that Dewey tried to overcome, e.g., he places too much reliance on traditional philosophical notions and values, and is too caught up in the nexus of the systems view of the world that may in fact destroy democratic participation.[3] By the same token, Dewey's conception of democracy may rest upon a kind of metaphysical naturalism (a kind of biologism) that is unacceptable for other reasons, and thus may be an inappropriate point of departure for a theory of radical democracy, especially at a time when evolutionary notions of social progress have little prima facie credibility.

So more recent developments within both the liberal and the radical democratic traditions may be required, if, as some suggest, the writings of Dewey and Habermas need to be surpassed in favor of more postmodernist ideas about democracy, dialogue, community, and pluralism.

Recent discussions[4] suggest that any marriage between liberalism and participatory democracy needs to be radicalized along a number of fronts. It will be useful to adopt the name "radical democracy" as a term of art for views which move in this direction. Here then, are some suggestions for what must be achieved if a model of radical democracy is to be developed:

a. It must be based on certain postmodernist insights about dialogue, philosophy, rationality, so as to avoid elitism and to build in the idea that democracy requires dialogue and debate, indeed contestation.
b. It must "resituate" notions such as self, community, plurality, and justice within a conceptual orbit that takes account of postmodernist discussions of difference and "otherness."
c. It must understand community as rooted in difference and plurality, not in unity, at least the unity in which all cows are black. The idea of social experimentation, of politics without a "ground," must be radicalized.
d. It must develop ideas about politics that reject the epistemological and moral frameworks of modern philosophy, especially those regarding "truth," "universality" and "rationality." Politics must not be rooted in epistemology.

I do not wish to thematize every aspect of these programmatic claims. There is already a growing body of literature[5] in any case. My aim here is just to sketch an overall approach that can reconcile elements of, or recent glosses on, liberalism with some form of participatory democracy in order to round out my argument. Details must wait for another occasion.

Step 1. Develop an antifoundationalist, post-metaphysical conception of liberalism that takes dialogue and practice, the construction of a "well-ordered society," as the aim of democratic politics.

This step has been taken by John Rawls and Michael Walzer, despite other differences between them.[6] The key ideas here are:

a. Politics is independent of philosophy.
b. Dialogue is pragmatic, not philosophical, i.e., not constrained by philosophical standards or theories of truth, knowledge, rationality.
c. Politics aims at consensus geared to the issues of the day.
d. Experts do not play a decisive role in democratic practice.
e. Some form of pluralism—of voices, perspectives, etc.—must exist, and not be reduced to any sort of unity that obscures or eliminates the differences, even though an "overlapping consensus" should be a goal.
f. Politics takes place against the background of ongoing dialogue and interpretation about our common history, since, as Benjamin Barber recently argued, democracy must be historicized if it is to work.

Step 2. Liberalism must take the next step, and move in the direction of postmodernism. Not only is politics independent of philosophy, democracy is incompatible with philosophy, which sees politics as rooted in epistemological criteria that rule out a constructivist view of society that has necessary democratic participation. In particular, the conception of "liberal neutrality" in John Rawls, Robert Ackerman and Ronald Dworkin may need to be abandoned, in favor of a more hermeneutical, even agonistic, conception of dialogue, such as that provided recently by Benjamin Barber.[7]

This step has been taken by Feyerabend,[8] Walzer and Barber,[9] and Rorty,[10] is present in Roberto Unger and Rawls,[11] and Jean-Francois Lyotard[12] and Jacques Derrida[13] can surely be read as moving in this direction.

The key insight here is that if citizens are to engage in dialogue to make democracy possible, the process and results must not be constrained or determined in advance by epistemological assumptions about knowledge, truth, rationality, method, and so on.[14] This would introduce the elitism that must, at all costs, be kept at bay. Moreover, if social experimentation is to be more than an empty phrase, citizens have to be free to develop whatever ideas and solutions the demands of the day suggest and to participate in a relatively uncoerced open dialogue.

Step 3. The pluralistic implications of these steps need to be embraced, not abandoned. This requires a discussion of whether Rawls's idea of a "well-ordered society," Rorty's notion of an existing consensus, and Ackerman's notion of a neutral dialogue may actually block more radical forms of social experimentation. Feyerabend's democratic relativism, Walzer's version of pluralism, Rorty's version of postmodernist liberal pragmatism, Rawls's version of Kantian constructivism may need a healthy dose of the sort of radical ideas about community, plurality, difference, and otherness developed of late by Derrida and Lyotard, as well as by feminists and others.[15]

In whatever forms it takes, pluralism requires that the existing consensus should never remain unchallenged. It needs to promote the idea that consensus and community are always essentially contestable, always makeshift, always rooted in diversity and plurality—never to aim at total unity or finality— and always the product of an uncoerced nonphilosophical tension among different voices. This again requires a pluralist approach to our own history and possibilities.[16]

Step 4. Plurality and community need to be rethought.

a. Plurality is the recognition of difference, of an epistemological perspectivism, of the need to preserve otherness at all costs. Feminist writers have explored this aspect of plurality, as have Lyotard and Derrida, and post-Marxists such as Ernesto Laclau and Chantel Mouffe, in their criticism of traditional Marxist notions of hegemony.
b. Community must be rethought to give pride of place to difference and plurality. A community must be based upon, indeed constituted by, the diversity of voices that give rise to an identity in difference that cannot be captured by the traditional notions of community as a unity. This Hegelian idea, suitably naturalized and then postmodernized, has arguably been the essence of radical democracy since the Sophists. Thanks to Lyotard, Laclau and Mouffe, Barber and Ariel Botwinick,[17] we may be in a position to reinvent these ideas.

Liberalism too often takes some "melting pot" idea of unity as a goal. What we need is a model of "community without unity,"[18] which takes plurality seriously, but which does not give up on ideals such as communication, justice, and agreement. Lyotard's notion of the differend, designed to prevent closure or unity, and his efforts to give Kant's discussions of aesthetic judgment a postmodernist political meaning, must be brought into the effort to develop models of radical democracy. Justice and community are always "ideas" without content that stand for the unexpressible and indeterminate hope for justice and community, with no telos or final resting place.[19] But ongoing debate about the meaning of "American democracy" must always be in play, since our future possibilities, as opposed to any "telos," are in important ways a function of how we interpret this notion.

Step 5. The insights of post-Marxists such as Laclau and Mouffe mesh with these proposals. An attempt is made to combine liberalism, Marxism, feminism, postmodernism, and democratic socialism, by developing a thoroughly historicist, pragmatic, post-metaphysical notion of "radical democracy" that takes the ideas of social experimentation, plurality, and the constitution of society to its limits, much as Roberto Unger's work on social theory does. Questions of justice, community, participation, plurality must all be reworked from the ground up within the sort of postmodern framework sketched here, in tandem with continuous efforts to appropriate a usable American past.

Step 6. Despite the disparities between the idea of radical democracy and the realities of the new world order/postindustrial society, with its technocratic, market-oriented politics (privatization, etc.), some developments may be signs of better things to come. Debates about post-Fordist flexibility[20] suggest that economic democracy and workplace democracy may become more and more necessary. The new populism, although not without its dangers, even its antidemocratic ideas about race, class, and gender, is still a step in the right direction, since it rejects elitism and takes dialogue and debate seriously. The debates involving the "cultural wars" make dialogue and participation, and perhaps eventually consensus or at least civility, real possibilities, in some ways even necessary. Hopefully, the climate will allow for more productive dialogue, more consensus, perhaps even the overcoming of obstacles to genuine pluralistic and radical democracy, e.g., sexism, racism, Social Darwinism, homophobia, etc. The emphasis on local involvement, on electronic town meetings, on the kind of participation Ross Perot generated, may be healthy signs that enough "backyard revolutions"[21] may eventually make a difference. At least we can hope that, under the pressure of postmodern conditions, more participation will become necessary and will eventually be seen as desirable.

NOTES

1. See David Beetham, "Beyond Liberal Democracy," *Socialist Register* 14 (1981); Samuel Bowles and Herbert Gintis, *Democracy and Capitalism* (New York: Basic Books, 1986).
2. Robert Westbrook, *John Dewey and American Democracy* (Ithaca: Cornell University Press, 1990).
3. See Thomas McCarthy, "Complexity and Democracy: On the Seductions of Systems Theory," in McCarthy, *Ideals and Illusions* (Cambridge: MIT Press, 1991); Danilo Zolo, *Democracy and Complexity: A Realist Approach* (College Park: Pennsylvania State University Press, 1992).
4. See William E. Connolly, *Identity/Difference* (Ithaca: Cornell University Press, 1991); John S. Dryzek, *Discursive Democracy* (New York: Cambridge University Press, 1990); Joshua Cohen, "The Economic Basis of Deliberative Democracy," *Social Philosophy and Policy* 6 (1989): 25–50; and idem, "Deliberation and Democratic Legitimacy," in *The Good Polity*, ed. Alan Hamlin and Philip Pettit (Cambridge: Blackwell's, 1989), 17–34; Onora O'Neill, "The Public Uses of Reason," *Political Theory* 15 (1988): 523–51.
5. For some important discussions of contemporary liberalism, see Stephen Mulhall and Adam Swift, *Liberals and Communitarians* (Cambridge: Blackwell's, 1992); Georgia Warnke, *Justice and Interpretation* (Cambridge: MIT Press, 1992); Ian Shapiro, *Political Criticism* (Berkeley: University of California Press, 1989).
6. John Rawls, "The Idea of an Overlapping Consensus," in Rawls, *Political Liberalism* (New York: Columbia University Press, 1993); "The Domain of the Political and Overlapping Consensus," in ibid. For critical discussion of Rawls' political liberalism, see Shapiro, Warnke, Mulhall and Swift, works cited above. See also Chantel Mouffe, "Rawls: Political Philosophy without Politics," *Philosophy and Social Criticism* 13 (1987): 105–23.
7. Benjamin Barber, *An Aristocracy of Everyone* (Ballantine Books, 1992).
8. Paul Feyerabend, *Science in a Free Society* (New York: Verso, 1979).
9. Barber, op. cit.; Michael Walzer, *Criticism and Interpretation* (Cambridge: Harvard University Press, 1990).
10. Richard Rorty, "The Priority of Democracy to Philosophy," in his *Philosophical Papers* (New York: Cambridge University Press); idem, *Contingency, Irony, and Solidarity* (New York: Cambridge University Press, 1989); idem, "Antirepresentationism, Ethnocentrism and Liberalism," introductory essay to *Philosophical Papers*, vol. 1, *Objectivity, Relativism, and Truth* (New York: Cambridge University Press, 1991), 1–20; and idem "Philosophy as Science, as Metaphor, and as Politics," in *The Institution of Philosophy*, ed. Avner Cohen and Marcelo Dascal (LaSalle: Open Court, 1989), 13–35. For criticism, see Christopher Norris, *Uncritical Reason* (Amherst: University of Massachusetts Press, 1992); and

Jo Burrows, "Conversational Politics: Rorty's Pragmatist Apology for Liberalism," in *Reading Rorty*, ed. Alan Malachowski (Cambridge: Blackwell's, 1989), 322–38; Ernesto Laclau, "Community and Its Paradoxes: Richard Rorty's 'Liberal Utopia,'" in *Community at Loose Ends* (Minneapolis: University of Minnesota Press, 1991), 85–99.

11. Roberto Unger, *Social Theory*, 3 vols. (New York: Cambridge University Press, 1987); and Robin W. Lovin and Michael J. Perry, eds., *Critique and Construction* (New York: Cambridge University Press, 1990); Rawls, "The Idea of Public Reason," op. cit.

12. See John Keane, "The Modern Democratic Revolution: Reflections on Jean-Francois Lyotard's *la condition postmoderne*," *Chicago Review* 35 (1987): 4–19.

13. See Jacques Derrida, *The Other Heading* (Bloomington: Indiana University Press, 1992); idem, *Spectres of Marx* (New York: Routledge, 1994).

14. Ariel Botwincik, *Postmodernism and Democratic Theory* (Philadelphia: Temple University Press, 1993).

15. See Carole Pateman, "Feminism and Democracy," in *Democratic Theory and Practice*, ed. Graeme Duncan (New York: Cambridge University Press, 1982), 204–17; idem, *Participation and Democratic Theory* (New York: Cambridge University Press, 1983). Nancy Fraser, "On Actually Existing Democracies," in *Habermas and the Public Sphere*, ed. Craig Calhoun (Cambridge: MIT Press, 1992); Nancy Fraser and Linda Nicholson "An Encounter between Feminism and Postmodernism," in *Universal Abandon?* ed. Andrew Ross (Minneapolis: University of Minnesota, 1987); "Solidarity or Singularity: Richard Rorty between Romanticism and Technocracy," in *Reading Rorty*, ed. Malichowski op. cit.

16. Botwinick, op. cit.

17. See works cited above.

18. See William Corlett, *Community without Unity* (Durham: Duke University Press, 1989).

19. See Jean-Francois Lyotard, *The Differend* (Minneapolis: University of Minnesota Press, 1989).

20. See Barry Smart, *Conditions of Postmodernity* (New York: Routledge, 1992); John Keane, op. cit.

21. See Harry C. Boyte, *Community Is Possible* (New York: Harper and Row, 1984); and Sara M. Evans and Harry C. Boyte, *Free Spaces* (Chicago: University of Chicago Press, 1990); see also Thomas E. Cronin, *Direct Democracy* (Cambridge: Harvard University Press, 1989); Anne Phillips, *Engendering Democracy* (College Park: Pennsylvania State University Press, 1991); Peter Bachrach and Ariel Botwinick, *Power and Emancipation* (Philadelphia: Temple University Press, 1991).

Part III

LIBERAL THEMES

Chapter 7

Liberalism and Elitism in Perspective

This brief chapter sums up the argument so far, to prepare the way for a more systematic and thematic discussion of liberalism in this part and to set the stage for a survey of some contemporary issues in part 4. The main thesis of the book is not new. It is that modern liberalism systematically undermines participatory democracy by limiting "democracy" to the political sphere and by construing political democracy to mean little more than voting for representatives who come from one or another ruling elite. Benjamin Barber, Alan Wolfe, C. B. MacPherson, Andrew Levine, S. Bowles and H. Gintis, Thomas Spragens, and others have made this argument. Barber's formulation is representative. He says this:

> We suffer, . . . not from too much but too little democracy. . . . From the time of de Tocqueville, it has been said that an excess of democracy can undo liberal institutions. . . . [Rather] an excess of liberalism has undone democratic institutions: for what little democracy we have had in the West has been repeatedly compromised by the liberal institutions with which it has been undergirded and the liberal philosophy from which its theory and practice have been derived.[1]

My investigation of modern liberalism has not focused on the conflict between democracy and capitalism or the connections between the latter and liberalism. Instead, I have tried to uncover the basic philosophical and sociological roots of the tension between liberalism and democracy by exploring the key assumptions and aspirations of modern liberalism, in its three ideal-typical forms: Millian liberalism, Weberian (romantic) liberalism, and Durkheimian (corporate) liberalism.

The focus of my argument is on the ways in which liberalism in philosophy, the social sciences, theories of culture and education, and American political theory undermines participatory democracy by defending what Barber calls "thin democracy." Democracy becomes either a morally neutral functional and organization concept, as in Durkheim and the corporate liberals, or a morally neutral battleground of competing gods and demons, in which democracy is itself but one private value that is only valid as an instrument for other ends, e.g., the preservation of privatized liberal-humanist values, or as a Madisonian device for keeping the iron cage at arm's length (Weber).

Since my argument is that modern liberalism is on the horns of a dilemma between elitism and democracy, I will begin with some brief remarks about elitism and its connection with the liberal thin conception of democracy.

Liberal elitism takes two forms, which often overlap or have a synergistic effect that reinforces thin democracy. The first type of elitism is cultural elitism. One can find this model in Mill, Arnold, the cold war, end-of-ideology liberals (the so-called New York Intellectuals), Trilling, Bell, Hook and, more recently, Rorty. On this view, thin democracy is preferable to radical or participatory democracy because the latter undermines high culture and results in mass society. The tyranny of the majority is the main fear. One can already see this in Kant, who argues for enlightenment from "the top down." One sees it in Mill, who weaves the conservative-liberalism of Tocqueville with the romantic elitism of Coleridge to defend a ruling class of cultural elites who will educate the masses for thin democracy, but also convince them to listen to their betters. He also advocates a weighted voting system to give the knowledge elite more representation.

The master argument of this view is that the need for a cultural elite, the need to preserve high culture and humanist values against mass democracy, must allow "culture" to subdue "anarchy," in Arnold's words. What the cold war liberals called "the theory of mass society" is just another name for this Mill-Arnold strategy.

Since the liberal cultural elites are convinced that most people are irrational and immature, the politics of mass society requires a theory of thin democracy: a minimal level of democratic participation and the defusion of mass culture, i.e., consumerism and narcissism, seen as the result of cultural modernism and the efforts of some high modernists to break down the liberal distinction between culture and politics and use radical literature and art to foment a revolution against capitalist bourgeois society.

The theory of the democratic elite, which Schumpeter and others extract from Weber's discussion of modern society, his existentialist conception of values and the resulting need for a charismatic political realist to prevent anarchy and limit the stranglehold of modern bureaucracy, leads to the idea that thin democracy should allow citizens to vote for competing elites, since classical democracy presupposes that people are rational and that we do not have a Weberian world. Schumpeter, following Kant and Weber, believes that after exercising their right to vote for the elites who will control them, they must, in the words of both Kant and Weber, "shut up and obey."

Later in this century, the cold war liberals invoked the end-of-ideology thesis, and various versions of liberalism—interest group liberalism, behavioralism, pluralism, empirical democratic theory, piecemeal social engineering—to solve the Weberian problem of the wars of gods and demons under the aegis of the end-of-ideology, "vital center" liberalism formulated by Schlesinger, Hartz, Richard Hofstadter, and Boorstein in an effort to silence radical criticism of the existing order, and in order to defend McCarthyism but save themselves from the charge that there were no differences between liberals such as themselves and Communists. In so doing, they distanced themselves from those forces within modern American liberalism, e.g., Randolph Bourne and Lewis Mumford, whose radical criticisms of capitalism and consumerism were congenial to the radical movements that began with populism and extended to social democracy and the radical culture movements in the 1920s, 1930s, and 1960s. In my judgment, it was the New Left, and not the liberals, who inherited the democratic tradition.

The role of the liberal cultural elite was to glorify America, dismiss European influences as un-American, anti-enlightenment, and antihumanist, and to argue that America was and always has been "liberal," so that political disagreements were only disagreements about means. This justified the end-of-ideology piecemeal engineering approach to politics and the various embodiments of the theory of the democratic elite mentioned earlier.

On top of all this, the cold-war liberals, notably Hook, Bell, Lipset, Parsons, argued that McCarthyism was the culmination of the populist and radical criticism of elitism and liberal enlightenment rationality; McCarthyism was seen as a manifestation of mass society. By viewing populism as conservative and antisemitic, participatory democracy becomes the devil: McCarthyism and the radical right are its latest and most dangerous manifestations. The attack on liberal elitism and thin democracy by members of the adversary culture reinforced the end-of-ideology thesis and the war against participatory democracy by liberals since the end of World War II, and is now being defended by Bell, Rorty, Fukuyama, and so-called neoliberals such as Robert Reich who proclaim the worldwide victory of liberalism, at least in principle. The end-of-history thesis of Fukuyama is the globalization of Bell's end-of-ideology thesis, designed to justify the postindustrial order of the knowledge elite and the global market.

But these results are not entirely due to the influence of liberal cultural elitism. A Durkheimian influence is evident, e.g., in Bell, in communitarians such as Michael Sandel and Robert Bellah. Civil religion must be recovered to prevent adversary culture—modernism, narcissism, radicalism, consumerism—from destroying capitalism, bourgeois society, and the market, the only forces of rational enlightenment progress. The growth of new and virulent forms of Social Darwinism and the Protestant work ethic, with the attendant increase in repression in all aspects of life, is the outgrowth of these developments.

More fundamentally, we see in them the culmination of corporate liberalism, which is the outgrowth of the second version of modern liberal elitism, the idea of the knowledge elite. This view, already found in Mill's insistence that the experts in social science and political economy be given more votes and more power than anybody else, came into its own at the beginning of the present century. As America became more industrialized and modernized, it turned into a Weberian iron cage. Corporate liberalism emerged in this context. Accompanying the call for "efficiency and uplift" was the rise of professionalization, in the social and behavioral sciences, and in the helping professions (under the aegis of Taylorism), for instance, and the growth of the modern American university. The early Progressives, e.g., Croly and

Lippmann, called for "mastery" over "drift," Lippmann's surrogates for Arnold's "culture" over "anarchy." They called for a knowledge elite, a group of Saint Simonian experts who should be morally neutral and objective, or at least guided by an ethos of enlightenment reformism, who would turn the United States into an integrated corporate state. Democracy became a functional, organizational procedure to maintain the dynamic equilibrium of the system to adjust. Parsons's functionalism is the end result of this development.

One can trace the history of this idea. The Progressives, the rise of administrative science, Taylorism, the notion of the managerial elite, of the politics of expertise, are but embellishments on it. The political realism of Weber, Morgenthau, and Henry Kissinger hooks up with the idea of the managerial elite, and eventually with end-of-ideology liberalism, to give us the idea of the totally administered state. The history of twentieth-century America is the history of how the views I have been discussing have systematically undermined participatory democracy, social criticism, and democratic culture, in favor of thin democracy, social engineering, and the politics of adjustment and efficiency.

What justifies the liberal allegiance to thin democracy? What motivates it is perhaps clear: a distrust of the average person. I think one justification for thin democracy is the idea that liberalism and liberal values take priority over democracy, so that democracy is seen at best as a means or expedient for promoting liberalism. Moreover, liberals such as Russell treat liberalism as an embodiment of scientific method, of the ethics of fallibilism, and thus of pragmatism. It follows that for liberals, democracy's existence rests upon contingent empirical considerations. Combined with the Weber-Rorty idea that liberal practices require and admit of no foundations, we get the result that democracy cannot be defended in any strong sense. If empirical considerations show that liberal values can be best achieved by a ruling elite, or that "too much" democracy threatens these liberal aims, so much the worse for democracy.

Of course, what is not tentative is that liberalism is the only rational political position, and that whatever liberal elites decide is privileged, a view defended by Mill and by Rorty, who makes liberalism the only possible conception of politics. But, as many critics have pointed out, liberalism is actually totally apolitical, which is why it can only defend thin democracy, and only in the most tentative manner.

Moreover, as I have already said, democracy is limited to the political sphere, not culture, the workplace, or the household. In the university reformists were dismissed and acceptable criticism was marginalized to academic controversies about expert opinion, once the modern social sciences became professionalized and became part of the modern university.[2] The idea of a democratic culture, found in Bourne and Mumford, and in the radical movements of the 1920s, 1930s, and 1960s, and Dewey's radical idea of democracy as a way of life, which supports participatory democracy in politics, have never been part of the mainstream liberal agenda.

Modern liberalism has advocated a top-down elitist strategy since Kant. This is what liberal education is all about. Educate the masses, lift them up, civilize them, prepare them for democracy, but also make sure they know who their betters are, and why they must shut up and obey them, if they want a democracy for the people, but not by them, which just will not work. Indeed, by invoking the pessimism about the intelligence and maturity of the masses and their opinions, found in Graham Wallas and Freud, elitists from Lippmann and Lasswell to Bell have paved the way for the conclusion implicit in liberal doctrines: even thin democracy is part of the problem, indeed, the greatest problem. Enter Huntington, Bell, Fukuyama, the neoliberals, on the one hand, and the New Right's version of populism, on the other, mix them with growing voter apathy and anger over what one recent writer calls "the betrayal of democracy,"[3] and the liberal elitist theory of mass society becomes a self-fulfilling prediction. If we add to this what Lyotard calls "the mercantilization of knowledge," and the incorporation of the modern university, the marginalization or destruction of the liberal arts and sociology—the two traditional sites of genuine criticism—how are we to seriously evaluate the claim of Fukuyama and Rorty[4] that liberalism has triumphed?

The so-called end-of-history thesis, echoed by Rorty, that liberalism has won a worldwide victory, at least "in theory," may seem preposterous in light of what has been going on in this country and in Europe for the past twelve years. But on my view they are right. Liberalism, in its neoliberal guise, which is indistinguishable from the corporatism of Reagan-Bush-Thatcher, has won a major victory. This is why democracy, especially participatory democracy, is on the verge of extinction, if it is not already dead. Democracy is dying *because* liberalism *has* triumphed.

It does not follow that radical democracy needs to reject everything in the liberal-humanist tradition, e.g., doctrines about liberty, autonomy, freedom of speech. Nor are we faced with the need to go in the conservative direction of the liberal communitarians or the neoliberals. We can, I believe, incorporate the insights of those radical elements in the liberal tradition—from Bourne, from Dewey, even from Rorty—marry them to the more radical democratic-socialist, populist, radical traditions from the 1920s, 1930s, and 1960s, and move toward a conception of radical democracy that combines their insights with those of radical democrats such as Walzer, Carde Pateman, and Barber, of post-Marxists such as Laclau and Mouffe, and of postmodernists such as Lyotard and Derrida, whose work arguably paves the way for a radical democracy that combines the insights of radical liberalism, Marxism, democratic socialism, feminism, and postmodernism.

NOTES

1. Benjamin Barber, *Strong Democracy* (Berkeley: University of California Press, 1984), xi.

2. Mary Furner, *From Advocacy and Objectivity* (Lexington: University of Kentucky Press); Dorothy Ross, *Origins of American Social Science* (New York: Cambridge University Press, 1990).

3. William Greider, *Who Will Tell the People: The Betrayal of Democracy* (New York: Simon and Schuster, 1991).

4. Francis Fukuyama, *The End of History and the Last Man* (New York: Macmillan, 1992); Richard Rorty, *Contingency, Irony, and Solidarity* (New York: Cambridge University Press, 1989).

Chapter 8

Liberalism, Science, and Society

Several dimensions of the interrelations between liberalism and science require more systematic discussion, in order to further the discussion of the elitist themes I have been exploring.

The following topics will be discussed in this chapter:

a. liberalism and the Enlightenment;
b. liberalism and the scientific ethos;
c. liberalism and the fact-value distinction;
d. science and elitism.

In chapter 9 I will elaborate further on the liberal view of culture and education.

Patrick Moynihan articulates the dark side of liberalism in a paper called "Liberalism and Knowledge." He puts it this way:

> As should be perfectly evident, social-science knowledge, like scientific knowledge, poses problems for democracy. (It being, for example, a particularly perverse quality of many social situations that solutions are what may be termed "counterintuitive." That is to say the operation of the system is such that the "common-sense" solution to a problem is exceedingly likely to be wrong. There are good reasons for this, as they can be demonstrated. But only to a small number of persons. What then to do with the popular will?) Concentrated knowledge is a form of concentrated power and creates, simply, the elite condition. . . . One way to look at American democracy is to see it not so much as democracy, but rather a society with an unprecedently large and varied assortment of elites. The people are asked which elites will govern them for which purposes.[1]

Moynihan is rehearsing Schumpeter's revisionist conception of democracy, the so-called theory of the democratic elite. In this chapter and the next I want to explore the ramifications of this version of liberalism.

LIBERALISM AND THE ENLIGHTENMENT

It is common wisdom that modern liberalism is associated with the eighteenth-century Enlightenment.[2] For the present purposes, the Enlightenment emphasizes the following themes:

a. Knowledge is power.
b. Ignorance is the root of human misery.
c. Knowledge, particularly science, and scientific method can relieve the human estate through continuous applications to society, indeed, to human problems in general, e.g., through some form of utilitarian or cost-benefit analysis.
d. Human beings are hard-wired to be selfish. So education must induce people to act altruistically to promote their enlightened self-interest. This will either directly (as in Bentham and Mill) or indirectly (as in Adam Smith) promote social well-being, where society is conceived on a Newtonian model.[3]
e. Humanity will progress as science allows us to replace institutions and practices that are nonscientific with those which are scientific, i.e., a scientific civilization is necessary (if not sufficient) for human progress.[4]

These doctrines already pit the common opinions and experience of the "uneducated" against the authority of a knowledgeable elite. The French thinkers, Saint-Simon, Comte, Durkheim, are the most zealous advocates of this view, which goes back to Francis Bacon and extends to the present.[5] I am not questioning entirely the wisdom of this Enlightenment idea. But it paves the way for the notion of expertise in society, and thus for the view that the masses are ignorant and incapable of much, if any, self-governance, at least none that is not "from the top down." At the same time, it serves as an aura that enshrines the professional as both more knowledgeable than, and, *ipso facto*, morally superior to, the average person.[6] The presumption is that the "expert" always knows best, and is either on higher moral grounds than others, or is making "objective," "morally neutral" scientific judgments, which therefore cannot be questioned by the nonexpert.

The issues are obviously very complex. I am only arguing against the presumption that the expert is all knowing and all good, and in favor of democratic participation of some sort, even in matters requiring expertise.[7] The general problem, certainly for liberal democracy, but also for participatory democracy, is to recognize the existence of a knowledge elite, and perhaps also a cultural elite, while also allowing for democratic participation across the board. This connects up with a second problem: steering a fine line between the kind of "organized skepticism" or "fallibilism" that is supposedly typical of liberal democracy and the scientific ethos—conceived of as an ideal microcosm of democracy—and the kind of dogmatism that one is prone to if one really believes that scientific doctrines and methods are privileged over everything else in all domains. In still other terms, the issue is about the limits of tolerance within liberal doctrines and practice, which I discussed briefly in connection with Mill. Does liberalism rule out doctrines and practices, e.g., those associated with participation, and thus limit tolerance? How does one determine when a matter has been "sufficiently settled" so as to justify restrictions on tolerance and thereby, perhaps, participatory democracy? If, for instance, a community wants creationism taught, should this be disallowed because it is demonstrably a false doctrine? If not, must democratic participation lead to irrational action? If so, is this the price we must pay for democracy? This is the conflict between Plato and Aristotle on theoretical knowledge vs. practical wisdom. In more recent terms, e.g., in Rorty, it is the problem of antifoundationalist pragmatism (social practices) vs. epistemology as the ground of politics.

LIBERALISM AND THE SCIENTIFIC ETHOS

There exists a good deal of literature on this topic.[8] According to one view, made famous by Robert Merton, Michael Polanyi, and Karl Popper, the virtues that guide the scientific community—tolerance, open-mindedness, fairness, "organized skepticism"—define the "open society" and turn the scientific community into a model, indeed a microcosm, of a liberal democracy. But this picture has recently been challenged, by Thomas Kuhn, Paul Feyerabend, and others.[9] I do not wish to enter these debates here. My point is rather that this scientific ethos, that of the "open society," raises once again the questions about tolerance, skepticism, and expertise. On the one hand, as we saw in connection with Russell, if liberalism is reduced to the application of scientific method to society, participation becomes at best a contingent and very conditional value. On the other hand, organized skepticism can become nihilistic, and may in fact destroy the conditions needed for any sort of communal discussion or action.[10]

One way to get between the horns of this dilemma is to follow Rawls and Walzer,[11] Feyerabend,[12] Rorty,[13] and Lyotard,[14] and break the connection between philosophy (epistemology and metaphysics, in particular) and politics. In even stronger terms, it may be necessary to argue that philosophy and participatory democracy are at odds.

Another option, the one I associate with John Dewey and Jurgen Habermas[15]—and this can be assimilated, up to a point, with the more radical view of the first option—is to find ways of reconciling expertise and participatory democracy. From the point of view of the problem of elitism, the practical problem is obvious: At what point does participatory involvement become, in Ludwig Wittgenstein's phrase, "an engine idling"?

A third option, which I will discuss at length, is the dominant response of the modern liberal tradition, as well as other advocates of the ruling-elite or managerial-elite idea, namely to limit democracy by turning politics into either a branch of applied science or technology or else a field of competition for various ruling elites or "interest groups." The liberal values of knowledge, rationality, and cost efficiency conspire to marginalize democratic participation, because (a) modern problems require expert knowledge, or at least a level of intelligence and rationality allegedly not available to the general populace; and (b) the general populace is emotionally and psychologically immature, i.e., most people are irrational as well as (relatively) unintelligent, so that their opinions cannot be trusted. This view, which shares a great deal with modern conservatism[16] takes two basic forms, which I have been calling "romantic" (Weberian) liberalism, and "corporate" (Durkheimian) liberalism.

LIBERALISM AND THE FACT-VALUE DICHOTOMY

One very important factor that generates the dilemma of modern liberalism centers around the relations among science, knowledge, and morality. The so-called fact-value dichotomy illustrates the issues.

On the view of scientific method that underlies modern liberalism's epistemology, scientific doctrines and methods provide the best or the only embodiments of "rational" activities. Scientific knowledge is privileged. Science gives us knowledge that is "objective," value neutral, beyond subjective interpretation and distortion, that is a universally valid set of doctrines, arrived at by an objective, neutral, rational method that eliminates bias, ideology, wishful thinking, etc.

But what about values, value judgments, morality, and, by extension, the political? The epistemology of liberalism, a mixture of British empiricism, Continental rationalism and its variants (including, as I suggested earlier, the existentialism of Weber and the anti-foundationalist postmodernism of Rorty) gives rise to the following dilemma. If morality is to be "rationally grounded," it must fall within the orbit of the scientific canon. Moral judgments must be supportable by science, or else relegated to the realm of opinion, which (on this view) means the realm of "the subjective." At the very least, morality would have to be understood on a very different model of rationality, which becomes more difficult to articulate under the influence of positivism and behaviorism, and in any case yields at best a formal, empty notion of morality, usually along Kantian lines (procedural justice and the morally neutral state, for instance).

The first alternative, that morality be assimilable to empirical science, is developed by utilitarianism and behaviorism, the forerunners of end-of-ideology, piecemeal engineering politics, as well as so-called political realism, all characteristic of liberalism in the twentieth century. If one starts with the "naturalistic" assumption that "the good" can be defined empirically, e.g., as "pleasure," or in terms of rational choice theory and its variants (as in theories of economic democracy and empirical democracy),[17] morality boils down to cost-benefit analysis, that is, to an applied science or technology. Legislation, for instance, then becomes a task for "experts," or at least a knowledge elite, whose aim is to promote the general welfare. The opinions of those affected, let alone their voices, becomes either irrelevant at best or harmful, on this view, whose only constraint is the bottom line. This is why writers such as B. F. Skinner think that democracy is irrelevant to social engineering.[18]

This naturalistic approach to morality gives rise to the technocratic elite mentality. Indeed, Durkheim's naturalistic versions of the "science of morals"—a Comtean mixture of positivism and Hegelianism—provides a theoretical foundation for the managerial-elite idea. The decisions of policy scientists and others are not value judgments, but are morally neutral, objective scientific findings.

The second possibility I will consider is the "noncognitivism" of writers such as Weber and Russell, as well as many positivists, whom they influenced. The crux of this position is contained in the following argument: Only science provides knowledge; moral judgments—basic, categorical, ultimate judgments—fall outside the scope of science; therefore they fall outside the scope of knowledge; therefore they are "mere" opinions, expressions of subjective preferences or personal tastes. Thus, since science can neither prove nor disprove the claim that genocide is immoral, it is merely a matter of opinion that it is; and the opinion that it is not is of equal weight, is equally rational, and has equal moral force. In effect, this view also makes politics morally neutral by neutralizing conflicting values, in good Madisonian fashion.

As a result of this view, connected as it is with the policy sciences, and with the idea that all the sciences are morally neutral, we get a cluster of ideas: the political realism of Weber, Hans Morgenthau, and Henry Kissinger,[19] as well as the various forms of end-of-ideology, piecemeal engineering conceptions of liberalism. This influential view has no place for dialogue, let alone participation—except for "morally neutral" experts, of course. Morality and politics can mean nothing more than the manipulation of public opinion or coercion, if it does not amount to top-down social engineering. This ignores Aristotle's distinction between technical and practical knowledge,[20] which is needed to provide an alternative notion of rationality and politics, and which arguably supports the sort of radical participatory democracy that liberalism sets aside.

The only resources of politics for this version of liberalism become

a. government by experts;
b. government by force or manipulation;
c. government by a charismatic leader or strong president[21] who functions with the aid of science advisors, a strong bureaucracy, and a passive or at least cooperative legislature;
d. piecemeal social engineering, interest group politics, etc., that is some version of "consensus politics," which just assumes that everyone who counts (Rorty's "we liberal intellectuals") agrees with the "liberal idea." That is, the "ultimate values" are given, and tacitly accepted by everyone. This is the "genius of American politics" for cold war liberals and end-of-ideology proponents.[22]

Participatory democracy is not part of the picture, even though the "organized skepticism," the epistemological outlook behind piecemeal social engineering, with its aversion to both philosophy and ideology, can be just as readily used to support participatory democracy.[23]

The second main option on the "science-values" issue is to develop other models of rationality. Several of these are important for this discussion. First, consider the option made famous by Kant: treat values as purely formal, modeling rationality on logic and mathematics—consistency and universality are the essence of the rational. This option supports the liberal doctrines of the morally neutral state and procedural justice, and renders science and morality/politics to unrelated activities: they belong to different spheres, and so are irrelevant to each other. I think these aspects of modern liberalism raise serious worries. My concern here is that they do not always promote dialogue and discussion, although various writers in the liberal tradition, e.g., Rawls and Ackerman,[24] develop important, but not entirely unproblematic, notions of political dialogue within this framework.

A second alternative, more promising for democratic participation, is derived from Aristotle's notion of practical knowledge and is taken up by Dewey, Habermas, and other advocates of participatory democracy. To some extent Kant's approach can and has been connected to this model, since Kant's notion of the Kingdom of Ends, his version of Rousseau's conception of participatory democracy, has an influence on the traditions of democratic socialism that influenced Dewey and Habermas. But there are vast differences between the Kantian and the Deweyan-Habermasian notion of dialogue and rationality, the latter of which is tied to a communicative ethics that defines democracy as participation in all areas of life.[25] One important difference is that the liberal notion of "spheres of culture"—science/knowledge, aesthetics/feeling, morality/politics—puts a Kantian-Weberian straitjacket on the various departments of life, disconnects science and morality, politics and art, and canonizes the fact-value distinction. All this reinforces what Walzer calls the "liberal art of separation." But then the spheres of art and science are relegated to the experts, and politics often is, too—to technocrats, for instance. Participatory democracy and democratic culture then fall between the cracks.

SCIENCE AND ELITISM

Elitism takes a variety of forms. In perhaps its most straightforward version, it amounts to the view that some people are better or superior to others because of birth, rank, economic status, education, role, deed, breeding, etc. The sort of elitism that is relevant to modern liberalism takes two forms: cultural elitism and the elitism associated with knowledge and expertise, in other words, science, technology, applied science, and so on.

Cultural elitism is captured in the views of writers such as Matthew Arnold, Lionel Trilling, T.S. Eliot, Nietzsche, and Alan Bloom, and is embodied in what is often known as the "canon" of Western literature (the focus of the current political correctness debates). The ideas of "high culture," "highbrow culture," "classical culture" are the vehicles that govern the teaching of the humanities in higher education and justify it in social terms.[26] Until the rise of the modern university at the beginning of the present century, this high culture was available only to the social, economic, and political elite, at places such as Princeton, Yale, and Harvard.

The attempt to democratize higher education, together with the rise of the modern university,[27] involved the notion that the canon could, indeed should, be transmitted to the masses, at least in small (controlled) doses. This would lift them up and prepare them for life in the modern world, e.g., for some sort of self-governance. In fact, it was the sort of self-governance we have seen in Mill: to recognize the wisdom of the cultural elite, whose top-down influence would control the extent of democratic participation.

Of course, the rise of the notion of mass society and of the crowd during the nineteenth century—in Soren Kierkegaard, Nietzsche, Mill, Arnold, Ferdinand Tonnies, Gustav Le Bon, Ortega Y Gassett, William Clifford, Spencer, and others—raised doubts about the extent to which the masses were capable of imbibing the classical tradition. The "revolt of the masses" now becomes a problem. High culture is now a counterweight to democracy, as in Arnold's *Culture and Anarchy*.

Liberalism is ambivalent about these issues, as we have already seen. Liberal thinkers such as Mill[28] wanted to preserve the tradition of high culture, even if in modified form (e.g., with the elimination of Latin from the curriculum.)[29] Yet they believed that the average person should have the opportunity to be exposed to it. At the same time, part of the fear associated with the tyranny of the majority was the fear that mediocrity and leveling—not to mention socialism—would destroy high culture. In the cultural Marxism of the Frankfurt School, the same fear, that the "mass culture industry" would deflect the proletariat from its true course, is evident.[30] The democratization of culture, to use Karl Mannheim's phrase,[31] becomes one of the great problems of the twentieth century.

The German notion of *Bildung*, or self-cultivation, one expression of the high culture ideal, pushes liberal thought in an elitist direction, and runs into conflict with the aim of political democracy, given the anxieties over the fate of high culture. This manifests itself in Mill's ambivalences: a loyalty to the notion of self-cultivation that he takes over from the romantics does not always sit well with his political democracy. This is why the latter is limited, and why his proposal for proportional voting and representation (in keeping with the Hare Plan) amounted to what one writer has called "a victory for the elites."[32]

The second type of elitism is associated with science, technology, expertise in the areas of management, social engineering, the policy sciences, economics, and so on. Liberalism moves in the direction of the idea that the liberal program of enlightened, rational government for the benefit of the masses can only succeed if knowledge provides the basis for action. This is, of course, a perfectly acceptable idea in the abstract. But we have to ask what "knowledge" and "action" mean and explore the ramifications of liberalism in this area.

"Action" clearly means utilitarianism and cost-benefit analysis for liberals who accept the free market, as well as the "new" welfare-state liberals who flourished beginning in the late nineteenth century in England,[33] France,[34] and the United States. Modern circumstances require a class of experts. "Knowledge," thanks to philosophical movements such as positivism, comes to be identified with science and its applications. The elitist values of liberal humanism become relegated to other spheres, notably the private and/or the aesthetic. (Witness the marginalization of music and art in elementary schools.) Politics becomes the province of the knowledge elite, as opposed to the culture elite. If we add the rise of the modern research university and the growth of professionalization, we move toward a society in which politics becomes problem solving. Indeed, a part of the liberal reformist programs was the goal of eliminating politics altogether. Some critics have even defined liberalism as apolitical.[35]

But then what becomes of the idea of politics as discussion and consensus by citizens? Can there be democracy in an age where expert knowledge becomes a *sina qua non* for rational action? Can education—science education, technological literacy—prepare and qualify the nonexpert for democracy? In theory, and often in practice, yes. This is why science is not inherently elitist, unless we define "elitism" to mean any view that overrides untutored prejudice.

But in practice, often despite the best intentions, there is a growing tension between the reliance on science and participatory democracy. The masses were seen as lazy and stupid by Freud, e.g., in his *Civilization and Its Discontents* and *The Future of an Illusion*. Freud was appropriated by writers in this country, especially after World War I (e.g., Lasswell, Graham Wallas, and Lippmann at the turn of the century).[36] In addition, the psychological-testing movement and the use of IQ tests reinforced Freud,[37] adding violence and irrationality to the antidemocratic litany. The growing demands of a corporate state and the belief that public opinion is irrational (Lippmann)[38] feed into the ruling-elite versions of liberalism. The liberal doctrines of value neutrality and of the moral neutrality of the state, combined with the missionary spirit of the elite idea, result in the notion that government is for the people, but cannot be by them. Social control, efficiency, order, and adjustment in the name of dynamic equilibrium and progress become the watchwords of liberalism. The reformist zeal of the early social scientists and liberal Protestants is not always lost; but is now to be achieved by "objectivity" rather than "advocacy."[39] Too much mass participation only gets in the way of liberal order.

NOTES

1. See Patrick Moynihan, *Coping* (New York: Random House, 1977), 259–72; see also Peter Bachrach, *The Theory of the Democratic Elite* (Boston: Little, Brown, 1967).

2. Anthony Arblaster, *The Rise and Decline of Western Liberalism* (Cambridge: Blackwell's, 1984); J. G. Merquior, *Liberalism Old and New* (New York: Twyne Publishers, 1991); Steven Seidman, *Liberalism and the Origins of European Social Theory* (Berkeley: University of California Press, 1984); Richard Bellamy, *Liberalism and Modern Society* (College Park: Pennsylvania State University Press, 1992).

3. See Sergio Cremaschi, "Adam Smith: Skeptical Newtonianism, Disenchanted Republicanism, and the Birth of Social Science" in *Knowledge and Politics*, ed. M. Dascal and O. Gruengard (Boulder: Westview, 1989), 83–110.

4. See Barbara Goodwin, *Social Science and Utopia* (Boston: Unwin, 1978).

5. Frank Fischer, *Technocracy and the Politics of Expertise* (Newbury Park, CA: Sage, 1990).

6. Thomas Haskell, ed. *The Authority of Experts* (Bloomington: Indiana University Press, 1984); Charles Derber, William A. Schwartz, and Yale Magrass, *Power in the Highest Degree* (New York: Oxford University Press, 1990).

7. See M. Groggins, ed. *Governing Science and Technology in a Democracy* (Knoxville: University of Tennessee Press, 1987); Richard B. Day, Ronald Beiner, and Joseph Masciulli, eds., *Democratic Theory and Technological Society* (San Francisco: Sharpe, 1988); David Dickson, *The New Science of Politics* (Chicago: University of Chicago Press, 1989).

8. For the *locus classicus* to this literature, see Robert K. Merton, *Science, Technology, and Society in Seventeenth Century England* (New York: Harper, 1970); and idem, *The Sociology of Science* (Chicago: University of Chicago Press, 1973). The debates generated by Merton, and the criticisms and alternatives, are well summarized in Michael Mulkay, *Science and the Sociology of Knowledge* (Boston: Unwin, 1979).

9. See Thomas Kuhn, *The Structure of Scientific Revolutions*, 2d ed. (Chicago: University of Chicago Press, 1962); idem, *The Essential Tension* (Chicago: University of Chicago Press, 1977); Paul Feyerabend, *Science in a Free Society* (New York: Verso, 1979); and idem, "Democracy, Elitism, and Scientific Method," *Inquiry* 22 (1980): 3–18.

10. Thomas Spragens, *Reason and Democracy* (Durham: Duke, 1990), Ch. 3.

11. John Rawls, *Political Liberalism* (New York: Columbia University Press, 1993); Michael Walzer, "Philosophy and Democracy," op. cit.

12. Feyerabend, *Science in a Free Society*, op. cit.; idem, "Historical Background," introduction to vols. 1 and 2, *Philosophical Papers* (New York: Cambridge University Press, 1981) 2: 1–33; idem, "Notes on Relativism," in *Farewell to Reason* (New York: Verso, 1987), 19–90.

13. See Richard Rorty, "The Priority of Democracy to Philosophy," in *Reading Rorty*, ed. Alan Malochowski (Cambridge: Blackwell's, 1990).

14. See John Keane, op. cit.; and Jean-Francois Lyotard, *Just Gaming* (Minneapolis: University of Minnesota Press, 1984).

15. See Robert J. Antonio and Douglas Kellner, "Communication, Modernity, and Democracy in Habermas and Dewey," unpublished typescript; John Dewey, *The Public and Its Problems* (New York: Holt, 1927); Jurgen Habermas, *Theory of Communicative Action*, 2 vols. (Boston: Beacon, 1982, 1986); idem, *Philosophical Discourse on Modernity* (Cambridge: MIT Press, 1989).

16. See Norman Wintrop and David W. Lovell, "Varieties of Conservative Theory," in *Liberal Democratic Theory and Its Critics*, ed. Norman Wintrop (London: Croom Helm, 1983); Don DeBats, "Liberal Democratic Theory in America," in ibid.; and Norman Wintrop, "Liberal-Democratic Theory: The New Liberalism," in ibid.

17. See e.g., Anthony Downs, *An Economic Theory of Democracy* (New York: Harper and Row, 1957); Russell Hardin, "Rational Choice Theories," in *Idioms of Inquiry*, ed. Terence Ball (Albany: SUNY Press, 1987), 67-91; *Empirical Democratic Theory*, op. cit.

18. B. F. Skinner, *Beyond Freedom and Dignity* (New York: Knopf, 1971).

19. See Stephen P. Turner and Regis A. Factor, *Max Weber and the Dispute about Reason and Value* (New York: Routledge, 1984); Michael Joseph Smith, *Realist Thought from Weber to Kissinger* (Baton Rouge: Louisiana State University Press, 1990).

20. Hans-George Gadamer, *Reason in the Age of Science* (Cambridge: MIT Press, 1982); Jurgen Habermas, *Theory and Practice* (Boston: Beacon, 1973).

21. See Robert Eden, op cit.

22. See Louis Hartz, *The Liberal Tradition in America* (New York: Harcourt, 1955); Joyce Appleby, *Liberalism and Republicanism in the Historical Imagination* (Cambridge: Harvard University Press, 1992); Arthur Schlesinger, Jr., *The Vital Center* (New York: Houghton, Mifflin, 1949); Daniel Boorstein, *The Genius of American Politics* (Chicago: University of Chicago Press, 1953); William J. Newman, *The Futilitarian Society* (New York: George Braziller, 1961); James P. Young, *The Politic of Affluence* (Boston: Chandler, 1968); Marion J. Morton, *The Terrors of Ideological Politics* (Cleveland: Case Western Reserve University Press, 1972).

23. Ariel Botwinick, *Postmodernism and Democratic Political Theory* (Philadelphia: Temple University Press, 1993); Sheldon Wolin, *The Presence of the Past* (Baltimore: Johns Hopkins University Press, 1989); and idem, "Why Democracy?" *Democracy* 1, no. 1 (1981): 3–5; Benjamin Barber, *Strong Democracy* (Berkeley: University of California Press, 1984); Walzer, "Philosophy and Democracy," op. cit.

24. John Rawls, "The Idea of an Overlapping Consensus," *Oxford Journal of Legal Studies* 7, 1 (1987): 1–25; idem, "The Domain of the Political and Overlapping Consensus," *New York University Law Review* 64 (1989): 233–55; idem, "The Theory of Justice: Political, not Metaphysical," *Philosophy and Public Affairs 14* (1985): 223–51; idem, "The Independence of Moral Theory," *Proceedings and Addresses of the American Philosophical Association* 48 (1975): 5ff.; idem, "The Idea of Public Reason," in his *Political Liberalism*, op. cit.

25. James F. Bohman, "Communication, Ideology, and Democratic Theory," *American Political Science Review* 85 (1990): 93–109.

26. See Walter Feinberg, *Reason and Rhetoric* (New York: Wiley, 1975); Clarence J. Karier, J. Paul Voilas, and Joel Spring, eds. *Roots of Crisis* (Chicago: Rand McNally, 1973).

27. Laurence Veysey, *The Emergence of the American University* (Chicago: University of Chicago Press, 1967). etc.

28. See John Stuart Mill, "Civilization," in *Essays on Politics and Culture*, ed. Gertrude Himmelfarb (New York: Anchor, 1963).

29. Knights, op. cit.

30. Alan Swingwood, *The Myth of Mass Culture* (New York: St. Martin's, 1977). A more recent discussion can be found in Stanley Aronowitz, "Is Democracy Possible?" in *The Phantom Public Sphere*, ed. Bruce Robbins (Minneapolis: University of Minnesota Press, 1993), 75–90; and his *Roll over Beethoven* (Wesleyan/New England University Press, 1993).

31. Karl Mannheim, "The Democratization of Culture," in *From Karl Mannheim*, ed. Kurt Wolff, (New York: Oxford University Press, 1971), 271–345.

32. P. B. Kern, op. cit.

33. See Richard Bellamy, ed., *Victorian Liberalism* (New York: Routledge, 1992).

34. William Logue, *From Philosophy to Sociology* (DeKalb: Northern Illinois University Press, 1983).

35. See Barber, op. cit., and Charles A. McCoy and John Playford, eds., *Apolitical Politics* (New York: Crowell, 1967).

36. See Harold Lasswell, *Psychopathology and Politics* (New York: Viking, 1930); Graham Wallas, *Human Nature and Politics* (New York: Macmillan, 1908); idem, *The Great Society* (New York: Macmillan, 1914); Walter Lippmann, *Public Opinion* (New York: Macmillan, 1922).

37. Michael Sokal, ed., *Psychological Testing in American Society: 1890–1930* (New Brunswick: Rutgers, 1987); John O'Donnell, *The Origins of Behaviorism* (New York: New York University Press, 1985).

38. Lippmann, op. cit.

39. Mary Furner, *From Advocacy to Objectivity* (Lexington: University of Kentucky Press, 1975); William Gerber, *American Liberalism* (Chicago: G. T. Hall, 1975).

Chapter 9

Liberalism, Culture, and Education

The liberal view of culture, made canonical by Kant and Weber, defended recently by Habermas and Rorty,[1] divides culture into spheres: art, science, politics/morality. These spheres of existence (Kierkegaard's phrase) sometimes map on to the liberal division between the private and the public, e.g., morality and art may be privatized. Or else we get the "art for art's sake movement," which relegates art to the (public) museum, and thus divorces it from life experience.

More significantly, the liberal conception of culture divides knowledge from values, aesthetics from politics. It leads to, or at least reinforces, a technocratic, "value free" notion of politics as piecemeal social engineering. It sustains the views of liberal cultural critics, who drive a wedge between literature and politics, *Bildung* and utilitarian reform, which then get relegated to their separate spheres, the private and the public. Such a view cannot have much sympathy with Dewey's notion of democracy as a pervasive and ubiquitous cultural phenomenon; nor with a notion of democratic participation that seeks to overcome the narrowness of instrumental politics by developing a notion of dialogue that breaks down the spheres of modernity.

Liberal elitism, as I indicated in chapter 8, takes two basic forms[2]: the knowledge/technocratic elite and the cultural elite. These two ideal types are not mutually exclusive. First, because membership in the two groups often overlaps. Second, because the leitmotif of modern liberalism makes sure "the best and the brightest" are in control, and provides the common thread that unites these two stands of the liberal elite. The linchpin of this unification is twofold: the humanist tradition of high culture and the liberal conception of social engineering.

In this chapter the following themes will be discussed:

a. the idea of the liberal clerisy and the role of liberal education;

b. the rise of the technocratic elite, the modern professions, and the new universities, and their effects on higher education, reformist politics, and liberal education;
c. the notion of mass society and the liberal elite reaction to it;
d. liberal education, neutrality, and the corporate state, as well as the end of ideology and the decline of the public intellectual: liberalism and pragmatism.

The guiding force behind the "liberal clerisy" idea[3] is the classical humanist tradition. According to this tradition, self-cultivation or education must ennoble the spirit by bringing it into contact with the "best that has been thought and said." This would be done by the cultural and intellectual elite and—through education—the younger members of this elite.

In the nineteenth century two events forced a modification of this ideal. The first event was the rise of modern democratic societies. The second was the secularization of culture, which did not bode well for the traditional aristocratic elites, in either culture or politics.

The problem was aggravated by the worry about the masses, in both politics and culture. The prospect of the tyranny of the majority in both spheres prompted Mill, as we have already seen, to introduce the ideas of Tocqueville and Coleridge into his work, and to develop an early version of the theory of the democratic elite.[4]

But (virtually) *all* modern liberals have wanted to have it both ways, as Irving Howe points out in his paper "Literature and Liberalism."[5] Political democracy, even in its limited form, had to be combined with the continued dominance of the classical humanist tradition, and thus of its clerisy.

The solution, at least in theory, was straightforward. Educate the masses, or at least the middle class, into the high-cultural tradition, and thus prepare them for democracy by lifting them up spiritually. This would offset the fears surrounding democracy, partly because the middle class would provide a counterweight to the masses at the low end of the social scale. So the old aristocracy would be replaced by a new, more vital elite, so that "culture" would be able to prevent "anarchy"—which clearly means too much popular democracy, as well as socialism.

Yet, as Howe points out, matters are not that simple. For classical humanism is not obviously compatible with the political egalitarianism of modern political democracy, even if we recognize that some liberals have believed otherwise. My suspicion is that Richard Rorty's version of liberalism can be read, in part, as the culmination of liberal attempts to deal with the dilemma posed by the liberal juxtaposition of inegalitarianism in high culture and the political egalitarianism of civic culture. Howe takes Trilling's remarks concerning this dilemma to represent the attitude of contemporary American liberal intellectuals. According to Trilling, most of "us" "are in our social and political beliefs consciously liberal," yet the great writers in the European modernist tradition of classical humanism "are indifferent to, even hostile to, the tradition of democratic liberalism.[6]

One way out of his dilemma, favored by cold-war liberals such as Trilling, Bell, and Rorty, was the end-of-ideology thesis. If European cultural elites do not favor liberal democracy, get rid of their influence, e.g., by marginalizing or "privatizing it," as Rorty does to defuse its radical political content. (This inspires the attacks on cultural radicals we still witness in Rorty and in, e.g., the political correctness controversy.) But it is really the conservative cultural elites (influenced by more conservative classical liberals such as Constant, Tocqueville, and Arnold) who were antidemocratic. It is the cultural critics in this tradition that Trilling, Bell, and others lionized when they attacked "the adversary culture." The leftist cultural critics in Europe and America (e.g., in the 1930s) were not antidemocratic, but anticapitalist. Some were cultural elitists; but many were not. As I will briefly indicate below, their attempt to democratize culture, anathema to many Marxists and liberals—and which sometimes coincides with a conservative version of "populism"—was the driving force behind much of the literary and cultural activity of home-grown U.S. radicals in this century.[7] The liberal elites' worries about democratic culture echo Mill's fears that political democracy would lead the masses to embrace socialism. The liberals took this to be a sign of how irrational the masses were, which justified severe limitations on popular democracy.

Another liberal strategy is to defend a sharp public-private distinction, relegate cultural elitism to the latter and democratic egalitarianism to the former, and then hope that education would allow the cultural elite to infuse humanist values and "new vocabularies" into the public sphere—or rather the hollow shell of what little remains of it. This is Rorty's approach.

By the end of the nineteenth century, humanists were fighting for their social roles, as the modern research universities, the professionalization of academics, social workers, etc., emerged in the United States and elsewhere.[8] The modern technocratic elite begins to appear. It is not long before the knowledge elite, including its liberal proponents, e.g., the Progressives, take center stage. Now science and technology will solve many, if not all, social problems. The technocratic elite, moreover, will now perform the Arnoldian role; only now the catchwords are "drift and mastery" instead of "anarchy and culture."[9] The idea is the same; the elite changes. Democracy will not be defined as the right of people to vote for competing elites. Liberal education still flourishes during this period, and continues to play its Mill-Arnold role.[10]

In his classic history of the modern American university,[11] Laurence Veysey discusses three competing models of higher education: the vocational, the research-service, the liberal-culture model. Two factors need to be mentioned here. First, there is the growth of professionalism, in the name of "efficiency, uplift and order."[12] Second, the movements to democratize education and culture, which began at the end of the nineteenth century, require attention.

The professionalization of the academic disciplines, especially the social and behavioral sciences, philosophy, and English,[13] put a premium on specialization, turf, prestige, and gave the members of the old elite a secularized role; it also provided a vehicle for upward mobility for the "best and the brightest." Nonacademic professionalization, e.g., engineering,[14] social work, various branches of applied psychology, and human resource management (i.e., Taylorism) also provided upward mobility for the lower and middle classes.

At the same time, reformism, let alone radicalism, was either squashed or channeled into elitist control, by the expedient of limiting professional and academic debates to issues which only "expert" opinion could address. In addition, the professionalization of the middle class instilled an ethos of obedience to expert authority, and thus helped undermine participatory actions.[15] Liberal culture now moves in the direction of education for the corporate state, thus sealing the connections between the two liberal elites, while establishing priority to the technological version of elitism.[16]

Although English departments[17] developed courses designed to educate the average college student into the canon, liberal-culture still remained elitist. But as the influence of the liberal-cultural elite waned, their role was mainly narrowed to instilling in the elite among their students a kind of noblesse-oblige attitude toward the masses.

The democratization of the universities via the Morrill Act, the Hatch Act, and the creation of the land grant colleges and universities, involved conflicts with the liberal culture. The aim was to combine classical liberal education with training in a practical art, say, engineering or agriculture, although the liberal culture was seen as both elitist and impractical. So while education was being democratized, the more populist and "pragmatic" advocates of these trends distrusted liberal culture. So neither side, the vocationalists or liberal culture, moved far enough in the direction of the sort of democratic culture that Dewey was extolling, which aimed to harmonize expertise, practice, and democracy.

Liberal culture looked askance at vocational education. But it also was largely unsympathetic to the research-service model, begun by Harvard's Eliot, to wed scientific research to public service. Eliot's intent was in many respects democratic, even though later developments in the sciences, and among universities, science, government, and business, allowed elitism to win its victory, too.[18]

The liberal culture of the university was also not particularly in favor of what later came to be called "adversary culture", nor even of democratic culture, which had made significant headway in the nineteenth century.[19] In addition to its dislike for lowbrow and even middlebrow culture,[20] many advocates of "liberal culture" (notably Irving Babbitt) were quite conservative; in fact, Babbitt is the forerunner of Alan Bloom and William Bennett.

Further, the rise of consumerism and consumer culture, of mass society and the culture industry, and the liberal disillusionment with human nature in the wake of World War I, conspired to a view that advocated government by experts.

The liberal culture, the newly emerging social and policy sciences and their cultures, in effect agreed with this ethos, although they disagreed on many other things, including which elite culture should be in control.

In response to these attitudes, a variety of cultural, social, and political movements, ranging from the very radical (socialism, Marxism) to radical liberal to populist, including the works of Bourne, Mumford, and Van Wyck Brooks, made valiant efforts to overcome capitalism, individualism, cultural and political elitism, capitalist-consumer culture, and technocracy, beginning in the 1890s, and continuing to at least the New Left counterculture of the 1960s.[21]

One large issue here concerns the nexus of modernism, capitalist culture and democracy, and the liberal culture's thinking on these matters, as well as on the issue of reform, and even radical change.

The notion of mass society has been treated from three perspectives: conservative, radical (mainly Marxist, democratic socialist, and populist), and liberal.

1. For the conservative, from Babbitt and Eliot to Bloom and Bennett, the "masses" are dangerous because they are ignorant, hedonistic, and irrational. On this view, the cultural elite must prevent anarchy by educating their own numbers into the mysteries of high culture, traditional religion, and the aristocratic ideals that are needed to preserve culture and keep the barbarians at bay.

The new populism, often of the right, defended recently by Christopher Lasch,[22] meshes only too well with this conservative vision of democratic culture. Daniel Bell and other so-called liberals (Lasch, for instance) believe that modernist culture leads to consumerism and narcissistic rebellion, and is plump for a Durkheimian solution: revise the old-time religion, in the form of a new Protestant work ethic, in order to overcome the modernist rebellion against capitalist culture and the market.[23]

2. The radical view of mass culture, most vociferously defended by the Frankfurt School,[24] is also elitist. The masses have been lulled into an acceptance of consumer culture, narcissism, kitsch, all in the interest of capitalism. Fascism is the highest stage—the culmination—of capitalist culture. Only high culture can pave the way for a critique of capitalist society and for revolution and utopia. But high culture has become a commodity, used to sell toilet paper.[25] Moreover, the mass-culture, mass-communication industries put in place of genuine culture pulp novels, Hollywood movies, etc., which all embody the ideology of consumer capitalism and bourgeois American values, all of which the masses have imbibed. Only "genuine people's democracy" and a strong countercultural movement can democratize culture and society.

By "populism" I mean not only the conservative populism mentioned above, but a more leftist, radical movement that grew out of late nineteenth-century populism[26] and efforts in the direction of democratic culture in a variety of areas,[27] which in some cases included a wholesale critique of modernity.[28] One can perhaps assimilate many of the radical and reformist movements in the literature and culture of the 1920s and 1930s, perhaps even of the 1960s, to these developments. Perhaps the so-called anti-Stalinist Left, including some of the work of the New York Intellectuals, also fit in here, at least up to a point.[29]

I take the thrust of these movements to be the search for a truly democratic culture and literature, participatory democracy, a usable American past (Van Wyck Brooks), and a united effort against capitalist society. These movements, whose history in relation to the liberal and Marxist traditions in the United States is complex and not unambiguous, may be revived again in the form of postmodernist efforts to reject the distinction between high culture and pop culture, in tandem with a new vision of intellectuals and democracy.

Here it is enough to point out that these American radical movements, while to a great extent Marxist, did not, in general, share the cultural elitism of either the Frankfurt School or conservatives such as Babbitt and Paul Elmer More, or of the liberal cultural elites. In this regard they may be part of the "third way" between capitalism and Marxism that James T. Kloppenberg charts in his *Uncertain Victory*.[30]

3. The liberal cultural guardians did not all have the same attitude towards mass society; but they did, I think, share a common analysis of it.[31] Mass culture is the manifestation of the dark side of modern democracy, painted by Tocqueville, Mill, Ortega, and others. Consumerism, hedonism, the simple-minded stupidity of the masses, as embodied in populism and its own form of adversary culture—fundamentalism, nativism, antisemitism, etc.—are all manifestations of the revolt of the masses against rational order, viz. liberal ideas and practices. The politics of mass society[32] breeds McCarthyism and the Radical Right, and thus the rejection of everything liberal intellectuals stand for.

Daniel Bell, as we have seen, links these developments to cultural modernism—the culture of rebellion, which stems from the same roots as consumer culture, once the Protestant ethic that binds capitalism and culture together in Durkheimian fashion loses its force. The culture of narcissism is the result.

Other liberals, e.g., Edward Shils,[33] have a more sanguine outlook on these developments: mass society becomes an integrated democratic culture; consumerism and mass culture integrate those on the "periphery" into the "center," which is good for democracy. But this "vital center" requires an end-of-ideology attitude, especially to block, indeed, denigrate, reformists and radicals who are not as sanguine about the alleged benefits of liberal America.

Since "modernism" is an essentially contested concept,[34] both Bell and Shils put a defensible twist on the relations among modernist culture, mass society, and democracy. For my purposes, the differences are relatively unimportant.

The issue of the role of the intellectual in modern democracy comes into the picture here. I do not want to rehearse the vast literature on this topic,[35] but to focus on the issues of reform vs. radical criticism, on the liberal view of education as both ideologically neutral and reformist, and on various liberal-reformist views of social criticism. I will conclude this chapter with a brief discussion of the role of the public intellectual in liberal culture.

The key issue concerns the notions of reform, revolution, and the limits of liberal critique. If we start with the idea that liberalism does not want revolution, we still are faced with the question of how radical can liberal social criticism be. Obviously, there is legitimate room for disagreement. What is not debatable, I think, is that, in fact, most liberals have not even tolerated radical *immanent* social criticism. One thinks here only of Dewey and Bourne, of Mumford and Van Wyck Brooks (assuming they are all liberals). But they are the exceptions that prove the rule.

In fact, we can identify several "liberal" attitudes toward radical social criticism and reform:

a. Bourne's radical liberalism;
b. Dewey's radical liberalism;
c. cold war liberalism;
d. Rorty's liberalism;
e. Walzer's liberalism.

For the moment, I want to concentrate on a and c.

One can identify a spectrum of liberal reformism, with correspondingly different attitude toward, indeed conceptions of, democracy, in modern America. Total revolution has never been part of the liberal tradition, even though liberalism's initial triumphs, and many of its subsequent effects, were both revolutionary and the result of revolution. I do not wish to enter the debates about the American Revolution and the founding of the country that focus around the works of Gordon Wood, Bernard Baylin, John Pocock, Joyce Appleby,[36] as important as these writings are to an understanding of American liberalism. However, I will shortly discuss the thesis of Hartz-Schlesinger-Boorstein[37] that liberalism (in its "Lockean" version) is the only American ideology, so that we are all liberals aiming at the preservation of a "vital center," since its aim is to show that radical reform and social/cultural criticism, and thus democratic participation, is both unnecessary and un-American.

The liberal rejection of "revolution" means rejection of Marxism and socialism, even though democratic socialism plays a vital part in much of liberal reformism in this century. The point is that liberalism promotes reform, no matter how radical, only within (not *of*) the existing framework, partly because of its meliorist, piecemeal approach to change—based on its epistemological fallibilism and pragmatism—partly because it maintains that immanent critique is the only acceptable form of critique. This means that change either requires new means to ends that are already in place—to prevent both wholesale skepticism and dogmatism—or involves closing the gap between our ideals and our practices. Both versions of immanent critique therefore rest upon the belief that our system is basically in order as it is; or at least is moving, slowly but surely, in the right direction, owing both to an Enlightenment faith in evolutionary progress and to good old American ingenuity. The engineering mentality—do not scratch where it does not itch, and then only relieve the itch by applying medicine locally—is a hallmark of epistemological fallibilism as well as American "practicality."

In this century two poles of liberal reformism can be found. The more radical pole of reformism had its heyday in the first decades of the century and in the New Left of the 1960s, the heir to these earlier movements. Liberals pushed two radical reformist programs, associated with the two types of liberal elitism discussed earlier: cultural elitism and technocratic elitism. But only the former plumped for radical democracy; the latter promoted the managerial elite. Eventually the end-of-ideology liberals of the cold war reject the early movement for radical democratic culture, and extend the Progressivist legacy of technocratic elitism through their own efforts. The result, to repeat, is a version of democracy that amounts to some form of interest group pluralism, designed to control "mass society," stifle "ideology" and serious social criticism, and promote piecemeal social engineering and conformity to the "vital center."

The activities of liberal muckrakers, e.g., the Progressives[38] and reformist social scientists,[39] were based upon the felt need for an industrial democracy, the desire to regulate big business, to promote welfare-state capitalism and social programs, to promote education and the social order.

In addition, there was a radical reformist movement of liberals and others, led by Bourne, Mumford, Van Wyck Brooks, Vernon Parrington, and Waldo

Frank,[40] whose aim was to retrieve an American usable past—from Herman Melville, Ralph Waldo Emerson, Walt Whitman—and to create a democratic national culture and a participatory democracy in keeping with populism, democratic socialism, the Jacksonian and Jeffersonian ideals of democracy and community. This movement was designed as a counterweight to the progressive version of liberal reform, to the extent that this latter was associated with scientism, technocracy, consumerism, an engineering mentality, and ignored culture, poetry, common experience, etc.—a charge they (wrongly, I think) leveled at Dewey and the pragmatists, especially after the support these figures gave to American involvement in World War I.[41]

One can see this conflict as an instance of the war between the two forms of liberal elitism: the technocratic and the cultural. But in this case, the cultural elites were promoting a democratic culture and a participatory democracy. In this respect their true heirs were the radicals of the 1930s and the 1960s, not the cold war liberal intellectuals or their followers, including Richard Rorty, whose liberal strategy involves trashing the more radical elements of even the liberal tradition. This suggests that liberal reformism must be wedded to the movements toward democratic culture and radical democracy that Bourne and his colleagues defended. In my judgment, Bourne and the others were right to criticize the thrust of the Progressive reformists, since democratic culture and participatory politics, including social criticism and reform, should not be based exclusively, even decisively, on the knowledge elite.

For Bourne[42] radical liberal reformism requires one to be a skeptic and a malcontent; but it is also wedded to the idea of an American "usable past." The smug conformism of Bourne's contemporary liberal intellectuals, echoed by the cold-war liberals and by Rorty, their lack of vitality and genuine criticism, were rejected. But so, too, was the anti-Americanism of much of American radicalism, as well as the Bloomian views of Bourne's contemporary cultural conservative, Irving Babbitt.

I am convinced that pragmatism and liberalism have the resources for radical criticism and reform, even though Dewey (perhaps) and Rorty (without any doubt) never push this radical potential to its limit, short of a wholesale rejection of America. But this sort of position requires us to reinvent the public intellectual. For reasons to be discussed, I think Bourne and Walzer are better exemplars of this type than Rorty, and sometimes even Dewey.[43]

I agree with Bourne (and Walzer) that we live in a time when social criticism must be infused with passion, anger, malcontentedness, spiritedness, even youthful enthusiasm, indeed excess, since we are becoming surrounded by too many "last men," and too many mean-spirited, cruel men and women. The tepid social criticisms of liberals like Rorty—Bourne calls it "timidity"—and the smugness of Irving Babbitt's heirs, whose notion of a community harks back to Spencer, and the excesses of some on the Left, who think they are making a political revolution by dominating English and comparative literature departments, and who, unlike the New Left of the 1960s, have no interest in the search for a usable past, make the need for radical-democratic liberal public intellectuals an urgent priority today.

Rorty sometimes exemplifies Bourne's (and Walzer's) worry that too much reliance on conventions and opinions, even—especially—those of liberal intellectuals, can be dangerously stifling. Unlike Bourne, Rorty wants to separate, rather than synthesize, the romantic/poetic and the political. Unlike Walzer, Rorty will not push the level of conversation beyond that of our current consensus, to press the question of, say, institutional racism. All he talks about is how we can change our vocabularies, which hardly gets at the deep-seated nature of institutional racism. How can one even raise this sort of general issue, if, as Rorty insists, there is nothing in between unacceptable metaphysical/theological criticism and concrete proposals for reform? Finally, Rorty takes the radical sting out of his liberal ironist. But Bourne rightly sees the need for such a sting if social criticism is to be effective.

I want to insist that we need to take up the more radical democratic tradition, the tradition of social criticism in Bourne, Dewey, and Walzer. For Rorty, only poets, teachers, and engineers play a social role. Public intellectuals cannot and (especially if they are philosophers) should not. Can we establish a democratic culture and radical democracy within these Rortyan constraints? I do not think so. At a time when the market is touted as the solution to all problems, when schools and universities are becoming part of corporate America, when free speech and debate are being stifled by both the extreme Left and the New Right, we need public intellectuals more than at any other time since Joseph McCarthy's heyday. We should be thankful for the work of feminists, postcolonialists, postmodernists, and liberals such as Walzer for revitalizing the radical democratic traditions of American history. One can only hope that current work on participatory models of democracy and community will have a significant impact on public life in the near future.

NOTES

1. Richard Rorty, *Contingency, Irony, and Solidarity* (New York: Cambridge University Press, 1989).

2. See Alan S. Kahane, *Aristocratic Liberalism* (New York: Oxford University Press, 1992); William V. Spanos, *The End of Education: Toward a Posthumanism* (Minneapolis: University of Minnesota Press, 1993).

3. Ben Knights, *The Idea of the Clerisy in the Nineteenth Century* (New York: Cambridge University Press, 1967).

4. Kahane, op. cit.; Peter Bachrach, *The Theory of the Democratic Elite* (Boston: Little, Brown, 1967).

5. Irving Howe, "Literature and Liberalism," in Howe, *Celebrations and Attacks* (New York: Harcourt, 1980), 239–54.

6. Ibid., 239.

7. John Patrick Diggins, *The Rise and Fall of the American Left* (New York: Norton, 1991); Douglas Tallack, *Twentieth Century America* (London: Longman, 1991); Andrew Jamison, *Seeds of the Sixties* (Berkeley: University of California Press, 1994); Alan Wald, *The New York Intellectuals* (Chapel Hill: University of North Carolina Press, 1987); Casey Blake, *Beloved Community* (Chapel Hill: University of North Carolina Press, 1990). On Populism, see Robert Goodwyn, *Democratic Promise* (New York: Oxford University Press, 1985); and Christopher Lasch, *The True and Only Heaven* (New York: Knopf, 1991); Russell Hanson, *The Democratic Imagination in America* (Princeton: Princeton University Press, 1985).

8. Laurence Veysey, *The Emergence of the American University* (Chicago: University of Chicago Press, 1967); Nathan Hatch, ed., *The Professions in American History* (Baltimore: Johns Hopkins University Press, 1987); Burton Bledstein, *The Culture of Professionalism* (New York: Norton, 1976).

9. Walter Lippmann, *Drift and Mastery* (New York: Holt, 1914).

10. Harvey Segal, *Technological Utopianism in American Culture* (Chicago: University of Chicago Press, 1985); Linda M. Steinman, *Made in America: Science, Technology and American Modernist Poets* (New Haven: Yale University Press, 1987).

11. Veysey, op. cit.

12. Samuel Haber, *Efficiency and Uplift* (Chicago: University of Chicago Press, 1964); Robert Wiebe, *The Search for Order* (New York: Hill and Wang, 1967).

13. See Bruce Kuklick, "The Professionalization of the Humanities," in *The Organization of Knowledge in Modern America: 1860–1920*, ed. A. Oleson and J. Voss (Baltimore: Johns Hopkins University Press, 1979); Gerald Graff, *Professing Literature* (Chicago: University of Chicago Press, 1988); Thomas Haskell, *The Emergence of Professional Social Science* (Urbana: University of Illinois Press, 1977).

14. See Donald Stabile, *Prophets of Order* (Boston: South End Press, 1984); Bruce Sinclair "The Engineers," in Hatch, op. cit.; Edwin Layton, *The Revolt of the Engineers* (Baltimore: Johns Hopkins University Press, 1967).

15. See Haskell, ed., *The Authority of Experts*, op. cit.; Bledstein, op. cit., Margali Sarfatti Larson, *The Rise of Professionalism* (Berkeley: University of California Press, 1977).

16. Henry Kariel, *The Decline of American Pluralism* (Stanford: Stanford University Press, 1967); and idem, *Frontiers of Democratic Theory* (New York: Random House, 1970); William Connolly, ed., *The Bias of Pluralism* (New York: Atherton, 1969).

17. Graff, op. cit.

18. Daniel Kevles, *The Physicists* (Cambridge: Harvard University Press, 1971).

19. See note 7 above for references.

20. Jane Rubens, *The Making of Middlebrow Culture* (Chapel Hill: University of North Carolina Press, 1992).

21. Blake, op. cit.

22. Lasch, *The True and Only Heaven*, op. cit.

23. Christopher Lasch, *The Culture of Narcissism* (New York: Norton, 1979).

24. Swingwood, op. cit.

25. Colin Campbell, *The Romantic Ethic and the Spirit of Consumerism* (Cambridge: Blackwell's, 1990).

26. Michael P. Federici, *The Challenge of Populism* (Westport, CT: Praeger, 1991).

27. Goodwyn, op. cit.; Kenneth Cmiel, *Democratic Eloquence* (Berkeley: University of California Press, 1990); Hanno Hardt, *Critical Communication Studies, Communication, History, and Theory in America* (New York: Routledge, 1991); John Roper, ed., *Democracy and Its Critics* (London: Unwin, 1989).

28. George Cotkin, *Reluctant Modernism* (New York: Twayne, 1992).

29. Alan Wald, op. cit.; Thomas Bender, *New York Intellect* (New York: Borzoi, 1987); Richard Pells, *Radical Visions and American Dreams* (New York: Harper, 1973).

30. James T. Kloppenberg, *Uncertain Victory* (New York: Oxford University Press, 1988).

31. Swingwood, op. cit.; Jeffrey Goldfarb, *The Cynical Society* (Chicago: University of Chicago Press, 1991).

32. Daniel Bell, ed., *The Radical Right* (New York: Anchor, 1963); Michael Paul Rogin, *The Intellectuals on McCarthy: The Radical Specter* (Cambridge: MIT Press, 1967); William Kornhauser, *The Politic of Mass Society* (New York: Free Press, 1959).

33. Edward Shils, "The Theory of Mass Society," in Shils, *Center and Periphery: Essays in Macrosociology* (Chicago: University of Chicago Press, 1975), 91–110.

34. Daniel Joseph Singal, ed., *Modernist Culture in America* (Belmont, CA: Wadsworth, 1991).

35. See George B. de Huszar, ed., *The Intellectuals* (New York: Free Press, 1960); Lewis Perry, *Intellectual Life in America* (Chicago: University of Chicago Press, 1984, 1989); Peter Coleman, *The Liberal Conspiracy* (New York: Free Press, 1989); Christopher Lasch, "The Cultural Cold War," in Lasch, *The Agony of the American Left* (New York: Vintage, 1966), 61–114; David A. Hollinger, *In the American Province* (Bloomington: Indiana University Press, 1985).

36. op. cit.

37. op. cit.

38. See Alan Dawley, *Struggles for Justice* (Cambridge: Harvard University Press, 1991).

39. See Furner, op. cit.; Dorothy Ross, *Origins of American Social Science* (New York: Cambridge University Press, 1991).

40. Blake, op. cit.

41. Blake, op. cit., Stuart I. Rochester, *American Liberal Disillusionment in the Wake of World War I* (College Park: Pennsylvania State University Press, 1971).

42. Randolph Bourne, *The Radical Will* (New York: Urizon, 1977); Christopher Lasch, *The New Radicalism in America* (New York: Vintage, 1965); Michael Walzer, *In the Company of Critics* (New York: Basic Books, 1988); Blake, op. cit.

43. Michael Walzer, *Interpretation and Social Criticism* (Cambridge: Harvard University Press, 1990); and idem, *In the Company of Critics* (New York: Basic Books, 1988); Russell Jacoby, *The Last Intellectuals* (New York: Noonday, 1987); Jamison, *Seeds of the Sixties* (Berkeley: University of California Press, 1994).

Part IV

CURRENT DEVELOPMENTS

Chapter 10

On Liberalism, Democracy, and Elitism Today

Francis Fukuyama's claim[1] that liberalism has won a worldwide victory, and that we are at the dawn of what Hegel called "the end of history," was popular in 1989. Today, after the 1994 elections, it is being claimed that liberalism is dead. Have things changed that much in five years? Or might both claims be right?

For Fukuyama, "liberalism" means classical, eighteenth-century free market capitalism and individual rights. But it is precisely this version of liberalism that is *not* dead, but which emerged triumphant in 1994. It is only "welfare state liberalism," not the liberalism that is today's conservatism and libertarianism, that he has died.

But it is not just welfare state liberalism that has died. Democracy, too, is on the verge of extinction, despite what pundits said about the "will of the people" in the 1994 elections. If "democracy" amounts to more than voting for mean-spirited candidates who blame the ills of this country on the poor and on the liberal elites, or against candidates who sound like Andrew Carnegie in "The Gospel of Wealth," then it seems to me that there is no evidence at all that democracy is alive, let alone thriving, in the United States (or anywhere else, for that matter) today.

What has, perhaps, died is a version of liberal democracy that combines the modern, welfare-state mentality with that of the liberal elite. Yet, what we have now is not populism, but rather a combination of a kind of cultural populism (the culture wars) and the same old liberal managerial-elite mentality that both liberals and today's conservatives endorse. The top-down management style of leadership that dominates governments, corporations, schools, universities, hospitals, Wal Mart, and just about everything else, is another chapter in the history of the corporate ideal that has influenced the United States for almost a hundred years.

In this book I have tried to tell the story of the liberal elite and its ambivalent relationship to democracy, and show why its decline, at least in the cultural sphere, does not pave the way for democratic participation. Today's conservatives are no more likely to favor participatory democracy than liberal elites have in the past, except in the cultural sphere, where popular democracy actually serves illiberal forces (racism, sexism, Social Darwinism, homophobia, to mention a few). Indeed, without clearly explaining the connections between Reaganomics and the culture wars, the liberals' loyalty to allegedly elitist cultural values will only reinforce the Republican view that it is these values (including the alleged liberal permissiveness, which get linked to the growing problems of crime and violence by the New Right), not a growing two-class economy, that are the cause of the problems the country now faces. (This is basically Daniel Bell's argument against cultural modernism in *The Cultural Contradiction of Capitalism.*[2])

What we need is an approach to democracy that avoids the elitism of modern liberalism and the retrograde ideals of culture and morality that the new conservatism favors, allegedly in the name of the will of the people. I have tried to indicate, especially in the last several chapters, what this kind of postmodernist participatory democracy might look like. But my primary aim has been to show why modern liberalism has not encouraged democracy, and in this part of the book, why contemporary conservatism fosters a cheap imitation of democracy in the name of right-wing populism.

As I see it, there are four political alternatives today. First, the right-wing populism of the new Republicans combines a faith in old-fashioned religious and moral values, and detests feminists, gays and lesbians, affirmative action, and believes in the Protestant work ethic; even at a time when more and more "workers" are losing their jobs, their pensions, their health insurance, the rich are getting richer, and the middle class is disappearing. For these people, the welfare state and the civil rights movements of the 1960s are the causes of this country's current problems.

Second, the current radical Left focuses on issues of class, race, gender, sexual orientation, multiculturalism, diversity, political correctness, and so forth. These groups embody Weber's wars of gods and demons with a vengeance. They have little interest in exploring ways in which diversity can be combined with unity of any sort. Although they undoubtedly abhor the latest waves of Social Darwinism and global capitalism, they are so caught up with what Nietzsche called "resenntiment"—vengeance against the past—that they often become fanatical purists, interested only in power for their own elites (largely at universities), forming alliances with corporate managers of the new university in order to acquire power, while burning their bridges with both leftist and liberal academics who happen to be white males and, increasingly, each other. (Witness growing tensions between Hispanics and African Americans on campuses.)

Third, there are the liberals, not just members of the Democratic party, who are floundering for programs and leadership. Today it seems that corporate liberalism is only a bit more humane than the corporatism of Reaganism. But the liberals differ from the New Right in the cultural sphere, since they by and large defend classical doctrines of privacy, choice, diversity. But in so doing they arguably aggravate the fragmentation being created by the culture wars, since they seem to have no notion of a common good, and do not even address the issue of reconciling diversity and unity in a multicultural society.

Fourth, there is the idea of a participatory democracy that combines Deweyan ideas of a democratic culture, in the family, the workplace, the university, with an attack on corporate capitalism in both its "neoliberal" and Reaganomic guises, and often talks about either workplace democracy or market socialism. On this view, which I favor, the other three available options are not democratic.

The New Right populism combines corporate liberalism with the Protestant work ethic. It wants to combine "family values" and traditional religion with a loyalty to corporate capitalism, and sees the "liberal elites" who favor diversity and protection from corporate greed as the devil. It has no objection to government interference in private life; indeed, "privacy" now means market capitalism. Our government and social institutions are becoming privatized while society is being pushed toward the white bread homogeneity of "Ozzie and Harriet." High-tech feudalism is being combined with Social Darwinism and a new work ethic. "Democracy" means little more than voting every two years. And this means people base political decisions on a combination of self-interest, anger, and fear, fueled by the media and by politicians who would not know a dialogue if they stumbled over it.

"Neoliberalism" combines corporate liberalism and managerial/technocratic elitism with a privatization of values in the culture sphere. So far as I can see, it is little more than Reaganism with a slightly greater human face in the economic sphere, combined with a total concession to the current fragmented cultural sphere in the name of the classical liberal ideal of privacy. Political democracy, for the neoliberal, does not exhibit any more concern for public dialogue (or for a renewed public sphere) than its corporate Republican counterpart. In fact, the neoliberal acceptance of the market, which differs very little from Reaganism, when combined with its indifference to the culture wars, may produce a new form of Weber's iron cage, which I have begun to think of as high-tech feudalism.

Both the populism of the Right and cultural Left are concerned with the culture wars. But there is no dialogue either within each of these cluster groups or between them. Indeed, there is little attempt at understanding on the part of the participants. Class warfare between traditional blue-collar workers and women and people of color is masked by the cultural wars; but nobody asks who benefits from a division among the poor and middle classes, or what the connections between the culture wars and the institutionalization of a two-class society are. So, if democracy requires understanding and dialogue, the rejection of elites, the welfare state, civil rights legislation, or whatever, do not guarantee democracy, any more than the victory of top-down management, privatization, and Reaganism do.

This book is concerned with the reasons why neither liberalism nor conservative populism promotes democratic participation. While the bulk of my argument concerns the conflicts between modern liberalism and democracy, part 4 focuses on the current populism of the Right as a reaction to liberal elitism. I shall argue that there is another alternative response, a conception of participatory democracy that preserves what is best in liberalism, including its defense of privacy and rejection of Social Darwinism, as well as democratic socialism and radicalism, while trying to come to grips with the current culture wars and the new two-class economy that neither neoliberals nor conservatives have adequately addressed. My view is that nothing will change for the better unless the story about this country's current malaise, which many voters have bought into, is openly debated and shown to be false, and until we create a climate in which participation in a multicultural society, where people aim at some consensus about the common good, provides a substitute for both liberal elitism and Reaganism, as well as the mean-spirited extremes of the Left and the Right that corporate capitalism has spawned.

In light of the 1994 elections in the United States, it is natural to ask whether "liberalism" is still alive, and whether democracy has finally won a victory over the elitist forces I have surveyed in the preceding chapters.

The issue is complicated. Not only is "liberalism" a term with many meanings; so is "democracy." If we add to these complexities questions about the meanings of "populism," the current scene threatens to become bewildering.

It may be helpful to begin with two hypotheses ("worldview" might be more apt) about our current malaise. Leaving aside for the moment anxieties about the new world order—the global market economy and postindustrial society—I want to focus on the state of the American economy and on the cultural wars. Conservatives tend to hold liberals responsible for both, and see the recent Republican election victories as a repudiation of New Deal liberalism and its successors, as well as the cultural and moral "permissiveness" spawned by the struggles of the 1960s for civil rights and against the Vietnam War. The current agenda of the cultural Left, on behalf of multiculturalism, political correctness, affirmative action, civil rights for gays and lesbians, and so on, is seen by the conservatives as the culmination of the 1960s counterculture, spearheaded by radicals of that time who are now "tenured radicals," and by their students.

The current attacks on the welfare system and what has been called "the war against the poor" are based upon the argument that the welfare state has aggravated the problems of the poor by making generations of poor people so dependent upon welfare that crime, illegitimacy, drugs, and so on, have increased significantly in the last twenty years, while there supposedly is little evidence to show that any of the social experiments spawned by liberalism have done the poor much good. In fact, in *The Bell Curve*,[3] Richard Hernstein and Charles Murray argue that such programs cannot work, since there is a provable correlation between native intelligence (genetics) and success, especially in a world in which information and knowledge are becoming the basis for the global economy.

What we need, according to this worldview, is a dismantling of the remnants of the New Deal, a return to rugged individualism, minimal government, traditional religion, and "family values." That is, the Republicans are in favor of the classical liberalism of the eighteenth and nineteenth centuries.

Is this worldview, which some people (perhaps too hastily) ascribe to the electorate who gave the Republicans political power in 1994, also a form of populism? Is it a form of populism that favors democratic participation? In what way was the recent election "democratic"? Is it a form of populism that harks back to the more conservative, even retrograde, populist movements of an earlier day, which were often antisemitic, anti-Black, America-firsters against the immigration of Eastern Europeans and others earlier in this century? (Proposition 187 in California has to be seen in this historical context.) If so, are liberal elitists correct in insisting that too much democracy is very dangerous? Or is the electorate dissatisfied with the extremes that liberal elitism has gone to, while at the same time not being as reactionary as first appears? Does the electorate still adhere to the values of democracy and fair play, and only reject what they take to be the excesses of multiculturalism, affirmative action, and so on? Perhaps. But is there a revolt against the excesses of corporate capitalism, or a recognition that the dismantling of the federal government in the name of local government also promotes diversity, perhaps a type of diversity not incongruent with multicultural diversity? Are old fashioned values seen as a bulwark against the heartlessness of the economy? Is a return to tradition the only alternative? Could public dialogue on this issue yield more positive options?

For their part, liberals have a worldview to explain our current malaise. They can point to the fact that during the 1980s, the decade of Reaganism, the top 4 percent of the population earned as much money as the bottom 51 percent[4]; and Reagan's dismantling of the government, all the deregulation, the theory of rational expectations, and the elimination of taxes on the wealthy helped transform America into a two-class society. He made it popular, even fashionable, to attack the poor, to trash the advances in civil rights for women and people of color, and he helped revitalize nineteenth-century Social Darwinism, which blamed the poor for their own failures and defended the view that came to be known as "the Gospel of Wealth"; let the wealthy make more money and everyone else will benefit. (Andrew Carnegie, in a well-known talk called "The Gospel of Wealth," advocated an early version of trickle-down economics and maintained that only great capitalists could realize Christ's ideas about helping the poor!)

Let me begin with certain obvious questions.

First, has either the liberal or the conservative worldview established any of its major causal hypotheses? Is it even clear what the hypotheses are? Does "permissiveness" cause an increase in crime? Or is crime the result of trickle-down economics and the growing number of unemployed and poor? Has the welfare system worsened the conditions of the poor? Did Reaganomics help them? So far as I can tell, neither liberals nor conservatives have established their main causal explanations.

Second, we must ask questions such as this: Who has benefitted from the welfare state? Only poor blacks? What about farmers? What about Chrysler Corporation? What about many of the same people who voted in favor of republican government in 1994? Who has benefitted from Reaganomics? Middle-class workers? What are the connections between the increase in crime, the cultural wars, and the stark economic realities of the 1980s and 1990s?

Perhaps it needs to be asked whether both liberals and conservatives have gone too far in attributing all of our nation's problems to the other side. Individual responsibility and hard work are certainly admirable. But is Social Darwinism and the practice of blaming the poor for just about everything that has gone sour really fair? By the same token, it seems to be undeniable that institutional and personal racism, sexism, and homophobia still pervade our society. And what about the current syndrome of victimization, of blaming white men for the world's evils, of endorsing the sometimes totally bizarre and counterproductive? Would more citizens listen if central issues about civil rights and the value of multiculturalism, rather than extremism (e.g., the view that all male-female sex is rape), were debated? It seems to me that neither conservatives nor liberals have a monopoly on either truth or stupidity.

This much being said, there are also common themes running through contemporary conservatism and "neoliberalism." First and foremost there is corporatism and elitism. Despite the appeal to "family values" and the old-time religion, conservatives are as caught up in corporate elitism as are the liberal elite. (In fact, the number of "liberals" in power can be counted on one hand. This country has not had a liberal president since Lyndon Johnson.) Top-down management ("Total-Quality Management") is everywhere. Corporate leaders downsize their operations by firing tens of thousands of their employees in the name of efficiency while giving themselves million-dollar raises. The leaders of the religious Right and their corporate allies talk as if they are just plain folks; but Pat Robertson and George Will are just as elitist as Bill Clinton and Robert Reich. Both liberals and conservatives are marching to the drum of *The Bell Curve* these days, despite Clinton's rhetoric. The new work ethic, while perhaps unavoidable in the new global economy, is accompanied by a new "search for order" that may yet make the ideas of efficiency and uplift of the modernization period of the 1890s–1920 pale by comparison. Privacy is being corroded, especially by conservatives who want the market to solve all problems, except those involving religion, morality, lifestyles, and family values. Drug tests, urine tests, genetic screenings, monitoring of the workplace, constraints on who one can date, and what one can say are all justified in the name of productivity, efficiency, and "moral values."

Liberals and conservatives talk a lot about punishment but very little about prevention, let alone the causes of our current crime wave. During the 1994 campaign, Democrats (for instance, in my own state of Iowa) tried to outdo conservative Republicans on issues such as the number of prisons they would build. The assumption that more prisons and more gas chambers will solve the problem of crime would be laughable if it were not so dangerously preposterous. It is unpopular to suggest that there is a connection between the fact that just about everyone in power has written off the poor and the increase in hate crimes, violence, drug addiction, and the expotential growth of the victimization industry. To be sure, not everybody who is poor evades all responsibility for self-improvement or engages in violent behavior. But in a society that seems to have written off the poor and in which (unlike the depression years of the 1930s) many people perceive a great unfairness in the current economy, it is not difficult to see why the least well off no longer accept the Calvinist ethos.

Nativism is rampant again. (Is it a coincidence that "nativism" is also the term used to denote "American firsters"?) Even academics are now claiming that genetics and physiology determine criminals, explain why men violate women, why some people are destined to be poor or rich or members of the "cognitive elite" (Charles Murray is hardly a *liberal* elitist!), why women's social roles are determined by the structure of the female brain, and so on. Partly in reaction to the extreme environmentalism of the 1960s, we now have a conservative ideology that even erstwhile liberals endorse in order to foreclose discussion about the causes and prevention of violence. Television shows drag the lowest order of human beings onto their programs so that people can forget how bad off they are when compared to the pathetic creatures on "Oprah" and "Donahue." "Hard Copy"-type shows and police shows give people a vicarious way of acting out their own violence and hatred, often against everybody and everything but the real culprit, namely greedy corporatism; yet, very little is said or done to address the causes of crime. This is not a new story. What is new is the growing mean-spiritedness of people, combined with a massive selfishness, greed, and heartlessness that we have not witnessed in a long time. On top of this, we are more and more prone to simple-minded solutions to very real problems, perhaps because we are too weak to face the truth. "Just say no" has about the same ring of reality as "let them eat cake" (or "more prisons will solve the crime problem"); yet, there is almost no attempt at any reasonable, realistic alternatives. Indeed, has there been anything resembling a public dialogue about any major issue? I can think of few, if any, examples.

As I shall argue in more detail in chapter 11, high culture is not doing much better than mass culture. (I doubt if this distinction does, or even should, make much sense any longer; but that is another issue.) Intellectuals are, by and large, caught up in ideological wars about postmodernism and the traditional canon. These are neither unimportant nor irrelevant to the issues I am discussing. On the contrary; they are crucially important. Academics of the Left, despite their general democratic intent, are, by and large, becoming elitist to the point of being irrelevant, perhaps because they feel impotent to engage in anything but campus politics; while conservative intellectuals do little more than defend tradition without even bothering to consider the realities of a fragmented and multicultural society. Their desire for a return to the good old-fashioned canon is the academic equivalent of returning to the days of "Ozzie and Harriet." It may be that the intellectual traditions and values of the West are still largely defensible. But to ignore the issues and arguments raised by multiculturalists and postmodernists—that is, the refusal to debate the issues, rather than calling names—is the intellectual equivalent of "just say no" as a solution to abortion, drugs, and crime.

Perhaps the problem is that we have too few intelligent people who are willing to try to speak the truth or get past ideological warfare. Perhaps we do not have enough people who can take the truth, or recognize it when they see it. Maybe our technological and managerial expertise has caused us to be unintelligent in the spheres of practical wisdom and open discussion. Perhaps many people are not interested in seeking the truth, or even reasonable consensus. (They have given up; things are too complicated; not many people really care about anything beyond their own noses.)

Another hypothesis comes to mind. Perhaps both liberalism and conservatism, perhaps even representative democracy as it has been practiced, are becoming outmoded in our current world, where multinationals and other corporations are not responsible to, or controllable by, anybody or anything, including governments, when the market has become our new god, and when government is perceived as the devil and the common good has become unintelligible to many people. Perhaps the Left has cried "wolf!" once too often. Perhaps the rhetoric of Reaganism has convinced too many of our citizens that everyone is selfish and greedy. If we do live in a postmodern, postindustrial global market, in a high-tech feudal world where each fiefdom is concerned only with itself, would it be surprising if the tried and true political philosophies that dominated the West (and, for well-known reasons, the world) for two hundred years are no longer relevant to our current scene?

But this may be premature. Postmodern conditions and the possibility of postmodern politics, postmodern democracy in particular, cannot be ruled out for the simple reason that we have not yet tried very hard. Recent work by a variety of writers, ranging from communitarians to postmodernists to advocates of participatory democracy, have been making important contributions. Feminists and defenders of multiculturalism see diversity and particularity as a strength that can renew our sense of community and the common good, albeit in much more complicated (multicultural) ways than traditional notions of community. In my optimistic moments, even the politics of 1994 may hold out hope for more genuine democracy, provided that we can move toward conditions where dialogue and debate, and not just name calling, are real possibilities. I do not have any novel suggestions for doing this.[5] But I do think that issues about education for democracy and civility need to be addressed before any genuine reforms can be proposed or evaluated. In the next chapter I want to take up some of these issues.

What I would like to suggest at this point is that we need to rethink the meaning of "democracy" today, since both liberal and conservative ideologies are becoming outdated by contemporary events. Indeed, the terms "Democrats" and "Republicans" are both misnomers today. Both political parties are in fact mirror images of each other, each a variation on modern liberalism. For the liberal Democrats, the cultural sphere is private and pluralistic, and the economic sphere requires some kind of public action. For conservative Republicans, the reverse is true: the economic sphere is totally privatized, while the cultural sphere is supposed to be public, i.e., accord with shared public values. But these values are both too narrow and too exclusive; and the Republican notion of civic virtue and the common good is today just as privatized as the liberal idea of community. Liberalism and conservatism today are both forms of classical liberalism, differing only in what is private and what is public, at least in principle. But in practice they have become virtually indistinguishable. Clinton, Reich, and other "new Democratics" (or neoliberals) are Reaganites about economics for most intents and purposes. And aside from some empty gestures to appease their traditional constituencies, Democratics are making the same noises about family values and so on, so that, as one wag recently put it, we now have two Republican parties in this country. Above all, thanks to liberalism and conservatism, the public sphere has disappeared. Liberal individualism and cultural elitism destroy the idea of public culture; the conservative efforts to reinstall an outdated public culture are dangerous and will not work, since they are too exclusive. Conservatives and neoliberals ("new Democrats") such as Clinton, Reich, and Tsongas want to "reinvent government" by privatizing it! The idea of the public realm, or the common good, which is at the heart of both classical democracy and the civic republican traditions, has been destroyed by its contemporary namesakes. Democratic participation rejects both of these current views, and seeks to restore these older traditions, which were pluralistic and multicultural almost by definition, in a postmodern context by maintaining that only a combination of greater economic democracy and a multicultural conception of community is a reasonable position for contemporary America.

Perhaps new forms or mechanisms of democratic participation would attract enough people on both the Left and the Right, despite many obvious differences between them. A concern for participation may override partisan and even ideological differences at this juncture in our history. If, for instance, more power is ceded to state and local governments by the new Congress, the way is at least open for more genuine citizen input, discussion, and collective action in a variety of settings (including the workplace). A growing realization that our country is in deep trouble, plus a dissatisfaction with politicians and all sorts of elites, may in fact create new forms of populism.

To be sure, what often passes for populism may be little more than the visceral responses of citizens to very real problems, perhaps based upon irrational biases and misinformation. So populism may err at the other extreme from elitism. My point here has been that democracy is committed to neither of these alternatives, despite its populist aspirations and its recognition of the importance of expertise in a democracy.

Education must take a lead in helping us distinguish between democracy and misinformed, mean-spirited public response. This is not to deny that the majority of citizens of a democracy can be mistaken and yet still be entitled to carry the day. But it is to insist upon a connection between democracy and intelligence, and thus between democracy and education. A recent cover story in *Time* attacking "hyperdemocracy"—the use of electronic media to provide quick but often thoughtless citizen responses to issues, together with the absence of any dialogue among people who are isolated with their computers at home—illustrates the point I am making about democracy, intelligence, and education.[6] But to do this, educational institutions, above all institutions of higher learning, must first put their own houses in order by rejecting *both* the corporate university *and* the notion that the main role of the university is to further political agendas of extremists on the Left or the Right. As I argue in the next chapter, the unholy alliance between corporate university administrators and political correctness extremists is ruining the universities of this nation.

Universities need to encourage the learning of citizenship, critical thinking, and dialogue, not just careers. They should not and cannot be engines for economic development or entrepreneurship or vehicles for foisting a radical cultural agenda on an unwilling public. They must lead the way to public debate, and convince people that democratic participation is vitally important to their future. They need to breed good will, civility, and a spirit of community.

At the same time, the notion that everybody needs and deserves a college or university degree, or that college is only a vehicle for a vocation, must be resisted, but not for the reasons advanced by Charles Murray. It is true that some people should not be in college, for a variety of reasons. But the main point is that we as a society need to move away from treating people without college degrees as worthless. Murray is right to insist that everybody has a contribution to make, and can lead a decent life. But what Murray does not insist upon is that our current economic stratifications and unemployment levels will not make it possible to move away from the "college or worthless" mentality that makes unwilling and unable people go to college just to get jobs, especially when none are available and when college is becoming prohibitively expensive in any case. Unless economic conditions and the cultural wars can be worked on in tandem to create a multicultural democracy that moves toward greater economic justice, this country is in for some very bad times indeed. So far as I can see, few political movements or ideologies that are key players on the current scene have even begun to address these issues. The important exceptions are those writings by feminists, participatory democrats, and communitarians (who are not, like MacIntyre, just old-fashioned traditionalists) whose views I sketched in chapter 6. In the next chapter I shall explore the ways in which a postmodernist participatory democracy can contribute to our educational institutions and thus to democratic renewal at the *fin de siecle.*

NOTES

1. Francis Fukuyama, *The End of History and the Last Man* (New York: Free Press, 1992).
2. Daniel Bell, *The Cultural Contradictions of Capitalism* (New York: Basic Books, 1974).
3. Richard J. Hernstein and Charles Murray, *The Bell Curve* (New York: Free Press, 1994).
4. See Donald Bartlett and J. B. Steele, *America: What Went Wrong?* (Kansas City: Andrews and McMeel, 1992); Kevin Phillips, *The Politics of Rich and Poor* (New York: Random House, 1990); and idem, *Arrogant Capital* (Boston: Little, Brown, and Company, 1994).
5. See Benjamin Barber, *An Aristocracy of Everyone* (New York: Ballantine Books, 1992).
6. Time, 23 January 1995, "Hyperdemocracy!" 14–21.

Chapter 11

On Democracy, Culture, and Education Today

Today we are witnessing the demise of the liberal ideal of higher education. While liberalism has bred elitism, it has also encouraged a process of democratization, which included ideas about the value of learning for citizenship and personal excellence, as well as for career preparation. In order to assess what must still be valued in this ideal, despite its now well-rehearsed weaknesses, it will be necessary to examine the two competing yet also strangely allied models of the university that are taking its place: the corporate-entrepreneur model and the political correctness–feel good model. Each of these models may also have something to be said for it. Perhaps by combining the virtues of these models we can move toward an ideal of the university that promotes democratic participation in a postmodern world.

THE LIBERAL MODEL

It is natural to begin with a quick review of the liberal ideal.[1] The main function of higher education is to ennoble the mind, by introducing students to the canon, or at least a sample of the best and the brightest, from Homer, Sophicles, Plato, and Aristotle, to Arnold, T. S. Eliot, and Thomas Mann. Such an education also prepares an individual for citizenship in a modern democracy, as well as for a career or a profession. Being acculturated into the canon, one is also immersed in the universal values and rational methods that distinguish Western heritage and manifest its intellectual and moral superiority over other traditions. Science in particular embodies these ideals in the modern world. Pure or applied research will both ennoble the mind and pave the way for useful applications that will help relieve the human estate and help humanity realize Enlightenment ideals of progress. Teaching involves imparting these ideals, including the ideals of impartiality, objectivity, and moral neutrality to students, who will thereby be exposed to the best that has been thought and written, or at any rate a subset of these ideas.

One feature of the liberal model that is worth some attention is the metaphor of the "marketplace of ideas." This capitalist image promotes the notion, expressed most forcefully in Mill's *On Liberty*, that a continuous process of open dialogue and debate—"sifting and winnowing"—will eventually promote the emergence of the truth. Science, as a democratic community writ small, is the exemplar of this ideal of "organized skepticism." The metaphor also reinforces the ideals of objectivity and value neutrality. Each competing idea is openly and fairly debated, given its strongest formulation, and considered only on its intrinsic merits.

It is not clear whether this model can work or should work. In practice, most academics are not, perhaps cannot be, this open-minded. As Abraham Kaplan once quipped, this ideal confuses being open-minded with being empty minded. Ideas that are incompatible with existing doctrines and methods are often dismissed out of hand. Students whose views differ from those favored by instructors are often not taken seriously, and are often browbeaten into submission. Revolutionary ideas that later turn out to be true are usually ridiculed at the outset. As a result, the notion of open dialogue is damaged.

On the other hand, the marketplace model often reinforces an inability or unwillingness to express an opinion or take a stand, since this is supposed to be incompatible with objectivity and neutrality. If students believe that gays are immoral, and if liberals believe that value judgments are either subjective or that some issues require never-ending debate—after all, there is always another twist on an argument in the offing—how can we ever settle an issue? Am I being dogmatic if I dismiss the view about gays out of hand? This sort of issue has come to haunt university campuses recently. On the one hand, hate speech is being censored, which seems to many in conflict with the sort of free speech that liberals cherish. On the other hand, if the preceding argument is applied to the case of hate speech, what if the gay bashers are right? As Mill would say, do we not risk losing the truth by censoring them?

My favorite example of this sort of conundrum is the ethics book that maintains the following three assertions:

a. There is an absolute moral truth.
b. We may not have any idea what it is, so that, for all we know, nobody has acted in accordance with it, yet.
c. Christian morality is obviously morally superior to that of the Hottentots.

(This is an old text!) This is the dilemma of liberal education and the marketplace-of-ideas approach to education in a nutshell: There are absolute truths, we may have an idea of what they are, we are approaching them, slowly if not surely, so that we can dismiss ideas that conflict with the best evidence and fairest debates whenever possible. But on issues where we are not sure (or which are not scientific) everything is equally up for grabs, including racism, sexism, ethnocentrism. The marketplace of ideas thus turns out to be another form of positivism: facts and theories in science are objective while everything else is a matter of opinion; or else we get the elitist view that "moral facts" and theories are scientific in some sense or other. The result is the same in either case. Thus, I have heard liberal social scientists claim, with a straight face, that since they cannot prove that genocide is immoral, it is merely a matter of opinion that it is not. By the same logic, it is merely a matter of opinion that gays and lesbians, women, and foreigners should have civil rights, or that war research is incompatible with the mission of a (liberal) university.

Before assaying some of the recent criticisms of the liberal ideals, let me sketch the corporate and political correctness alternatives.

THE CORPORATE MODEL

In the last five to six years universities have become top-down corporations, whose main goal is to generate funds through the establishment of research parks and university-corporate contracts for commercialized research. Teaching, especially undergraduate teaching, has become a peripheral concern. Education, what used to be called "higher learning," is at serious risk, for a variety of reasons:

1. The student as consumer model has turned the marketplace of ideas into the notion that students, as paying customers, should not have to listen to ideas they do not like; they can leave class without penalty, and faculty have to provide them with "alternative" assignments if the course material is "too controversial" to them. (Some policies require that students be forewarned of such controversial material, so they can opt out.) But what is "controversial"? Pornographic films (often involving gays)? A discussion of gay rights, abortion, or whatever in an ethics class? Evolutionary theory in a zoology class? Further, one now hears the argument that since students are paying customers, they should receive an A in all classes without having to work or measure up to academic standards. Pretty soon we can just have a student's parents write a $30,000 check to the alumni fund and receive a diploma and a list of jobs in the mail.

2. Administrators have become tyrants. They play zero-sum games with faculty, stifle open debate and free speech, build themselves plush offices while taking every penny from academic departments for themselves and for research parks, and then use accounting procedures that even Price Waterhouse could not decipher. They tell faculty they are not working hard enough, so that they need to continually devise new evaluation instruments, which guarantee that faculty do not get any real work done. They downsize academic units and narrow the "mission" of the university on the grounds of "efficiency," using the red herring that a university cannot be all things to all people. Indeed not. But what has it become, and for whom? Faculty are chastised for not having a communal spirit, while universities are becoming fiefdoms where each unit has to play zero-sum games with every other unit for funds, and where there is a war of all against all on campuses. More bureaucrats are then hired to deal with the problems created by top-down managers, while faculty get blamed for everything.

3. Scientific research has become totally bastardized. Money and competition with Japan have become top priority. Commericalized and

corporate-sponsored research, and knowledge as "real estate" or "intellectual property," are the current buzz words. (Lyotard calls this "the mercantilization of knowledge.") Professor-enterpreneurs would sell their souls to Mephistopheles without any prodding. There is more fraud, secrecy, and deception among scientists than ever. Undergraduates are now being sucked into this process of "professionalization," spending more and more time, at age nineteen or twenty, trying to publish papers to get into graduate school, and do not much care about expanding their intellectual horizons. English departments are becoming technical writing programs, or else they are divided by wars between technical writers, literature professors, and postmodernist critics. Philosophy departments are becoming service units to business, engineering, agriculture colleges, trying to teach ethics to thousands of very resistant students a semester, often without the benefit of extra tenured faculty. Temporary instructors, often the most devoted teachers, are treated like indentured servants, paid 50 percent less for a full load, and told they are lucky to have a job at all. Those researchers who do not play ball are out of the loop. Those who actually try to do research are often hamstrung by bureaucrats, who evidently are only interested in banking the overhead money, not in allowing the research to get done. Public universities are becoming privatized, and traditional missions to the citizens, for example, disseminating knowledge and expertise, are taking a back seat to corporate contracts. Corporations do not want knowledge to be given away. They want to own it, for obvious reasons. Commercialized research, biotechnology, and so on, are private property, owned by researcher-university-corporate teams. Since we live in an information-based economy, knowledge has become the fundamental economic commodity. Privatizing knowledge so that it can be sold for huge profits is what scientific research and universities are all about these days.

4. Perhaps the most insidious development in the corporate university is the alliance between corporate, trickle-down managerial elites and the most vociferous elements of the political correctness–feel good model of the university. Multicultural curricula and diversity, a campus with fewer hate crimes and and more women, people of color, international students, gays, etc., on the student and faculty are all admirable goals. But the alliance I am referring to is an alliance based upon nothing but power. University administrators want to minimize education, discussion, and criticism, marginalize the humanities, and retain student monies while appearing to be noble advocates of tolerance and diversity. Many political correctness activists are interested in power, in controlling the agenda of universities, in instituting courses and programs (very often legitimate, indeed necessary and important), and are undoubtedly convinced that white male liberal academics—but not, apparently, white male central administrators, whether liberal or not—are the number one enemy and obstacle. (This further fragments the Democratic left at a most inopportune time.) We therefore now have a situation in which university retention policies, and unwritten sexual harassment policies that define harassment to include any remark that makes anyone, for whatever reason or for no reason, feel uncomfortable in a "hostile" environment, are telling faculty and students that the educational mission of the university is not to upset anyone and to retain students at all costs. Students are not stupid; they are practiced customers.

Faculty members are not stupid, either. They realize (or are increasingly being made to realize, e.g., by their department chairs) that if students find a course too hard they will leave; if, for whatever reason, they find the environment "hostile," they—and their money—will leave. If a student wants to see her advisor at a time when the advisor is not in her office (she may even be in class), the student complains that she has a bad advisor. So now universities will institute mandatory advisor-evaluation forms, even while administrators admit that these student charges are often ridiculous. After all, we do not want the customer to go away dissatisfied, even if they are being grossly unfair. The upshot is that courses will have to be watered down and controversy eliminated. If a student finds a course difficult, faculty cannot say "work harder"; we must make the material easier. And what happens when these students, who have no sense of responsibility—many do not do the work or even care if they get bad grades—go out to get a job? Undoubtedly faculty will be blamed if these students cannot keep their jobs. Outcome assessments is the name of this game.

It is perhaps obvious what the corporate university does to the liberal ideal of education. It destroys it. But its destruction is also being accomplished from the other direction, namely from advocates of the political correctness–feel good model of the university, to which I now turn.

THE POLITICAL CORRECTNESS–FEEL GOOD MODEL

I have already indicated my sympathy for the goals of multiculturalism and diversity, and will later suggest ways in which these goals provide the means to inculcate more democratic participation in society. What I would like to focus on here is the educational agenda of the extreme political correctness–feel good advocates, both to bring up issues about the liberal ideal and as a backdrop for my discussion of democratic education. I want to focus on two issues in particular: teaching methods and course content; and diversity courses and multicultural curricula.

1. Methods vs. Educational Content. Perhaps not so ironically, the most vociferous advocates of hate-speech restrictions are in favor of absolute free speech when their agenda is in question. This typically takes two forms. One, faculty are now being told to trade off course content for a process that requires the instructor to use as many different styles of teaching as there are styles of learning. And how many is that? Am I required to become an expert in educational psychology and in a variety of cultures to do so? And do humanities and social-science instructors have to carry an unfair burden, since it is not clear whether mathematics, engineering, biochemistry, or physics can be expected to follow suit? Or are they? How would it work? Suppose I get a course roster with one hundred names for my ethics course. There are, let us say, ten different styles of learning spread out (let us suppose) among these one hundred names. (I am leaving aside problems with, say, dyslexic students here.) If I cannot think of the right ten teaching styles, or cannot use them very well, what do I do? Get help, I suppose. If the students come from ten different countries or

cultures, what do I do? If ninety students get bored while I teach the other ten according to their own learning style, what do I do? Do I give ten sets of "exams" (or whatever) three or four times a semester? (And what does my teaching assistant do?) Do I give out ten different course-evaluation forms? Do some students read texts, while others watch videos?

Again, there is some truth behind this sort of proposal. Lecturing may be ineffective; videos and computers may be better. But the problem is that our culture is already functionally illiterate. People do not read much or well, but do get inundated by MTV. How can we have a democratic culture then? If you do not read well, you cannot write well, think well, argue well, evaluate evidence, or have much of a conversation. On the other hand, one can easily get taken in by sound bites. Students already are so influenced by TV that they turn you off if you do not entertain them, or if you ask them to work harder. How will culturally disadvantaged or different students prosper if I do not get them to try other learning styles? Will the workplace have to follow suit? What about the course content? Should that take backseat to learning and teaching styles? For what purpose and with what results?

As a corollary to these proposals about "methods" there now is in place an ethos that applies the 12-step method used in groups like Alcoholics Anonymous to discussions, even in faculty groups. Everybody says their piece. Nobody can question or criticize bad arguments without being accused of being a typical, white male academic who cares only about empty abstractions, not personal experience or "real life." Nothing much gets said, let alone debated. Evidently debate, argumentation, and logic are white male instruments of domination. Students now do the same. They cannot stick to a topic, much less make a relevant point. They just say whatever pops into their heads. This form of feel-good narcissism may make people with hangups about being victims feel better; but it is a disaster for democracy and education.

2. Multicultural education and diversity. How will this feel-good style of conversation and the mania for "teaching and learning styles" promote multicultural education and diversity? It seems clear to me that they will not and cannot promote it, but will turn it into either a shouting match or a propaganda session. Indeed, if each person's own preferences and learning styles find those of others "hostile," what do we have to look forward to? More hate speech and insipid substitutes for dialogue and mutual understanding.

What is needed are courses that allow students to understand other cultures and to gain diverse perspectives on racism, sexism, homophobia, and xenophobia in all cultures, as well as an appreciation for a multicultural perspective on American history and contemporary problems. But as my colleague David Roochnik has pointed out, this will do little good since many of our students do not understand the "dominant" cultures of the West; they know little about American history; they cannot or do not wish to evaluate evidence or arguments with an open mind; nor do they appreciate the values of diversity and community. I am speaking here from personal experience; but this experience has been confirmed by just about every faculty member I know at a good number of institutions. The point is made with great clarity by Benjamin Barber in *An Aristocracy for Everyone: The Politics of Education and the Future of America*.[2] A culture without a sense of history can have no future but the kind we are now experiencing, dictated by corporations, technology, and managers and bureaucrats who have the vision of accountants. This will continue to spawn fringe groups, negativism, reactionary solutions to contemporary problems. Before students can appreciate Confucius, they need to be exposed to the Western tradition, to great works by women writers, Black writers, Hispanic writers. They also need to read books like Mill's *On Liberty* and be given some idea of what democracy is supposed to be. They need to study American history, the great issues that have molded our nation's past and that will play a role in fashioning our future. They need to learn what the idea of *e pluribus unum* means and be exposed to the notion that we are and always have been a "community of communities" (to borrow a phrase from Robert Nisbet). We need to focus on conflicts in classes, not ignore them. Students need to be exposed to the idea that dogmatism and nihilism are not the only possibilities, and the fallacy in the belief that whatever is not "provable" in science is automatically rubbish.

So while I am against cultural and political elitism,I do favor policies that will encourage students who want to get a broad education, an education that requires a background in history, American studies, philosophy, the social sciences, and literature, not just a smattering here and there. What we need is a renewal of a broad core curriculum for all undergraduates, no matter what they plan to major in or do for a living. When I was an undergraduate at Brooklyn College in the mid 1960s everybody took about two years of required courses. Today students start focusing on their majors and their careers when they are sophomores. This breeds more narrow-minded careerists who have neither the will nor the ability to participate in a democratic community except as experts for hire. We need to make college less expensive, since it is in the nation's interest to do so, and will cost us more in both human and monetary terms if we do not. (We will further institutionalize a two-class society of rich and poor as college becomes financially impossible for bright poor people.) We also should focus more on civic education and on the need to educate students for a multicultural world, that involves more than technical expertise. Finally, we must think about establishing other post-high school education and career options for those unable or unwilling to go to a university or college. As long as we can diminish the elitism that goes with expertise, this may not hurt. At any event, it is clear that our economic problems and cultural and political problems are inseparable. Even if liberal elitism is dead, we are still a very long way from democracy.[3]

In recent years, a number of authors have tried to develop ideas about education for democracy and democratic education that are based upon a rejection of the sort of Platonic assumptions that ground guardianship conceptions of politics, including the varieties of liberal elitism and liberal democracy. (Recall Kahane's observation, in my introduction, that liberal elitism preempts the democratic potential in humanistic ideals of education.) In particular, Jean Bethke Elshtain, Richard Bellamy, Amy Gutmann, and Benjamin Barber, try to develop models of democratic education based upon a Deweyan outlook, but taken in the sort of postmodernist direction espoused by Rorty. Gutman sums up this view as follows:

> The most distinctive feature of a democratic theory of education is that it makes a democratic virtue out of our inevitable disagreement. . . . The democratic virtue is that . . . we can publicly debate educational problems in a way much more likely to increase our understanding of education and each other than if we . . . (as Kant suggests) . . . "depend entirely upon the judgment of the most enlightened experts." The policies that result from our democratic deliberations will not always be the right ones, but they will be more enlightened—by the values and concerns of the many communities that constitute a democracy—than those that would be made by unaccountable . . . experts.[4]

Gutmann goes on to develop a model of democracy that involves dialogue, consensus, and the search for agreement while preserving differences, but without appeal to any foundational epistemological, political, or moral principles. I would suggest, in closing, that we need to see the positive value in this kind of postmodern approach to democracy and education in a multicultural society (and world) where utopian standards and metanarratives have no real purchase or general assent. It is time to move on to the positive potentials in such a view.

In today's world, a democratic culture and education must take into account the politics of recognition,[5] the positive value of diversity and multiculturalism combined, however, with a renewed emphasis on citizenship, community, dialogue, and a sense of experimentation. If postmodernism has anything to teach us, it is that both nostalgia for the old shibboleths and values, for instance, religion, simple-minded moral absolutism, solutions to problems that have no foundation in reality, as well as a blind faith in the value of science, technology, capitalist individualism and expertise need to be surpassed in favor of an emphasis on understanding, dialogue, social experimentation and a shared recognition that our social worlds are a product of human actions. In *Democracy in America*, Tocqueville admonishes his readers to accept the idea that new times call for new politics. Until we can figure out how to build a postmodern democratic society, our civilization will continue along its downward spiral.[6] Once we can make progress in the construction of democratic communities, perhaps liberal democracy can begin to redeem its democratic potential.

NOTES

1. See John Searle, "Storm over the University," in *Debating P.C.*, ed. Paul Berman (New York: Laurel, 1992), 85–124; see also idem "Postmodernism and the Western Rationalist Tradition," in *The Campus Wars*, ed. John Arthur and Amy Shapiro (New York: Routledge, 1994), 28–49.

2. Benjamin Barber, *An Aristocracy for Everyone* (New York: Ballantine, 1992); see also Frances Moore Lappe, *Rediscovering America's Values* (New York: Ballantine, 1990).

3. See William A. Henry III, *In Defense of Elitism* (New York: Doubleday, 1994).

4. Amy Gutmann, *Democratic Education* (Princeton: Princeton University Press, 1987), 11; see also Geraint Parry, "Making Democrats: Education and Democracy," in *Democracy and Democratization*, ed. Geraint Parry and Michael Moran (New York: Routledge, 1993), 47–68; Richard Bellamy, *Liberalism and Modern Society*

(College Park: Pennsylvania State University Press, 1992), ch. 5; Barber, *An Aristocracy for Everyone*; Jean Bethke Elshtain, *Democracy on Trial* (New York: Basic Books, 1995).

5. See Charles Taylor, "The Political Recognition" in *Multiculturalism and the Politics of Recognition*, rev. ed., ed. Charles Taylor (Princeton: Princeton University Press, 1994).

6. See Robert Hughes, *The Culture of Complaint* (New York: Oxford University Press, 1993), for a more detailed elaboration and defense of the sort of views I have sketched in chapters 10 and 11.

Bibliography

Aaron, Daniel. *Writers on the Left*. New York: Harcourt, 1961.

Abbott, Philip. *Furious Fancies*. Westport, CT: Greenwood, 1980.

Aken, William. *Technocracy and the American Dream*. Berkeley: University of California Press, 1977.

Alford, Robert F., and Roger Friedland. *Powers of Theory*. New York: Cambridge University Press, 1985.

Allen, Garland E. "The Role of Experts in Scientific Controversy." In *Scientific Controversies*, edited by H. Tristam Engelhardt and Arthur Caplan. New York: Cambridge University Press, 1987, pp. 169–202.

Anderson, Charles W. *Pragmatic Liberalism*. Chicago: University of Chicago Press, 1990.

Anderson, Perry. *A Zone of Engagement*. New York: Verso, 1992.

Antonio, Robert J., and Douglas Kellner. "Communication, Modernity, and Democracy in Habermas and Dewey." Typescript, 1992.

Appleby, Joyce. *Liberalism and Republicanism in the Historical Imagination*. Cambridge: Harvard University Press, 1992.

Arblaster, Anthony. *The Rise and Decline of Western Liberalism*. Cambridge: Blackwell, 1982.

Arendt, Hannah. *The Origins of Totalitarianism*. New York: Penguin, 1951.

Arnove, Robert, ed. *Philanthropy and Cultural Imperialism*. Chicago: G. T. Hall, 1980.

Aronowitz, Stanley. "Is Democracy Possible?" In *The Phantom Public*, edited by Bruce Robbins. Minneapolis: University of Minnesota Press, 1993, pp. 75–90.

Ash, Mitchell G., and William R. Woodward eds. *Psychology in Twentieth Century Thought and Society*. New York: Cambridge University Press, 1988.

Bachrach, Peter. *The Theory of the Democratic Elite*. Boston: Little, Brown, 1967.

Bachrach, Peter, and Ariel Botwinick. *Power and Emancipation*. Philadelphia: Temple University Press, 1991.

Baken, David. "Behaviorism and American Urbanization: 1870–1914." *Journal of the History of the Behavioral Sciences* 2 (January 1966).

Ball, Terence. "The Politics of Social Science in Postwar America." In *Recasting America*, edited by F. May. New York: Routledge, 1990, pp. 76–92.
Bannister, Roger C. *Sociology and Scientism*. Chapel Hill: University of North Carolina Press, 1983.
Barber, Benjamin. *An Aristocracy for Everyone*. New York: Ballantine Books, 1992.
______. *Conquest of Politics*. Princeton: Princeton University Press, 1989.
______. *Strong Democracy*. Berkeley: University of California Press, 1984.
Baritz, Loren. *Servants of Power*. New York: Wiley, 1960.
Barrow, Clyde W. *Universities and the Capitalist State*. Madison: University of Wisconsin Press, 1990.
Bartlett, Donald, and J. B. Steele. *America: What Went Wrong?* Kansas City: Andrews and McMeel, 1992.
Bates, Ernest Sutherland. "John Dewey: America's Philosophic Engineer." *Monthly Review* 122 (1933): 387–96.
Beetham, David. "Beyond Liberal Democracy." *Socialist Register* 13 (1981).
______. *Max Weber and the Theory of Modern Politics*. Cambridge, UK: Polity Press, 1985.
______. "Weber and the Liberal Political Tradition." In *The Barbarism of Reason: Max Weber and the Twilight of Enlightenment*, edited by Asher Horowitz and Terry Maley. Toronto: University of Toronto Press, 1994, 99–112.
Behler, Ernst. *Irony and the Discourse of Modernity*. Seattle: University of Washington Press, 1991.
Bell, Daniel. *The Coming of Post-Industrial Society*. New York: Basic Books, 1973.
______. *The Cultural Contradictions of Capitalism*. New York: Basic Books, 1974.
______. *The End of Ideology*. Rev. ed. Cambridge: Harvard University Press, 1989.
______. "Liberalism in the Post-Industrial Society." In Bell, *Winding Passages*. New York: Basic Books, 1983.
______. "Passion and Politics in America." *Encounter* 3 (1956): 54–60.
______. *The Radical Right*. New York: Anchor, 1964.
______. *The Winding Passage*. New York: Basic Books, 1980.
Bellah, Robert, ed. *Emile Durkheim on Morality and Society*. Chicago: University of Chicago Press, 1973.
Bellah, Robert, Richard Madesen, William M. Sullivan, Ann Swidler, and Steven M. Tipton. *The Good Society*. New York: Knopf, 1991.
Bellamy, Richard. *Liberalism and Modern Society*. College Park: Pennsylvania State University Press, 1992.
Bellamy, Richard, ed. *Victorian Liberalism*.. New York: Routledge, 1992.
Bender, Thomas. *New York Intellect*. New York: Borzoi, 1987.
Bendix, Reinhard, and Guenther Roth, eds. *Scholarship and Partisanship: Essays on Max Weber*. Berkeley: University of California Press, 1971.
Bernard, Luther Lee. "The Transition to an Objective Standard of Social Control." *American Journal of Sociology* 11 (1910–1911): 530–55.
Bernard, Luther Lee, and Jesse Bernard. *Origins of American Sociology*. New York: Crowell, 1943.
Berry, Wendell. *The Unsettling of American Agriculture*. San Francisco: Sierra Club Books, 1977.
Blake, Casey Nelson. *Beloved Community*. Chapel Hill: University of North Carolina Press, 1990.
Bledstein, Burton. *The Culture of Professionalism*. New York: Norton, 1976.
Blumenberg, Hans. *The Legitimacy of the Modern Age*. Cambridge: MIT Press, 1985.

Bohman, James F. "Communication, Ideology, and Democratic Theory." *American Political Science Review* 85 (1990): 93–109.
Boller, Paul F., Jr. *American Thought in Transition: The Impact of Evolutionary Naturalism*, 1865–1900. Chicago: Rand McNally, 1969.
Bologh, Roslyn Wallach. "Max Weber and the Dilemma of Rationality." In *Max Weber's Political Sociology*, edited by Ronald M. Glassman and Vatro Murvar. Westport, CT: Greenwood Press, 1984, 175–188.
Boorstein, Daniel. *The Decline of Radicalism*. New York: Random House, 1967.
______. *The Genius of American Politics*. Chicago: University of Chicago Press, 1953.
______. *The Lost World of Thomas Jefferson*. Boston: Beacon Press, 1948.
______. *The Republic of Technology*. New York: Harper and Row, 1978.
Bottomore, Tom. *Elites and Masses*. New York: Basic Books, 1964.
Botwinick, Ariel. *Postmodernism and Democratic Theory*. Philadelphia: Temple University Press, 1993.
Bourke, Paul F. "The Social Critics and the End of American Innocence, 1907–1921." *Journal of American Studies* 3 (1969): 57–72.
______. "The Status of Politics: 1909–1919." *Journal of American Studies* 8 (1974): 171–202.
Bourne, Randolph. *Radical Will*. Edited by Olaf Hanson. New York: Urizon, 1977.
Bowles, Samuel, and Herbert Gintis. *Democracy and Capitalism*. New York: Basic Books, 1986.
Boyer, Paul. *Urban Masses and Moral Order in America*. Cambridge: Harvard University Press, 1978.
Boyte, Harry C. *Community Is Possible*. New York: Harper and Row, 1984.
Brickman, William W. "Dewey's Social and Political Commentary." In *Guide to the Works of John Dewey*, edited by Jo Ann Boydston. Carbondale: Southern Illinois University Press, 1979, pp. 218–56.
Briggs, B. Bruce, ed. *The New Class?* New York: McGraw-Hill, 1979.
Brodsky, Garry M. "Politics, Culture, and Society in Marx and Dewey." In *Context over Foundation: Dewey and Marx*, edited by William Gavin. Boston: Reidel, 1988, 77–119.
Bruce, Robert V. *The Launching of Modern American Science*. Ithaca: Cornell University Press, 1985.
Bryant, Christopher. *Positivism in Social Theory and Research*. New York: St. Martin's Press, 1984.
Brzezinski, Zbigniew. *Between Two Ages*. New York: Viking, 1970.
Buenker, John, John Burnham, and Robert Cruden. *Progressivism*. Boston: Schenkman, 1977.
Bullert, Gary. *The Politics of John Dewey*. Buffalo: Prometheus Books, 1983.
Burke, Kenneth. "The Road to Indignation." *New Republic* 65, 18 February 1931, 13–15.
Burnham, John C. "On the Origins of Behaviorism." *Journal of the History of the Behavioral Sciences* 3 (1968): 143–51.
Burhnam, Walter Dean. *The Current Crisis in American Politics*. New York: Oxford University Press, 1982.
Burns, J. H. "J. S. Mill and Democracy, 1829–1861." In Mill: *A Collection of Essays*, edited by J. Schneewind. Notre Dame: Notre Dame University Press, 1969, 285–99.
Burns, Walter Demry. *The Current Crisis in American Politics*. New York: Oxford University Press, 1982.

Burrows, Jo. "Conversational Politics: Rorty's Pragmatist Apology for Liberalism." In *Reading Rorty*, edited by Alan Malachowski. Cambridge: Blackwell's, 1989, 322–38.

Buss, A. R., ed. *Psychology in Social Context*. New York: Irvington, 1979.

Buxton, William. *Talcott Parson and the Capitalist Nation-State*. Toronto: University of Toronto Press, 1985.

Callinicos, Alex. *Against Postmodernism*. New York: St. Martin's, 1990.

Camfield, Thomas M. "The Professionalization of American Psychology, 1870-1917." *Journal of the History of the Behavioral Sciences* 9 (1973): 66-74.

Campbell, Colin. *The Romantic Ethic and Spirit of Consumerism*. Cambridge: Blackwell's, 1990.

Campbell, James. "Dewey's Method of Social Reconstruction." *Transactions of the C. S. Peirce Society* 20 (1983–84): 263–93.

_____. "Dewey's Understanding of Marx and Marxism." In *Context over Foundation: Dewey and Marx*, edited by William Gavin. Boston: Reidel, 1988, 119–47.

_____. "Rorty's Use of Dewey." *Southern Journal of Philosophy* 21 (1984): 175–87.

Chamberlain, John. Farewell to Reform. London: Liverright, 1932.

Chandler, Alfred D. *The Visible Hand*. Cambridge: Harvard University Press, 1977.

Cmiel, Kenneth. *Democratic Eloquence*. Berkeley: University of California Press, 1990.

Cnudde, Charles, and Dean Neuberger eds. *Empirical Democratic Theory*. Boston: Markham Publishing Co., 1969.

Cohen, Joshua. "Deliberation and Democratic Legitimacy." In *The Good Polity*, edited by Alan Hamlin and Philip Petit. Cambridge: Blackwell's, 1989, 17–34.

_____. "The Economic Basis of Deliberative Democracy." *Social Philosophy and Policy* 6 (1989): 25–50.

Coleman, Peter. *The Liberal Conspiracy*. New York: Free Press, 1989.

Collins, Randall. *The Credential Society*. New York: Academic Press, 1990.

_____. *Three Sociological Traditions*. New York: Oxford University Press, 1985.

Connolly, William, ed. *The Bias of Pluralism*. New York: Atherton, 1969.

_____. *Identity/Difference*. Ithaca: Cornell University Press, 1991.

Corlett, William. *Community without Unity*. Durham, NC: Duke University Press, 1989.

Coser, Lewis. "Durkheim's Conservatism." In *Essays on Sociology and Philosophy*, edited by Kurt Wolff. Columbus: Ohio State University Press, 1960.

Cotkin, George. *Reluctant Modernism*. New York: Twayne, 1990.

Cowling, Maurice. *Mill and Liberalism*. New York: Cambridge University Press, 1961.

Cravens, Hamilton. "History of the Social Sciences." In *Historical Writing on American Science*, edited by M. Kohlstadt and M. Rossiter. Baltimore: Johns Hopkins University Press, 1986, 183–207.

_____. *The Triumph of Evolution*. Baltimore: Johns Hopkins University Press, 1988.

Cremaschi, Sergio. "Adam Smith, Skeptical Newtonianism, Disenchanted Republicanism, and the Birth of the Social Sciences." In *Knowledge and Politics*, edited by M. Dascal and O. Gruengard. Boulder: Westview Press, 1989, 83–110.

Cremin, Lawrence A. *The Transformation of the School*. New York: Vintage, 1961.

Crick, Bernard. *The American Science of Politics*. Berkeley: University of California Press, 1960.

Croly, Herbert. *Progressive Democracy*. New York: Macmillan, 1914.

______. *The Promise of American Life*. New York: Macmillan, 1907.

Cronin, Thomas E. *Direct Democracy*. Cambridge: Harvard University Press, 1989.

Crozier, Michel, Samuel P. Huntington, and Joji Watanuki. *The Crisis of Democracy*. New York City: New York University Press, 1975.

Crunden, Robert. *Ministers of Reform*. New York: Basic Books, 1982.

Curtis, Tom. "Bourne, MacDonald, Chomsky, and the Rhetoric of Resistance." *Antioch Review* 28 (Summer 1969): 245–52.

Dahl, Robert A. *Democracy and Its Critics*. New Haven: Yale University Press, 1989.

______. *Dilemmas of Pluralist Democracy*. New Haven: Yale University Press, 1982.

______. *Pluralist Democracy in the United States*. Chicago: Rand McNally, 1967.

______. *A Preface to Democratic Theory*. Chicago: University of Chicago Press, 1956.

D'Amico, A. "Analysis and Advocacy: Pragmatism and the Study of Politics." *Polity* 6 (1974): 193–208.

______. "Dewey and Marx: On Partisanship and the Reconstruction of Society." *American Political Science Review* 75 (1981): 654-66.

______. "Impractical America: Reconsideration of the Pragmatic Lesson." *Political Theory* 13 (1986): 83–104.

______. *Individuality and Community*. Tampa: University of Florida Presses, 1978.

______. "The Politics after Deconstruction: Rorty, Dewey, and Marx." In *Context over Foundation: Dewey and Marx*, edited by William Gavin. Boston: Reidel, 1988, 178–205.

Daniels, George. *Science in American Society*. New York: Knopf, 1971.

Dawley, Alan. *Struggles for Justice*. Cambridge: Harvard University Press, 1991.

Day, Richard P., Ronald Beiner, and Joseph Masciulli, eds. *Democratic Theory and Technological Society*. San Francisco: Sharpe, 1988.

DeBats, Don. "Liberal Democratic Theory in America." In *Liberal Democratic Theory and Its Critics*, edited by Norman Winthrop. London: Croom Helm, 1983.

Derber, Charles, William A. Schwartz, and Yale Magrass. *Power in the Highest Degree*. New York: Oxford University Press, 1990.

Derrida, Jacques. "The Contest of the Faculties." In *Logomachia: The Conflict of the Faculties*, edited by Richard Rand. Lincoln: University of Nebraska Press, 1992, 1–33.

______. *The Other Heading*. Bloomington: Indiana University Press, 1990.

______. *Spectres of Marx*. New York, Routledge, 1994.

Dewey, John. "Creative Democracy—the Task before Us." In *Classic American Philosophers*, edited by Max Fish. New York: Appleton, 1951, 389–95.

______. "The Ethics of Democracy." In *Dewey, The Early Works*. Vol. 1. Carbondale: Southern Illinois University, 1970.

______. *Freedom and Culture*. 1939. Carbondale: Southern Illinois University Press, 1969, 227–49.

______. *Individualism Old and New*. New York: Capricorn, 1930.

______. *Lectures on Psychological and Political Ethics: 1898*. Edited by Donald F. Koch. New York: Hafner, 1976.

______. *Liberalism and Social Action*. New York: Capricorn, 1935.

______. *Problems of Men*. New York: Philosophical Library, 1946.

_____. *The Public and Its Problems*. New York: Holt, 1927.
Dewey, John, and Arthur F. Bentley. *The Knower and the Known*. Boston: Beacon, 1949.
Dickson, David. *The New Science of Politics*. Chicago: University of Chicago Press, 1990.
Dietze, Gottfried. *Liberalism Proper and Proper Liberalism*. Baltimore: Johns Hopkins University Press, 1985.
Diggins, John Patrick. "Dewey on Peace and War." *American Scholar* 49 (1981): 213–30.
_____. "Ideology and Pragmatism: Philosophy or Passion?" *American Political Science Review* 64 (1970): 889–900.
_____. *Mussolini and Fascism: The View from America*. Princeton: Princeton University Press, 1972.
_____. *The Promise of Pragmatism*. Chicago: University of Chicago Press, 1993.
_____ *The Rise and Fall of the American Left*. New York: Norton, 1991.
Domhoff, William. *The Power Elite and the State*. New York: Aldine De Gruyter, 1980.
_____. *The Powers That Be*. New York: Random House, 1969.
Domhoff, William, and F. Ballard, eds. *C. Wright Mills and the Power Elite*. Boston: Beacon Press, 1968.
Downs, Anthony. *An Economic Theory of Democracy*. New York: Harper and Row, 1957.
Dryzek, John S. *Discursive Democracy*. New York: Cambridge University Press, 1980.
Duncan, Graeme. *Marx and Mill*. New York: Cambridge University Press, 1973.
Durkheim, Emile. *The Division of Labor in Society*. New York: Free Press, 1982.
_____. *Durkheim: Selections*. Edited by Anthony Giddens. New York: Cambridge University Press, 1979.
_____. *Moral Education*. New York: Free Press, 1961.
_____. *Professional Ethics and Civic Morals*. 1957. New York: Routledge, 1992.
_____. *The Rules of Sociological Method*. New York: Free Press, 1982.
_____. *Sociology and Philosophy*. New York: Free Press, 1974.
_____. *Suicide*. New York: Free Press, 1951.
Dworkin, Ronald. "The Foundations of Liberalism." In *Tanner Lectures on Values*. Vol. 11. Salt Lake City: University of Utah Press, 1990, 1–19.
_____. "Liberal Community." In *Communitarianism and Individualism*, edited by Shlomo Avineri and Avner de-Shalt. New York: Oxford University Press, 1992, 205–24.
_____. "Liberalism." In *Public and Private Morality*, edited by Stuart Hampshire. New York: Cambridge University Press, 1978, 113–42.
Eden, Robert. "Doing without Liberalism: Weber's Regime Politics." *Political Theory* 9 (1982): 379–407.
_____. *Political Leadership and Nihilism*. Tampa: University of Florida Press, 1989.
Ekrich, Arthur. *Progressivism in America*. New York: New Viewpoints, 1974.
Elshtain, Jean Bethke. *Democracy on Trial*. Yew York: Basic Books, 1995.
Erzahi, Yehuda. *The Descent of Icaraus*. Cambridge: Harvard University Press, 1991.
Etzioni, Amitai. *The Active Society*. New York, Free Press, 1968.
Etzioni-Halevy, Eva. *The Elite Connection: Problems and Potentials of Western Democracy*. Cambridge: Blackwell's, 1993.
_____. *Fragile Democracy*. Totowa, NJ: Transaction Publishers, 1989.

Eulau, Heinz, ed. *Behavioralism in Political Science*. New York: Atherton, 1969.
______. *Technology and Civility*. Stanford: Hoover Institution Press, 1977.
Evans, Sara M., and Harry Boyte. *Free Spaces*. Chicago: University of Chicago Press, 1990.
Factor, Regis A., and Stephen P. Turner. "The Limits of Reason and Some Limitations of Weber's Morality." *Human Studies* 2 (1979): 301–34.
Featherstone, Joseph. "John Dewey and David Riesman: From the Lost Individual to the Lonely Crowd." In *On the Making of Americans: Essays in Honor of David Riesman*, edited by H. Gans, N. Glazer, J. Gusfield, and C. Jencks. Philadelphia: University of Pennsylvania Press, 1979, 3–40.
Federici, Michael P. *The Challenge of Populism*. Westport, CT: Praeger, 1991.
Feinberg, Walter. *Reason and Rhetoric*. New York: Wiley, 1975.
Feyerabend, Paul. "Democracy, Elitism, and Scientific Method." *Inquiry* 22 (1980): 3–18.
______. "Historical Background." In *Philosophical Papers*. Vol. 2. New York: Cambridge University Press, 1981, 1–33.
______. "Notes on Relativism." In *Farewell to Reason*. New York: Verso, 1987, 19–90.
______. *Science in a Free Society*. New York: Verso, 1979.
Fine, Sidney. *Laissez Faire and the General Welfare State*. Ann Arbor: University of Michigan Press, 1967.
Fine, William. *Progressive Evolutionism and American Sociology: 1890–1920*. Ann Arbor: UMI Research Press, 1975.
Fischer, Frank. *Technocracy and the Politics of Expertise*. Newbury Park, CA: Sage Publications, 1990.
Fisher, Donald. "American Philanthropy and the Social Sciences: The Reproduction of a Conservative Ideology." In *Philanthropy and Cultural Imperialism*, edited by Robert Arnove. Chicago: G. T. Hall, 1980, 233–68.
Flacks, Richard. "The Sociology of Liberation Movements: Some Legacies and Lessons." In *Radical Sociologists and the Movement*, edited by Martin Oppenheimer, Martin J. Murray, and Rhonda F. Levine. Philadelphia: Temple University Press, 1990, 3–25.
Forcey, Charles. *The Crossroads of Liberalism*. New York: Oxford University Press, 1961.
Foucault, Michael. "Kant on Enlightenment and Revolution." *Economy and Society* 14 (1986): 88–96.
______. "What Is Enlightenment?" In *The Foucault Reader*, edited by Paul Rabinow. New York: Random House, 1984, 32–51.
Fowler, Robert Booth. *Believing Skeptics*. Westport, CT: Greenwood, 1978.
Fraser, Nancy. "On Actually Existing Democracies." In *Habermas and the Public Sphere*, edited by Craig Calhoun. Cambridge: MIT Press, 1992.
______. "Solidarity or Singularity: Richard Rorty between Romanticism and Technocracy." In *Reading Rorty*, edited by Alan Malachowski. Cambridge: Blackwell's, 1989.
Fraser, Nancy, and Linda Nicholson. "An Encounter between Feminism and Postmodernism." In *Universal Abandon?* edited by Andrew Ross. Minneapolis: University of Minnesota Press, 1987.
Freeden, Michael. *The New Liberalism*. New York: Oxford University Press, 1988.
Friedman, Richard B. "An Introduction to Mill's Theory of Authority." In *Mill: A Collection of Essays*, edited by J. B. Schneewind. Notre Dame: University of Notre Dame Press, 1969, 378–97.

Fukuyama, Francis. "The End of History." *The National Interest* 16 (Summer 1989): 3–18.

_____. *The End of History and the Last Man*. New York: Free Press, 1992.

Furner, Mary. *From Advocacy to Objectivity*. Lexington: University of Kentucky Press, 1975.

Gadamer, Hans-George. *Reason in the Age of Science*. Cambridge: MIT Press, 1982.

Gavin, William, ed. *Context over Foundation: Dewey and Marx*. Boston: Reidel, 1988.

Gerber, William. *American Liberalism*. Chicago: G. T. Hall, 1975.

Giddens, Anthony, ed. *Durkheim: Selections*. New York: Cambridge University Press, 1979.

_____. "Durkheim's Political Sociology." *Sociological Review* n.s. 1 (1971): 477–519.

_____. *Emile Durkheim*. New York: Penguin, 1978.

Gilbert, James. *Designing the Industrial State*. New York: Quadrangle, 1972.

_____. *Writers and Partisans*. New York: Wiley, 1968.

Ginzburg, Benjamin. "Against Messianism." *New Republic* 65, 18 February 1931, 15–17.

Goldfarb, Jeffrey. *The Cynical Society*. Chicago: University of Chicago Press, 1991.

Goldman, Harvey. *Max Weber and Thomas* Mann. Berkeley: University of California Press, 1988.

Goldstene, Paul. *The Bittersweet Century*. San Francisco: Chandler and Sharp, 1989.

_____. *The Collapse of Liberal Empire*. San Francisco: Chandler and Sharp, 1977.

Goodwin, Barbara. *Social Science and Utopia*. Boston: Unwin, 1978.

Goodwyn, Lawrence. *Democratic Promise*. New York: Oxford University Press, 1976.

Goodwyn, Robert. *Democratic Promise*. New York: Oxford University Press, 1985.

Gouinlock, James, ed. *The Moral Writings of John Dewey*. New York: Hafner, 1976.

Graff, Gerald. *Professing Literature*. Chicago: University of Chicago Press, 1988.

Graham, Keith. *The Battle of Democracy*. London: Harvester, 1986.

Greenstone, David J. "Group Theories." In *Handbook of Political Science*. Vol. 2, Micropolitical Theories, edited by Fred I. Greenstein and Nelson W. Polsby. Boston: Addison-Wesley, 1975, 243–319.

Greider, William. *Who Will Tell the People: The Betrayal of American Democracy*. New York: Simon and Schuster, 1992.

Grimes, Alan P. "The Pragmatic Course of Liberalism." *Western Political Quarterly* 8 (1956): 633–40.

Groggins, M., ed. *Governing Science and Technology in a Democracy*. Knoxville: University of Tennessee Press, 1987.

Gross, Bertram. *Friendly Fascism*. Boston: South End Press, 1980.

Gruber, Carol S. *Mars and Minerva: World War I and the Uses of Higher Learning in America*. Baton Rouge: Louisiana State University Press, 1975.

Gutman, Amy. *Democratic Education*. Princeton: Princeton University Press, 1987.

Haber, Samuel. *Efficiency and Uplift: Scientific Management in the Progressive Era*, 1890–1920. Chicago: University of Chicago Press, 1964.

Habermas, Jurgen. "Neo-Conservative Cultural Criticism in the United States and West Germany." In *Habermas and Modernity*, edited by Richard J. Bernstein. Cambridge: MIT Press, 1985, 78–94.

_____. *Philosophical Discourse on Modernity*. Cambridge: MIT Press, 1988.

_____. *The Structural Transformation of the Public Sphere*. Cambridge: MIT Press, 1988.

______. *Theory and Practice*. Boston: Beacon Press, 1973.
______. *The Theory of Communicative Action*. 2 vols. Boston: Beacon Press, 1984, 1987.
Hale, Matthew. *Human Science and Social Order*. Philadelphia: Temple University Press, 1980.
Halliday, R. J. *John Stuart Mill*. London: Unwin, 1976.
Hallowell, Robert. "Americanize America." *The New Republic* 65, 4 February 1931, 324–26.
Hamburger, J. *Intellectuals in Politics: John Stuart Mill and the Philosophic Radicals*. New Haven: Yale University Press, 1965.
Handy, Robert T. *The Social Gospel in America: 1870–1920*. New York: Oxford University Press, 1966.
Hanson, Russell. *The Democratic Imagination in America*. Princeton: Princeton University Press, 1985.
Hardin, Russell. "Rational Choice Theories." In *Idioms of Inquiry*, edited by Terence Ball. Albany: SUNY, 1987, 67–91.
Hardt, Hanno. *Critical Communication Studies, Communication, History, and Theory in America*. New York: Routledge, 1991.
Hartz, Louis. *The Liberal Tradition in America*. New York: Harcourt, 1955.
Haskell, Thomas, ed. *The Authority of Experts*. Bloomington: Indiana University Press, 1984.
______. *The Emergence of Professional Social Science*. Urbana: University of Illinois Press, 1977.
Hatch, Nathan, ed. *The Professions in American History*. Baltimore: Johns Hopkins University Press, 1987.
Hawthorn, Geoffrey. *Enlightenment and Despair*. New York: Cambridge University Press, 1976.
Hayek, Friedrich von. *The Road to Serfdom*. Chicago: University of Chicago Press, 1944.
Hays, Samuel. *Conservation and the Gospel of Efficiency*. Cambridge: Harvard University Press, 1959.
Held, David. *Models of Democracy*. Stanford: Stanford University Press, 1987.
Hennis, Wilhelm. *Max Weber: Essays in Reconstruction*. London: Unwin, 1988.
Henry, William A., III. *In Defense of Elitism*. New York: Doubleday, 1994.
Herrnstein, Richard J., and Charles Murray. *The Bell Curve*. New York: Macmillan, 1994.
Higham, John. *Strangers in the Land*. New Brunswick: Rutgers University Press, 1955.
Himmelfarb, Gertrude. *On Liberty and Liberalism*. New York: Knopf, 1974.
Hinkle, Roscoe C., and Gissela Hinkle. *The Development of Modern Sociology*. New York: Random House, 1954.
Hofstadter, Richard A. *The Age of Reform*. New York: Vintage, 1955.
______. *Anti-Intellectualism in American Life*. New York: Vintage, 1962.
______. *The Progressive Historians*. New York: Vintage, 1968.
______. *Social Darwinisn in American Thought*. Boston: Beacon Press, 1955.
Holden, Barry. *Understanding Liberal Democracy*. London: Philip Allan, 1988.
Hollinger, David A. *In the American Province*. Bloomington: Indiana University Press, 1985.
Hollinger, Robert. "The Limits of Tolerance: Mill vs. Feyerabend." *Southwest Philosophy Review* 2 (1985): 146–57.
______. *Postmodernism and the Social Sciences: A Thematic Approach*. Newbury Park, CA: Sage, 1994.

Holmes, Stephen. "John Stuart Mill: Fallabilism, Expertise, and the Politics-Science Analogy." In *Knowledge and Politics*, edited by M. Dascal and O. Gruengard. Boulder: Westview Press, 1989, 125–54.

Hook, Sidney. "The Centrality of Democracy." In *The American Pragmatists*, edited by Milton Konvitz and Gail Kennedy. New York: Meridian, 1960, 379–89.

______. "Civilization and Its Malcontents." *National Review*, 13 October 1989.

______. "The Justification of Democracy." In *The American Experience*, edited by Milton Konvitz and Gail Kennedy. New York: Meridian, 1960, 390–403.

Horowitz, Irving Louis, ed. *The New Sociology*. New York: Oxford University Press, 1964.

______. *The Rise and Fall of Project Camelot*. Cambridge: MIT Press, 1982.

Howe, Irving. "Literature and Liberalism." In *Celebration and Attacks*. New York: Harcourt, 1980, 239–54.

Hughes, Robert. *The Culture of Complaint*. New York: Oxford University Press, 1993.

Hughes, Thomas. *American Genesis*. New York: Viking, 1989.

Huntington, Samuel P. "American Democracy." In Michel Crozier, Samuel P. Huntington, and Joji Watanuki. *The Crisis of Democracy*. New York: New York University Press, 1975.

______. *American Politics: The Promise of Disharmony*. Cambridge: Harvard University Press, 1981.

______. "The Democratic Distemper." *The Public Interest* 25 (1962): 10–36.

______. Paradigms of American Politics: Beyond the One, the Two, and the Many." *Political Science Quarterly* 89 (1974): 1–26.

______. "Postindustrial Politics: How Benign Will It Be?" *Comparative Politics* 6 (1974): 163–91.

Huszar, George B. de, ed. *The Intellectuals*. New York: Free Press, 1960.

Israel, Jerry, ed. *Building the Organizational Society*. New York: Free Press, 1972.

Jacobs, S. *Science and British Liberalism*. London: Avebury, 1991.

Jacoby, Russell. *The Last Intellectuals*. New York: Noonday, 1987.

Jamison, Andrew. *Seeds of the Sixties*. Berkeley: University of California Press, 1994.

Janowitz, Morris. *The Last Half Century*. Chicago: University of Chicago Press, 1978.

Josephson, Matthew. "The Road to Indignation." *The New Republic* 65, 18 February 1931, 13–15.

Kahane, Alan S. *Aristocratic Liberalism*. New York: Oxford University Press, 1992.

Kant, Immanuel. *Contest of the Faculties*. Translated by Mary Gregor. Lincoln: University of Nebraska Press, 1992.

______. *Perpetual Peace and Other Essays*. Translated by Lewis White Beck. Indianapolis: Hackett, 1989.

______. *Political Writings*. 2d, enl. ed. Edited by H. Riess. New York: Cambridge University Press, 1991.

Kaplan, Sidney. "Social Engineers as Saviors: The Effects of World War I on Some American Liberals." *Journal of the History of Ideas* 16 (1956): 347–69.

Kariel, Henry. *The Decline of American Pluralism*. Stanford: Stanford University Press, 1967.

______. *Frontiers of Democratic Theory*. New York: Random House, 1970.

Karier, Clarence, J. Paul Violas, and Joel Spring, eds. *The Roots of Crisis*. Chicago: Rand McNally, 1973.

Karl, Barry. *Charles Merriam and the Study of Politics*. Chicago: University of Chicago Press, 1974.

______. *Executive Reorganization and Reform in the New Deal.* Cambridge: Harvard University Press, 1963.
______. *The Uneasy State.* Chicago: University of Chicago Press, 1981.
Kaufman-Osborn, Timothy V. "John Dewey and the Liberal Science of Community." *Journal of Politics* 46 (1984) 1143-1164.
______. "Pragmatism, Policy Science, and the State." *Journal of Politics* 48 (1986): 827–48.
Keane, John. "The Modern Democratic Revolution: Reflections on Jean-Francois Lyotard's *la condition postmoderne.*" *Chicago Review* 35 (1987): 4–19.
______. *Public Life and Late Capitalism.* New York: Cambridge University Press, 1984.
Kelso, William Alton. *American Democratic Theory: Pluralism and Its Critics.* Westport, CT: Greenwood Publishers, 1978.
Kennedy, David M. "The Progressive Era: An Overview." *Historian* 37 (1975): 453–68.
Kennedy, Gail, ed. *Pragmatism and American Culture.* Boston: Heath, 1952.
Kern, P. B. "Universal Suffrage without Democracy: Thomas Hare and John Stuart Mill." *Review of Politics* 34 (1972): 306–23.
Kevles, Daniel. *In the Name of Eugenics.* Berkeley: University of California Press, 1985.
______. *The Physicists.* Cambridge: Harvard University Press, 1972.
______. "Science." In *The Professions in American History*, edited by Nathan Hatch. Baltimore: Johns Hopkins University Press, 1987.
Kilker, Ernest. "Max Weber and the Possibilities for Democracy." In *Max Weber's Political Sociology*, edited by Ronald M. Glassman and Vatro Murvar. Westport, CT: Greenwood Publishers, 1984, 65–83.
Klansner, S., and V. Lidz eds. *The Nationalization of the Social Sciences.* Philadelphia: University of Pennsylvania Press, 1966.
Kloppenberg, James T. *Uncertain Victory.* New York: Oxford University Press, 1988.
Knights, Ben. *The Idea of the Clerisy in the Nineteenth Century.* Cambridge: Cambridge University Press, 1967.
Kornhauser, William. *The Politics of Mass Society.* New York: Free Press, 1959.
Kuhn, Thomas. *The Essential Tension.* Chicago: University of Chicago Press, 1977.
______. *The Structure of Scientific Revolutions.* 2d ed. Chicago: University of Chicago Press, 1962.
Kuklick, Bruce. "The Emergence of the Humanities." *South Atlantic Quarterly* 89 (Winter 1990): 195–206.
______. "The Professionalization of the Humanities," in *The Organization of Knowledge in Modern America: 1860–1920*, edited by A. Oleson and J. Voss. Baltimore: Johns Hopkins University Press, 1979.
Kurtz, Paul. "The Democratic Ethic." In *Journeys through Philosophy*, edited by Nicholas Capaldi, Eugene Kelley, and Luis E. Navia. Rev. ed. Buffalo: Prometheus Books, 1982, 285–301.
Kuznick, Peter J. *Beyond the Laboratory.* Chicago: University of Chicago Press, 1984.
Lachman, L. M. *The Legacy of Max Weber.* London: Heineman, 1970.
Laclau, Ernesto. "Community and Its Paradoxes: Richard Rorty's 'Liberal Utopia.'" In *Community at Loose Ends*, edited by Miami Theory Collective. Minneapolis: University of Minnesota Press, 1991, 85–99.

Lane, Robert E. "The Decline of Politics and Ideology in a Knowledgeable Society." *American Sociological Review* 31 (1966): 649–62.
Lapham, Lewis H. "Democracy in America?" *Harper's*, 9 November 1990, 47–56.
______. *The Wish for Kings: Democracy at Bay*. New York: Grove Press, 1992.
Lappe, Frances Moore. *Rediscovering America's Values*. New York: Ballantine, 1990.
Larson, Margali Sarfatti. *The Rise of Professionalism*. Berkeley: University of California Press, 1977.
Lasch, Christopher. "The Cultural Cold War." In Lasch. *The Agony of the American Left*. New York: Vintage, 1966, 61–114.
______. *The Culture of Narcissism*. New York: Norton, 1984.
______. *The New Radicalism in America*. New York: Vintage, 1965.
______. *The Revolt of the Elites and the Betrayal of Democracy*. New York: Norton, 1994.
______. "Toward a Theory of Post-Industrial Society." In *Politics in the Post-Welfare State*, edited by M. Donald Hancock and Gideon Sjorberg. New York: Columbia University Press, 1972, 36–50.
______. *The True and Only Heaven*. New York: Norton, 1991.
Lasswell, Harold. *Politics: Who Gets What, When, How*. New York: Meridian, 1951.
______. *Psychopathology and Politics*. New York: Viking, 1930.
Lasswell, Harold, and Abraham Kaplan. *Power and Society*. New Haven: Yale University Press, 1950.
Laursen, John Christian. "The Subversive Kant: The Vocabulary of 'Public' and 'Publicity.'" *Political Theory* 13 (1986): 584–603.
Lawson, Alan. *The Failure of Independent Liberalism*. New York: Capricorn, 1971.
Layton, Edwin. *The Revolt of the Engineers*. Baltimore: Johns Hopkins University Press, 1967.
Leiserson, Avery. "Charles Merriam, Max Weber, and the Search for Synthesis in Political Science." *American Political Science Review* 69 (March 1975): 175–85.
Letwin, Shirley. *The Pursuit of Certainty*. Cambridge, UK: Cambridge University Press, 1965.
Levine, Daniel. "Randolph Bourne, John Dewey, and the Legacy of Liberalism." *Antioch Review* 28 (Summer 1969): 234–44.
Lippmann, Walter. *Drift and Mastery*. New York: Holt, 1914.
______. *The Good Society*. Boston: Little, Brown, 1937.
______. *The Phantom Public*. New York: Harcourt, 1925.
______. *A Preface to Politics*. Boston: Mitchell Kennerley, 1914.
______. *Public Opinion*. New York: Macmillan, 1922.
Lipset, Seymour Martin. *Political Man*. Garden City: Anchor, 1963.
Logue, William. *From Philosophy to Sociology*. DeKalb: Northern Illinois University Press, 1983.
Lothstein, Arthur. "Salving from the Dross: John Dewey's Anarcho-Communism." *Philosophical Forum* n.s. 10 (1978): 55–110.
Lovin, Robin W., and Michael J. Perry, eds. *Critique and Construction*. New York: Cambridge University Press, 1990.
Lowi, Theodore J. *The End of Liberalism*. New York: Norton, 1979.
Lubove, Roy. *The Professional Altruist*. Cambridge: Harvard University Press, 1966.
Lustig, R. Jeffrey. *Corporate Liberalism*. Berkeley: University of California Press, 1984.

Lyons, Gene M. *The Uneasy Partnership*. New York: Russell Sage, 1969.
Lyotard, Jean-Francois. *The Differend*. Minneapolis: University of Minnesota Press, 1989.
______. "Judiciousness in Dispute: Kant after Marx." In *The Lyotard Reader*, edited by Andrew Benjamin. Cambridge: Blackwell's, 1989, 324–60.
______. *Just Gaming*. Minneapolis: University of Minnesota Press, 1984.
______. *The Postmodern Condition*. Minneapolis: University of Minnesota Press, 1984.
MacPherson, C. B. *Democratic Theory: Essays in Retrieval*. New York: Oxford University Press, 1975.
______. *The Life and Times of Liberal Democracy*. New York: Oxford University Press, 1977.
______. *The Real World of Democracy*. New York: Oxford University Press, 1966.
Manicas, Peter. "Dewey and the Class Struggle." In *Values in Twentieth Century America*, edited by A. Edel. Philadelphia: Temple University Press, 1988, 67–81.
______. "John Dewey: Anarchism and the Political State." *Transactions of the C. S. Peirce Society* 18 (1982): 133–58.
______. "John Dewey and the Problem of Justice." *Journal of Value Inquiry* 14 (1981): 279–91.
______. "Philosophy and Politics: A Historical Approach to Dewey and Marx." In *Context over Foundation*, edited by William Gavin. Boston: Reidel, 1988, 147–77.
Mannheim, Karl. "The Democratization of Culture." In *From Karl Mannheim*, edited by Kurt Wolff. New York: Oxford University Press, 1971, 271–345.
Martindale, Don. *The Scope of Social Theory*. Vol 1. Boston: Cap and Gown Press, 1984.
McCarthy, Thomas. "Complexity and Democracy: On the Seductions of Systems Theory." In McCarthy, *Ideals and Illusion*. Cambridge: MIT Press, 1991.
McCoy, Charles A., and John Playford Crowell, eds. *Apolitical Politics*. New York: Crowell, 1967.
Menand, Louis. "Man of the People." *New York Review of Books*, 11 April 1991, 39–44.
Merquior, J. G. *Liberalism Old and New*. New York: Twyne Publishers, 1991.
Merriam, Charles. *New Aspects of Politics*. Chicago: University of Chicago Press, 1925.
______. *The New Democracy and the New Despotism*. New York: McGraw-Hill, 1939.
Merriam, Charles, and W. Ogburn, eds. *Recent Social Trends in the United States*. 2 vols. New York: McGraw-Hill, 1933.
Merton, Robert K. *Science, Technology, and Society in Seventeenth Century England*. New York: Harper, 1970.
______. *The Sociology of Science*. Chicago: University of Chicago Press, 1973.
Meyer, Donald B. *The Protestant Search for Political Realism*. Berkeley: University of California Press, 1960.
Mill, John Stuart. "Civilization." In Mill, *Essays on Politics and Culture*. Edited by G. Himmelfarb. New York: Anchor, 1963.
______. "Democracy and Government." In *John Stuart Mill on Politics and Society*, edited by G. L. Williams. London: Harvester, 1976.
______. *Essays on Politics and Culture*, edited by G. Himmelfarb. New York: Anchor, 1963.

______. *Essential Works of J. S. Mill*. New York: Bantam, 1961.
______. *Philosophy of J. S. Mill*. Edited by M. Cohen,. New York: Modern Library, 1961.
Miller, James. *Democracy in the Streets*. New York: Simon and Schuster, 1975.
Mills, C. Wright. *The Power Elite*. New York: Oxford University Press, 1956.
______. *Power, Politics, and People*. New York: Oxford University Press, 1960.
Misgeld, Dieter. "Modernity, Democracy, and Social Engineering." *Praxis International* 7 (1987–88): 268–85.
Mommsen, Wolfgang. *The Age of Bureaucracy*. New York: Oxford University Press, 1964.
Mommsen, Wolfgang, ed. *Max Weber and His Contemporaries*. London; Unwin, 1987.
Mommsen, Wolfgang, and Jurgen Osterhammeleh, eds. *Max Weber and His Contemporaries*. London: Allen and Unwin,1987.
Moretti, F. "The Spell of Indecision." In *Marxism and the Interpretation of Culture*, edited by C. Nelson and L. Grossberg. Urbana: University of Illinois Press, 1988, 336–47.
Morton, Marion J. *The Terrors of Ideological Politics*. Cleveland: Case Western Reserve University Press, 1972.
Mouffe, Chantel. "Rawls: Political Philosophy without Politics." *Philosophy and Social Criticism* 13 (1987): 105–23.
Moynihan, Daniel Patrick. *Coping*. New York: Random House, 1977.
Mulhall, Stephen, and Adam Swift. *Liberals and Communitarians*. Cambridge: Blackwell's, 1992.
Mulkay, Michael. *Science and the Sociology of Knowledge*. Boston: Unwin, 1979.
Mumford, Lewis. "The Corruption of Liberalism." *New Republic* 74 (1940) 569–73.
Murphy, Arthur E. "John Dewey and American Liberalism." *Journal of Philosophy* 57 (1960): 420–36.
Napoli, Donald. *Architects of Adjustment*. Port Washington, NY: Kennikat Press, 1981.
Newman, William J. *The Futilitarian Society*. New York: George Braziller, 1961.
Niebhur, Rinehold. *Children of Light and Children of Darkness*. New York: Scribner's, 1944.
______. *The Irony of American History*. New York: Scribner's, 1952.
Nietzsche, Friedrich. *The Birth of Tragedy*. In *Basic Writings of Nietzsche*, edited and translated by Walter Kaufmann. New York: Modern Library, 1966.
Noble, David F. *American by Design*. New York: Knopf, 1977.
Noble, David W. *The End of American History*. Minneapolis: University of Minnesota Press, 1985.
______. *The Paradox of Progressive Thought*. Minneapolis: University of Minnesota Press, 1958.
______. *The Progressive Mind*. Chicago: Rand McNally, 1979.
Norris, Christopher. *Uncritical Reason*. Amherst: University of Massachusetts Press, 1992.
Novack, George. *Pragmatism vs. Marxism*. New York: Pathfinder, 1975.
Novick, Peter. *The Objectivity Question*. New York: Cambridge University Press, 1989.
Oberschall, Anthony. "The Institutionalization of American Sociology." In *The Establishment of Empirical Sociology*, edited by A. Oberschall. New York: Harper, 1972, 187–252.
O'Donnell, John M. *The Origins of Behaviorism*. New York: New York University Press, 1985.

O'Neill, Onora. "The Public Use of Reason." *Political Theory* 15 (1988): 523–51.
Osbun, Lee Ann. *The Problem of Participation*. Lanham, MD: University Press of America, 1985.
Page, Charles. *Class and American Sociology*. New York: Dial, 1940.
Parry, Geraint. "Making Democrats: Education and Democracy." In *Democracy and Democratization*, edited by Geraint Parry and Michael Moran. New York: Routledge, 1993.
______. *Political Elites*. Westport, CT: Praeger, 1969.
Pateman, Carole, "Feminism and Democracy." In *Democratic Theory and Practice*, edited by Graeme Duncan. New York: Cambridge University Press, 1983, 204–17.
______. *Participation and Democratic Theory*. New York: Cambridge University Press, 1983.
Pearce, Frank. *The Radical Durkheim*. London: Unwin, 1989.
Pells, Richard. *Radical Visions and American Dreams*. New York: Harper, 1973.
Perry, Lewis. *Intellectual Life in America*. Chicago: University of Chicago Press, 1984, 1989.
Phillips, Ann. *Engendering Democracy*. College Park: Pennsylvania State University Press, 1991.
Phillips, Kevin. *Arrogant Capital*. Boston: Little, Brown, 1994.
______. *The Politics of Rich and Poor*. New York: Random House, 1990.
Pickering, Donald K. *Eugenics and the Progressives*. Nashville: Vanderbilt University Press, 1968.
Popper, Karl. *The Open Society and Its Enemies*. 2 vols. New York: Harper, 1944.
______. *The Poverty of Historicism*. New York: Harper, 1957.
Prewitt, Kenneth, and Alan Stone. *The Ruling Elite*. New York: Harper, 1973.
Purcell, Edward. The Critics in Democratic Theory. Lexington: University of Kentucky Press, 1973.
Ratner, S., and J. Altman, eds. *John Dewey and Arthur F. Bentley: A Philosophical Correspondence, 1932–1951*. New Brunswick: Rutgers University Press, 1964.
Rawls, John. "The Domain of the Political and Overlapping Consensus." *New York University Law Review* 64 (1989): 233–55. Reprinted in Rawls, *Political Liberalism*. New York: Columbia University Press, 1993.
______. "The Idea of an Overlapping Consensus." *Oxford Journal of Legal Studies* 7 (1987): 1–25. Reprinted in Rawls, *Political Liberalism*, New York: Columbia University Press, 1993.
______. "The Idea of Public Reason." In Rawls, *Political Liberalism*. New York: Columbia University Press, 1993, 212–54.
______. "The Independence of Moral Theory." *Proceedings and Addresses of the American Philosophical Association* 48 (1975): 5–22.
______. "The Theory of Justice: Political, Not Metaphysical." *Philosophy and Public Affairs* 14 (1985): 223–51.
Reich, Robert B. "Policy Making in a Democracy." In *The Power of Public Ideas*, edited by Robert Reich. Cambridge: Harvard University Press, 1988, 123–56.
Rejai, M., ed. *Decline of Ideology?* New York: Atherton, 1971.
Ricci, David. *Community Power and Democratic Theory*. New York: Random House, 1971.
______. *The Tragedy of Political Science*. New Haven: Yale University Press, 1984.
Rice, Daniel F. *Reinhold Niebhur versus John Dewey*. Albany: State University of New York Press, 1993.

Richter, Melvin. "Durkheim's Politics and Political Sociology." In *Essays on Sociology and Philosophy*, edited by Kurt Wolff. Columbus: Ohio State University Press, 1960, 170–210.

Riesman, David. *Thorsten Veblen*. New York: Scribner's, 1953.

Robson, John M. *The Improvement of Mankind*. Toronto: University of Toronto Press, 1961.

Rochester, Stuart I. *American Liberal Disillusionment in the Wake of World War I*. College Park: Pennsylvania State University Press, 1971.

Rogin, Michael Paul. *The Intellectuals and McCarthy: The Radical Specter*. Cambridge: MIT Press, 1967.

Roper, John, ed. *Democracy and Its Critics*. London: Unwin, 1989.

Rorty, Richard. "Anti-Representationalism, Ethnocentrism, and Liberalism." In Rorty, *Objectivity, Relativism, and Truth, Philosophical Papers*. Vol. 1. New York: Cambridge University Press, 1991.

______. *Consequences of Pragmatism*. Minneapolis: University of Minnesota Press, 1982.

______. *Contingency, Irony, and Solidarity*. New York: Cambridge University Press, 1989.

______. "Contingency of Community." *London Review of Books* 8 no. 13 (24 July 1986): 1–4.

______. "Education without Dogma." *Dissent* 36 (Spring 1989): 198–204.

______. "Epistemological Behaviorism and the De-transcendentalization of Analytic Philosophy." In *Hermeneutics and Praxis*, edited by Robert Hollinger. Notre Dame: University of Notre Dame Press, 1985, 89–121.

______. "Foucault/Dewey/Nietzsche." *Raritan*. 9 (Spring 1990), 1–8.

______. "Freud and Moral Reflection." In *Pragmatism's Freud: The Moral Disposition of Psychoanalysis*, edited by Joseph H. Smith and William Kerrigan. Psychiatry and the Humanities, vol. 9. Baltimore: Johns Hopkins University Press, 1986, 1–27.

______. "Habermas and Lyotard on Postmodernity." *Praxis International* 4 (1984): 32–44.

______. "The Humanistic Intellectual." In *Viewpoints*. Washington, DC: American Council for Learned Societies Occasional Papers, no. 10, 1989, 9–12.

______. "Method, Social Science, Social Hope." In Rorty, *Consequences of Pragmatism*. Minneapolis: University of Minnesota Press, 1982, 191–210.

______. "The Opening of American Minds," *Harper's* 269 (July 1989) 18–21.

______. *Philosophy and the Mirror of Nature*. Princeton: Princeton University Press, 1979.

______. "Philosophy as Science, as Metaphor, and as Politics." In *The Institution of Philosophy*, edited by A. Cohen and M. Dascal. LaSalle: Open Court Press, 1989, 13–33.

______. "Postmodernist Bourgeois Liberalism." *Journal of Philosophy* 80 (1983): 583–89. Reprinted in *Hermeneutics and Praxis*, edited by Robert Hollinger. Notre Dame: University of Notre Dame Press, 1985, 214–21.

______. "A Post-Philosophical Politics?" Interview with Danny Postel. *Philosophy and Social Criticism* 17 (1990): 199–204.

______. "The Priority of Democracy to Philosophy." In *Reading Rorty*, edited by Alan Malachowski. Cambridge: Blackwell's, 1989, 279–302.

______. "Thugs and Theorists." *Political Theory* 16 (1989).

______. "Two Cheers for the Cultural Left." *South Atlantic Quarterly* 89 (Winter 1990): 227–34.

Rosenberg, Charles E. *No Other Gods*. Baltimore: Johns Hopkins University Press, 1976.
Rosenblum, Nancy. *Another Liberalism*. Cambridge: Harvard University Press, 1987.
Rosenthal, Joel. *Righteous Realists*. Baton Rouge: Louisiana State University Press, 1991.
Ross, Dorothy. "The Development of the Social Sciences." In *The Organization of Knowledge in Modern America: 1860–1920*, edited by A. Oleson and J. Voss. Baltimore: Johns Hopkins University Press, 1979, 107–39.
______. *Origins of American Social Science*. New York: Cambridge University Press, 1991.
Ross, E. A. *Social Control*. 1901. Boston: Beacon Press, 1959.
Rothenberg, Randall. *The Neo-Liberals*. New York: Simon and Schuster, 1984.
Rothman, David. *Conscience and Convenience*. Boston: Little, Brown, 1980.
______. *The Discovery of the Asylum*. Boston: Little, Brown, 1971.
Roucke, Joseph S., ed. *The Making of Middlebrow Culture*. Chapel Hill: University of North Carolina Press, 1992.
______. *Social Control for the 1980's: A Handbook for Order in a Democratic Society*. Westport, CT: Greenwood Publishers, 1987.
Russell, Bertrand, "Philosophy and Politics." In Russell, *Unpopular Essays*. London: Unwin, 1968, 3–25.
Russett, Cynthia Eagle. *The Concept of Equilibrium in American Thought*. New Haven: Yale University Press, 1966.
Sandel, Michael. "Democracy and Community: A Public Philosophy for American Liberalism. *New Republic*, 22 February 1988.
______. "The Political Theory of the Procedural Republic." In *The Power of Public Ideas*, edited by Robert B. Reich. Cambridge: Harvard University Press, 1988, 109–22.
Sartori, Giovanni. *The Theory of Democracy Revisited*. New York: Chatham House, 1987.
Scaff, Lawrence A. *Fleeing the Iron Cage*. Berkeley: University of California Press, 1989.
Schlesinger, Arthur, Jr. *The Vital Center*. New York: Houghton, Mifflin, 1949.
Schmitt, Carl. *Political Romanticism*. Cambridge: MIT Press, 1986.
Schneewind, J. B., ed. *Mill: A Collection of Essays*. Notre Dame: University of Notre Dame Press, 1969.
Schumpeter, Joseph A. *Capitalism, Socialism, and Democracy*. New York: Harper and Brothers, 1942.
Schwedinger, H., and J. Schwedinger. *Sociologists of the Chair*. New York: Basic Books, 1974.
Searle, John. "Postmodernism and the Western Rationalist Tradition." In *The Campus Wars*, edited by John Arthur and Amy Shapiro. New York: Routledge, 1994, 28–49.
______. "Storm over the University." In *Debating P.C.*, edited by Paul Berman. New York: Laurel, 1992, 85-114.
Segal, Harvey. *Technological Utopianism in American Culture*. Chicago: University of Chicago Press, 1985.
Seidelman, David. *The New Republic*. Westport, CT: Praeger, 1986.
Seidelman, S., and R. Harpham. *Disenchanted Realists: Political Science and the American Crisis*, 1884–1994. Albany: SUNY Press, 1985.
Seidman, Steven. *Liberalism and the Origins of European Social Theory*. Berkeley: University of California Press, 1984.

Seybold, Peter J. "The Ford Foundation and the Triumph of Behavioralism in American Political Science." In *Philanthropy and Cultural Imperialism*, edited by Robert Arnove. Chicago: G. T. Hall, 1980, 268–304.

Shalin, Dmitiri N. "G. H. Mead, Socialism, and the Progressive Agenda." *American Journal of Sociology* 93 (1988): 913–51.

Shapiro, Ian. *Political Criticism*. Berkeley: University of California Press, 1989.

Shapiro, William. "The Nietzschean Roots of Max Weber's Social Science." Ph.D. diss., Cornell University, 1978.

Shils, Edward. "The Theory of Mass Society." In Shils, *Center and Periphery: Essays in Macrosociology*. Chicago: University of Chicago Press, 1975, 91–110.

Sinclair, Bruce, "The Engineers." In *The Professions in American History*, edited by Nathan Hatch. Baltimore: John Hopkins University Press, 1987.

Singal, Daniel Joseph, ed. *Modernist Culture in America*. Belmont, CA: Wadsworth, 1991.

Skinner, B. F. *Beyond Freedom and Dignity*. New York: Knopf, 1971.

Skinner, Quentin. "The Empirical Theorists of Democracy and Their Critics: A Plague on Both Their Houses." *Political Theory* 1 (1973): 287–306.

Sklar, Martin. "Woodrow Wilson and the Political Economy of U. S. Liberalism." In *A New History of Leviathan*, edited by R. Radosh and M. Rothbard. New York: Dutton, 1972.

Skorupski, John. "Liberal Elitism." In *Liberalism, Citizenship, and Autonomy*, edited by David Milligan and William Watts Miller. London: Avery, 1992, 134–53.

Smart, Barry. *Conditions of Postmodernity*. New York: Routledge, 1992.

Smith, Dennis. *The Chicago School: A Liberal Critique of Capitalism*. New York: St. Martin's, 1988.

Smith, Dusky Lee. "Scientific Liberalism: Ward, Galbraith, and the Welfare State." In *Politics in the Post-Welfare State*, edited by M. Donald Hancock and Gideon Sjoberg. New York: Columbia University Press, 1972, 51–65.

______. "Sociology and the Rise of Corporate Liberalism." *Science and Society* 38 (1974): 401–18.

Smith, Mark C. *Social Science in the Crucible*. Durham: Duke University Press, 1994.

Smith, Merritt Roe. "Technology, Industry, and the Idea of Progress." In *Responsible Technology: Impact of Technology on Society*, edited by Kevin B. Byrne. Nobel Lectures, no. 21. New York: Harper, 1986, 1–28.

Smith, Michael Joseph. *Realist Thought from Weber to Kissinger*. Baton Rouge: Louisiana State University Press, 1990.

Sokal, Michael. "Origins of the Psychological Corporation." *Journal of the History of the Behavioral Sciences* 16 (1981): 54–67.

Sokal, Michael, ed. *Psychological Testing in American Society: 1890–1930*. New Brunswick: Rutgers University Press, 1987.

Somit, Albert, and Joseph Tanenhaus. *The Development of American Political Science*. New York: Irvington Publishers, 1982.

Somjee, A. H. *The Political Philosophy of John Dewey*. New York: Teacher's College Press, 1968.

Soule, George. "Hard-Boiled Liberalism." *New Republic* 65, 21 January 1931, 261–65.

Spanos, William. *The End of Education: Toward a Posthumanism*. Minneapolis: University of Minnesota Press, 1993.

Spragens, Thomas. *The Irony of Liberal Reason*. Chicago: University of Chicago Press, 1982.

_____. *Reason and Democracy*. Durham: Duke University Press, 1990.
Spring, Joel. *Education and the Rise of the Corporate State*. Boston: Beacon Press, 1972.
Stabile, Donald. *Prophets of Order*. Boston: South End Press, 1984.
Steinman, Linda M. *Made in America: Science, Technology and American Modernist Poets*. New Haven: Yale University Press, 1987.
Swingwood, Alan. *The Myth of Mass Culture*. New York: St. Martin's, 1977.
Tallack, Douglas. *Twentieth Century America*. London: Longman, 1991.
Talmon, J. L. *The Origins of Totalitarian Democracy*. Westport, CT: Praeger, 1952.
Taylor, Charles. "Multiculturalism and the Politics of Recognition." In *Multiculturalism*, edited by Amy Gutman. Rev. ed. Princeton: Princeton University Press, 1994.
Thomas, William. *Mill*. New York: Oxford University Press, 1984.
Thompson, Dennis F. *John Stuart Mill and Representative Government*. Princeton: Princeton University Press, 1976.
Tichi, Cecilia. *Shifting Gears*. Chapel Hill: University of North Carolina Press, 1987.
Tobey, Ronald. *The American Ideology of National Science: 1919–1930*. Pittsburgh: University of Pittsburgh Press, 1971.
Touraine, Alain. *The Post-Industrial Society*. New York: Random House, 1971.
_____. "What Is Daniel Bell Afraid Of?" *American Journal of Sociology* 77 (1972): 469–73.
Turner, Stephen P., and Regis A. Factor. "The Disappearance of Tradition in Weber." *Midwest Studies in Philosophy* 15 (1990): 400–24.
_____. *Max Weber and the Dispute about Reason and Value*. New York: Routledge, 1984.
Turner, Stephen P., and Jonathan Turner. *The Impossible Science: An Institutional Analysis of American Sociology*. Newbury Park, CA: Sage Publishers, 1990.
Ulmen, G. L. "The Sociology of the State: Carl Schmitt and Max Weber." *State, Culture, and Society* 1, no. 2 (1985): 3–57.
Unger, Roberto. *Social Theory*. 3 vols. New York: Cambridge University Press, 1987.
Veysey, Laurence. *The Emergence of the American University*. Chicago: University of Chicago Press, 1967.
_____. "The Plural Organized Worlds of the Humanities." In *The Organization of Knowledge in Modern America: 1860–1920*, edited by A. Oleson and J. Voss. Baltimore: Johns Hopkins University Press, 1979, 51–106.
Vidich, Arthur, and Sanford Lyman. *American Sociology*. New Haven: Yale University Press, 1985.
Wald, Alan. *The New York Intellectuals*. Chapel Hill: University of North Carolina Press, 1987.
Wallas, Graham. *The Great Society*. New York: Macmillan, 1914.
_____. *Human Nature and Politics*. New York: Macmillan, 1908.
Walzer, Michael. *Interpretation and Criticism*. Cambridge: Harvard University Press, 1990.
_____. *In the Company of Critics*. New York: Basic Books, 1988.
_____. "Philosophy and Democracy." In *What Should Political Theory Be Now?* edited by John Nelson. Albany: SUNY Press, 1983, 75–99.
Warnke, Georgia. *Justice and Interpretation*. Cambridge: MIT Press, 1992.
Warren, Mark. "Max Weber's Liberalism for a Nietzschean World." *American Political Science Review* 82 (March 1988): 32–50.

Waxman, Chaim I., ed. *The End of Ideology Debate*. New York: Funk and Wagnalls, 1968.

Weber, Max. *Economy and Society*. 2 vols. Berkeley: University of California Press, 1978.

———. "Politics as a Vocation." In *From Max Weber*, edited by Hans Gerth and C. Wright Mills. New York: Oxford University Press, 1946.

———. "Science as A Vocation." In *From Max Weber*, edited by Hans Gerth and C. Wright Mills. New York: Oxford University Press, 1946.

Weinberg, Julius. *Edward Alsworth Ross and the Sociology of Progressivism*. Madison: University of Wisconsin Press, 1972.

Weinstein, James. *The Corporate Ideal in the Liberal State*. Boston: Beacon Press, 1972.

Weinstein, Michael A. "Western Liberalism Goes Postmodern: Rorty's Pragmatism." *Canadian Journal of Political and Social Theory* 9 (1986): 10–19.

Westbrook, Robert B. *John Dewey and American Democracy*. Ithaca: Cornell University Press, 1991.

Wiebe, Robert. *The Search for Order: 1877–1920*. New York: Hill and Wang, 1967.

Wiener, M. J., ed. *Humanitarianism or Control*? Houston: Rice University Press, 1981.

Williams, G. L., ed. *John Stuart Mill on Politics and Culture*. London: Harvester, 1976.

Wilson, Edmund. "Appeal to Progressives." *New Republic* 65, 14 January 1931, 234–38.

Wintrop, Norman. "Liberal-Democratic Theory: The New Liberalism." In *Liberal Democratic Theory and Its Critics*, edited by Wintrop. London: Croom Helm, 1983.

Wintrop, Norman, and David W. Lovell. "Varieties of Conservative Theory." In *Liberal Democratic Theory and Its Critics*, edited by Norman Wintrop. London: Croom Helm, 1983.

Wolfe, Alan. "Sociology, Liberalism, and the Radical Right." *New Left Review* 128 (1981): 3–27.

Wolin, Sheldon. *The Presence of the Past*. Baltimore: Johns Hopkins University Press, 1989.

———. "Why Democracy?" *Democracy* 1, no. 1 (1981): 3–5.

Young, James P. *The Politics of Affluence*. Boston: Chandler, 1968.

Zolo, Danilo. *Democracy and Complexity: A Realist Approach*. College Park: Pennsylvania State University Press, 1992.

Index

About the Author

ROBERT HOLLINGER is Associate Professor of Philosophy at Iowa State University. He is author of *Postmodernism and the Social Sciences: A Thematic Approach* and coeditor, with David Depew, of *Pragmatism: From Progressivism to Postmodernism* (Praeger, 1994).

ISBN 0-275-95334-3
90000>
EAN
9 780275 953348
HARDCOVER BAR CODE